DETERMINED
NORMAN
WHITESIDE
THE AUTOBIOGRAPHY

with Rob Bagchi

headline

First published in 2007 by
HEADLINE PUBLISHING GROUP

I

Cataloguing in Publication Data is available from the British Library

Hardback ISBN 978 0 7553 1596 3
Trade paperback ISBN 978 0 7553 1597 0

Typeset in Centaur MT by Palimpsest Book Production Limited,
Grangemouth, Stirlingshire

Career statistics compiled by Jack Rollin

Printed and bound in Great Britain by
Mackays of Chatham Ltd, Chatham Kent

Headline's policy is to use papers that are natural, renewable and recyclable products and
made from wood grown in sustainable forests. The logging and manufacturing processes
are expected to conform to the environmental regulations of the country of origin.

HEADLINE PUBLISHING GROUP
An Hachette Livre UK Company
338 Euston Road
London NWI 3BH

www.headline.co.uk
www.hodderheadline.com

To my family who have loved and supported me to this day,
and with whom I look forward to the future:
Ma Aileen, Da Norman, brothers Ken and Hughie,
Julie, Della Beau, Blaine, Clodagh, Denise and Gabriel.

CONTENTS

FOREWORD

Saturday 18 May 1985, Queen's University Belfast Student Union bar. It's 0–0 in the FA Cup final between Manchester United and Everton and United's Kevin Moran has become the first player ever to be sent off in the final. To be fair, in today's modern game the same tackle would see him sent to Coventry, an outcome not good whatever way you look at it. With 10 minutes of extra time remaining, Everton look like making their advantage tell when suddenly Mark Hughes, with a beautifully weighted pass, releases one Norman Whiteside. Bearing down on Everton's last defender, Norman bamboozles him with an early prototype of the crossover before curling a left-footed peach of a shot from twenty yards past the reach of the world's greatest goalkeeper, Neville Southall, and into the right-hand corner. Cue pandemonium in Belfast, Salford, Wembley and all over the world.

At just twenty years and eleven days old, but looking thirty-five, Whiteside has won the Cup. Not for the first time United fans everywhere are thinking, 'Cometh the hour, cometh the Norman.'

The first time I met Norman I was speechless, literally. It was in 1993 and I'd blagged my way into the players' lounge at Old Trafford. Rambling incessantly to Gary Pallister and Steve Bruce I was suddenly introduced to the big man and was dumbstruck. I wanted to speak, I tried to speak, but the only words that formed in my mind were, 'I love you Norman. I've always loved you and I always will.' It seemed a bit early in our relationship to confess this so I just stood there, mute and gormless.

It's not difficult to explain why I was in such a state. Norman was my hero. It's impossible to overestimate the positive impact he's had on Northern Ireland's recent history. From a footballing perspective, he's a legend. Others before him had been labelled the next George Best but Norman alone dealt with that impossible expectation. No one will ever play football like George but they had more in common than coming from the same place, playing for the same club and enjoying the occasional glass of sherry. Both could shoot with either foot, were strong in the air, never shirked a challenge and could turn on a sixpence.

But Norman was his own man and many of his achievements outshone even George. At seventeen he was the youngest player to appear in a World Cup during those heady days of España '82; in Mexico '86 he scored our first goal of the tournament, and in the 1982–3 season he was the youngest player to score in both the League Cup and the FA Cup finals.

There was, however, another similarity with George. Raised in Loyalist Belfast, they were both vehemently non-sectarian. During the decades of the bloodshed and despair they were idolised by both sides of the community and offered a vital alternative to the global perception of Northern Ireland. But like George it's for the football Norman will be remembered.

A giant of a man at seventeen, he ran like a train and scored blistering goals: the unstoppable volley against Arsenal, the goal of the season against Everton and definitively the quarter-final hat-trick against West Ham – a header, one with the right, then a thundering penalty with the left.

I'll also remember the generous, funny, loyal friend who during the curtain call of a play I was recently in was the first to rise, clapping and cheering. Pure theatre, pure class, pure Norman.

James Nesbitt
June 2007

ACKNOWLEDGEMENTS

Each book is a team effort and so, particularly in football, is each life. I would like to pay tribute to those in addition to my family who made the story both possible and so enjoyable. Thanks, in no particular order, go to all those who have helped me in my career: Bob Bishop for sending me to Old Trafford; Jim McGregor, the physio with the healing touch who also inspired my podiatry; Bet and Tom Fannon, my landlord and landlady in the early days; and Norman Davis, the best kitman in the world.

The managers and coaches – Ron Atkinson, Billy Bingham, Sir Alex Ferguson, Colin Harvey, Howard Kendall, Dave Sexton, Syd Owen, Eric Harrison and Jimmy Curran.

Those influential people from my schooldays: Willy 'Oxo' Williamson, Herbie 'Honey' Artt, Victor 'The Coalman' Anderson, my Edenbrooke teacher Heather Mulligan, and special thanks to the current Edenbrooke head teacher, the remarkable Betty Orr, and her husband John.

The infamous drinking pals and purveyors of hospitality including, Robbo, Big Paul, Viv Anderson, Mike Milligan, Peter 'Sleepy' Clavin, Clodagh Buckley, Michael Prophet, Phil 'Magic' Fenton, Jimmy Nesbitt, The Roebuck, The Orange Tree, Ming and the team at the Tai Pan.

For their longstanding kindness and support, thanks to Geoff, 'Moet' Mason, and to all of my friends too many to mention by name.

Thanks are also due to special agent David Luxton who got the ball rolling and whose wise counsel, skill, humour and cardigan kept our spirits up. At Headline I am grateful to David Wilson, Lorraine Jerram and Juliana Foster for their invaluable input and patience. Finally, I'd like to thank Rob Bagchi for helping me put this book together over several civilised afternoons in Belfast, Altrincham, Hale and London and he would like to note the gratitude he owes to Alison Kirby, Eden, Saral and Angela Bagchi.

CHAPTER ONE

WHAT BECOMES
OF THE
BROKEN-HEARTED?

Once upon a time . . . isn't that how fairytales begin? And I had
been told often enough that this was supposed to be a fairy-
tale, one that had taken a kid from the back streets of Belfast
to the Theatre of Dreams, Wembley and the World Cup. So
I couldn't help asking, as I sprawled on my bed in our dream
house on that glorious mid-June morning in 1991, what the
hell had happened to the happily ever after? Usually I'd lie for
hours in silence in our bedroom, staring out at the trees and
the sky above Charcoal Woods, lost in mental rehearsal for the
forthcoming match, picturing the runs I would make, almost

feeling the beautiful, familiar sensation of the ball on the instep of my left foot, joyfully preparing to express myself on the stage where I felt most comfortable. But not today.

The duvet is over my head and my eyes are burning from the tears that just won't stop. Where have the tears come from? Of Manchester United's three amigos, Paul McGrath, Bryan Robson and me, it's Paul who is supposed to be the deep one, Bryan the resilient one and me the happy-go-lucky one. But these aren't the tears of a clown. It's not self-pity. It's grief and fear. Grief for a career and a future I've lost and fear of how I'm going to manage without it. I'm twenty-six years old, half my lifetime away from the normal retirement age, and the dream is over. In that gorgeous Cheshire house, hiding under a feather quilt, the man-boy, the Shankill Skinhead, Rambo, Roy of the Rovers, Stormin' Norman the Scousebuster lies slumped and I am torturing myself with a question that scares the life out of me: what am I going to do now?

Perhaps it would be better if I could identify someone to blame, a person around whose neck I could hang the responsibility for my situation. My medical file is an inch thick, but I know that, when I leaf through it, a scapegoat won't easily emerge. All the specialists, all the operations, all the rehabilitation programmes are logged in intricate detail, but the advice I took was given with the best intentions, as first United and then Everton fought to save and prolong my career. So whose fault is it? The larcenous faith healer who stole my speed? The Preston North End youth player who caught me with a tackle so innocuous I couldn't even remember it the morning after the game? The surgeons who operated on my right knee so often over ten years that it may have been better if they'd sewn in a zip? The coaches and managers who hurried me to resume playing? The solace I found in booze when injured that my critics contend stopped me from recovering properly? Or the Everton trainee who carelessly clattered my standing leg when tackling me from behind in a practice match on 20 September 1990 – a rash challenge, but one that I have to accept was not malicious, even though it began the nine-month wait for the verdict I accepted yesterday? They all add up, but it's too complicated for simple answers. Talent, time and chance took me to the heights, but they have also brought me low. So while I lie here in panic and rail at my misfortune, I also know it's no use pointing fingers: accidents will happen. Indeed, if anyone is to blame for the way I feel this morning, it's me.

You see, I am not being forced to quit. In fact I could have squeezed another two years' pay out of Everton, from the best contract of my life, if I'd had the stomach for it. Stringing them along, I could have hobbled about in the reserves on one leg, hoping for a miracle, hopping between spells in the operating theatre to flush my knee out and the gym. It could have taken me through to 1993, at least giving myself time to adjust to a life without football.

My wife, Julie, my family and friends don't want me to give up, seeing it more as giving in. Even Howard Kendall, Everton's manager, whose desire to see 'a fit Norman Whiteside' had rung in my ears since his return to the club the previous autumn, wasn't pushing me towards the door. And only a few weeks ago, in my snooker room downstairs, my absolute pride, I'd entertained my old mentor, Ron Atkinson, as he outlined, in his

customary, sparkling sales-patter, a lifeline: a 'pay-as-you-play'
deal at Sheffield Wednesday.

None of those well-meaning people, however, have endured
nine operations in as many years, with the certainty of several
more to follow. None of them have gone out to train or play
in the knowledge that one mistimed tackle would put them in
a wheelchair before they reached forty. None of them have
spent months like a caged animal with the physio, gradually
building up muscles to compensate for the joint's frailty, only
to feel a twinge five minutes into their first comeback practice match. The twinge confirms a nagging doubt that the latest
operation has fundamentally failed. None of them had known
how it felt to be me at my best and then suffer years of pain
trying to stay at that level. If a return to that peak was clin-
ically impossible, how was I now to reconcile myself to carrying
on if I could no longer do myself justice? I may be many
things, but I'm not a coward. No, the courageous and noble
decision was to walk away, quite literally while I still could.

But being honourable, brave and rational is no consolation.
I can still look at myself in the mirror, but what's the point
of that if I can't get out of bed? If all you've ever wanted to
do is play football and all you've ever done *is* play football,
where do you turn to when football is finished for you? God?
No, I'd had a religious spell, but I'd long since put my bible
away. The bottle? Well, I love a drink, but I'm not one of life's
maudlin boozers and I know there are no answers there. Family
and friends? Their love and concern is palpable and I know it
supports me, but I feel so alone that no one can touch me
today. I'll stay in bed then, the footballer's haven where we

4

spend so many of our days resting up before and after games. Tomorrow I'll try to get up and face facts, but today, on the cusp of my professional career, stumbling into my new, uncertain life, I think I'll hole up right here in this sanctuary and wait for the tears to run dry.

The odd thing about my bed-in was the shock I felt at being finished, something that suddenly hit me, despite months of discussing it and thinking of nothing else. It was like knowing someone with a fatal illness and it not mattering how logically prepared and steeled for their death you were. The emotional tidal wave still knocks you sideways when the end comes. The day before, I had been sitting in Howard Kendall's office at Bellefield, Everton's training ground, with the manager, club secretary Jim Greenwood and Gordon Taylor of the Professional Footballers' Association, thrashing out a settlement. The long meeting took on a very jovial air when, as was Howard's custom, out came the corkscrew, and my career was jollied along towards the knacker's yard during an afternoon spent alternately negotiating, reminiscing and what was known at Everton as 'wine-tasting'.

It had been eight months since my last operation and though I had left Arrowe Park Hospital on the Wirral determined to continue, it hadn't escaped me that this, my first procedure while at Everton, was also the first time a new consultant had treated my knee for six or seven years. At United, the specialist I was sent to see had perhaps got used to the ugly state it was in and knew how to micromanage it, cleaning it out and sending me back to the club until more bits flaked off the bone and made the joint swell up to the size of a swede. Although

Everton's surgeon, Mr Johnson, had read the reports and pored over the X-rays, when he cut me open he was the first doctor for years to train a fresh pair of eyes on the state my knee was in. The other surgeons had repeatedly patched me up since I was sixteen and although I accept that the familiarity that had bred over such a long relationship did not mean that they were not professional and frank with me, they were probably inclined to break bad news gently. Mr Johnson had no such inhibitions and in September 1990 it was he who first mentioned the possibility of a wheelchair. Like most football players, I have selective hearing when it comes to bad news and I tried my best to ignore him.

Fast forward to mid-1991, though, and I had to accept that being fit enough to play regularly was something that was never going to come back. I had managed four and a half reserve games, had come on as a sub at Coventry in the second game of the season and had even had an hour of first-team football at Plough Lane in the 1990–1 season. Wimbledon's spartan, half-empty stadium would not exactly have been my venue of choice at which to bow out. I found I could cope with playing for the stiffs, because there's a world of difference between reserve-team football and First Division matches and if you've got half a brain and know what you're doing you can take it quite easy-ozy by letting the ball do the work and you can dictate the play by sitting in a small pocket of the pitch and becoming the hub of distribution, like an American football quarter-back. I even enjoyed it; my lack of mobility gave me an obstacle to overcome and I loved a challenge to grapple with. Pretty soon, however, I began to realise that if there was nothing at the end of a period of daily rehabilitation other than the prospect of an hour here and half an hour there with the reserves, then I was wasting my time.

Without doubt ego is involved too. I had standards as a player and if they were not going to be met then I couldn't face going on. It's not for me to criticise those who take the option of continuing until they drop, their love of the game taking them down the pyramid until only age or dignity can stop them, but this was something I barely considered. But I must have been told a thousand times that although my knee wasn't up to the top flight there was no reason to suggest I couldn't do a job at semi-pro level, or even as far up as the Second Division. Perhaps I'd been spoilt, but a descent down the leagues wasn't for me — you can love the game and still walk away from it. I wouldn't have lacked motivation, as white-line fever would have compelled me to want to win as soon as I got on to the pitch, yet the player trotting out would not have been me and I didn't want fans paying to watch a team I was in and going away asking: 'Do you remember when he used to be good?' Instead, just after Everton had resumed pre-season training and I had given the knee one last chance in a series of lacklustre laps and kickabouts, I rang the PFA and asked them about the procedure for ending one's career. That's how I came to be sitting in Howard's office as the corks popped, getting pleasantly out of it as I signed an agreement with the club to terminate my contract.

The wine had its usual effect and we carried on drinking late into the night at a testimonial dinner before I went home to be hit by the full repercussions of my decision the following morning. It was then that I found I'd lost my brave face. I must have spent hours there weeping, but nothing was resolved by the time Julie finally coaxed me out of bed. For a while at least, it remained our secret and it was not until I was approached by a reporter in Northern Ireland a few days later that the story broke. I'd been running summer soccer schools outside Belfast with my friend Peter McBurney for about four years and I was in the middle of an exercise when I noticed the journalist on the touchline. When I finished up and went over to talk to him and was asked to confirm the rumour that he had heard, I remember watching our daughter Della toddling about so cheerfully after a ball as I began to speak. It was an unsettling reminder of how carefree I myself had been before the burden of injury had consumed me entirely. Maybe I looked a bit wobbly, I don't know, but I was aware that Julie came closer to us, perhaps to show that Whiteside had been forced to give up one team, but retained the support of the only one that counted.

My wife says she was fighting back the tears when the words came out of my mouth that, reluctantly, yes, I had retired from professional football. I was obviously downbeat, but tried to explain as dispassionately as I could the medical reasons and the long months of agonising over the decision. The way it was written up hinted at regret, but he was sympathetic and conveyed the sense, I think, that it was the mature thing to do and was a sober (ha!) acceptance of the inevitable. I can't say that telling the press made it any more real, because I hadn't been in denial about it for ages. If anything it cranked up the fear as it became clear to me that the period between us knowing and the world being informed that I had now finished was the only opportunity I would have to indulge my unhappiness, anger and confusion. My pride meant that I had to show that I could pick up the pieces. The only problem I had was that I still didn't have a clue how I was going to do it and, even more pressingly, what on earth I was going to do for money until the insurance pay-out was finalised.

I realise now that I had been preparing subconsciously for the end for quite some time. Each spring, I had made sure that I applied for some course or other to fill up time in the close season and by 1991 I had been through the Football Association centre at Lilleshall three times to pick up my coaching diploma and my A and B coaching badges. Partly, of course, it was merely commonsense to assume that my career wouldn't last and, moreover, I had been told by United's physiotherapist, Jim McGregor, not to expect a long career shortly after the 1985 FA Cup final. At the time I had thought it was a bizarre thing to say to a twenty-year-old, but my desire to pick up qualifications while still playing indicates that his warning must have registered. There was also the fact that players of my generation always took it for granted that we would have to work once we had stopped playing, so I always knew that the day would come when I would have to do something else for a living. But all the groundwork you do and the bravado and bluster you adopt down the pub about the transience of your career doesn't make you feel any better when that dreaded day dawns.

As I racked my brains to come up with a solution, it didn't take me long to dismiss the thought of going into coaching full time. Although I had passed the right exams and did not doubt I had the skills required to do it, I was far from convinced that I had the right character. I'm all right with kids and enjoy working with them, honing their development, but I was not so sure then that I had the patience to coach more senior players. I am certain of that now. Communication can be difficult for me because football came so naturally. It's like the game is my native tongue, something I'm fluent in, a knowledge I take for granted. However many coaching qualifications I had managed to accrue to put some sparkle on my CV, I still found it hard to help manufacture players who did not have the innate ability or instinctive grasp of how to play that I was used to. Technically, I know what to do to put on a high-quality, functional training session, but I become frustrated too easily by the exhaustive and repetitive drills some professional players need to improve their game in painfully small instalments. I admire enormously those who have the patience for it, but I knew myself well enough to understand that this tantalising prospect of being able to stay in football, if I had asked any of my former team-mates now in management to do me a favour, could not have provided a long-term future of fulfilment.

The more pressing the requirement to make a decision became, the more troubled I felt, but, looking back, I am quite proud that I was never so desperate that I clutched at the straw offered by coaching. Sure, it would have given me a way out, but I'm glad I recognised that I was temperamentally unsuitable for it. However, knowing what you don't want to do is not the same thing as knowing what you do want to do. All you're really doing is narrowing your options, hoping that you'll be left with one that leaps out at you and says, 'Follow me to the rest of your life.' I couldn't see myself going down the stock post-career route of opening my own business — a pub or a shop — and carving a career in the media pre-BSkyB was rarer than a Frenchman's steak. No, the more I ruled things out, the more I felt backed into a corner, scared to make the wrong decision that would define my life for the next forty years.

So I found myself asking the question, 'What do I do if I've got nowhere to go today?' The answer seemed to be to stay at home, play with my two-year-old daughter and go back to bed at regular intervals. Perhaps it was depression, I don't know, but it seems more like shock and profound disappointment. Left to my own devices, I would have come through it eventually, I am sure, but I have to give enormous credit to Julie, who was suffering with her own feelings of loss and trepidation, for snapping me out of it. At first, she sat at the end of the bed and just listened, but in time she began to ask a series of gently probing questions. Not how are we going to pay the mortgage but did I want to stay in the game? How could I achieve that? What areas was I specifically interested in? What path would we need to take to get to where I wanted to be in five years' time? And when I kept coming back to the same things, that I did indeed want to stay in football if possible and that my long track record of injuries and rehabilitation and the thousands of hours I had spent chatting with Jim McGregor and Everton's physio, Les Helm, had sparked a curiosity about the medical side that far outstripped my interest in theory and tactics, my once-muddled mind at last became focused. 'Right,' she said after weeks of conversation, 'it's up to you to go and do something about it.'

What I did, in many ways, was the hardest thing I've ever done. I had never been fazed by any challenge that football threw up: play against Brazil in the World Cup; walk out in front of a crowd of 100,000; try to stop Diego Maradona going past you; take on the League champions in extra-time of the FA Cup final when you've got ten men and score the winning goal; kick the Kop's favourite son at Anfield and have 50,000 Liverpool fans advocating your execution; or face an enraged Sir Alex Ferguson the morning after a bender when he's had hours to digest the intelligence brief he's got from United's army of spies around the Cheshire pub circuit. All these things I had done and they were a doddle compared to taking the first steps towards a new life, because I felt at home in a football environment and had always been confident my ability would cash the cheques my instinct wrote. Now, however, I was heading into the unknown. When all I'd experienced before was bounding uncannily quickly from one stage to the next – landing an apprenticeship, First Division debut and World Cup all in the space of twelve months – it was baby steps from here on in.

I had been such a regular patient and inhabitant of Jimmy McGregor's physiotherapy room that one of the ways I fought boredom was to take a keen interest in my treatment. Because, disastrously, I had once ceded control of my rehabilitation to someone whose 'cure' I had cause to regret, ever since I was sixteen I had demanded some input into my care. The only way I could stop being bamboozled by Latin tags and becoming a passive object on which the doctors could practise their expertise was to learn as much as I could about what was happening to me. Jim played a vital role in this, first by explaining properly, then, picking up on my interest and concern, setting me home-work. Whenever I was out for a few weeks, I'd go home each night after the remedial work with anatomical diagrams showing the muscles, tendons and bones and their physiological function. I found it fascinating and was always ready for Jim's quiz the following morning. Unwittingly, by trying to relieve the tedium of one of his charges with his characteristic good humour and kindness, Jim had given me something to latch on to in my darkest moment. If playing was ruled out for phys-ical reasons and coaching for temperamental ones, there were only intellectual paths left to take and, as unlikely as it may sound, physiotherapy offered the hope of giving me a stimu-lating second chance in football. If I wasn't exactly the lame man throwing away his crutches and dancing a double jig when my future path became clear to me, I did at last get out of bed with the sense of purpose that had been mislaid for far too long.

Before I could even dream about doing the degree course that would enable me to pursue my new-found ambition, however, I had to go back to school, since, a cupboard full of cups and medals apart, I had nothing to show for my previous brush with education. It was the physical act, in September 1991, of going for the first time into a classroom packed with fifteen-year-old students that made me realise how my life had changed. Although the average international footballer's lifestyle fifteen years ago was nothing like as luxurious as it is today, I have to admit that we were still remarkably pampered. I don't mean that we couldn't do anything for ourselves, just that we were used to being mollycoddled. This went from the basic stuff like not having to bother with tickets and passports if we were going abroad, as these would be looked after by the club, to the frankly ridiculous custom that when we got out of the bath at Old Trafford after a match we wouldn't have to dry ourselves off, as one of the attendants would take care of towelling us down. Of course I could survive without any of that, but it is an example of the culture shock I faced when I left behind a decade spent with two of the so-called 'Big Five' clubs and six weeks later walked through a door marked 'GCSE English' at South Trafford College.

Mature students are generally pretty conspicuous among a group of kids in their mid-teens anyway, but imagine what it was like for me in a United-mad area. I was already pretty raw and sticking out like the proverbial sore thumb hardly helped matters. Starting again was the toughest thing I've ever done and I found that the constant recognition was by far the most difficult part. Fame sticks to you long after you've finished doing what brought it in the first place and on many occasions it gives you a lovely warm feeling when people come up to you and tell you what you've meant to them. But at other times, and in college especially, fame stripped of the purpose that endowed it on you is like the Emperor's new clothes: everyone's staring at you and you're stark naked. On my first day, my class-mates started nudging each other and gradually their murmured questions grew increasingly audible. 'Is that Norman Whiteside?' 'Surely not?' 'It is, you know.' It made me uneasy, so I furiously leafed through my course notes, trying to mask my anxiety, a case of 'Please stop gawping. I'm just like you. I'm not a celebrity.'

The following week it became even more excruciating when students from other classes started to gather outside our door, peering in through the glass porthole, making me feel like a goldfish in a bowl. I couldn't wait to escape for lunch, when I'd meet up with Julie and Della or sometimes just hide in the car to get away from people for an hour. That period didn't last long though, and while I never truly blended in, since I was more than a decade older than the others, I grew less uncomfortable as I became a more familiar face around the place. Some students would bring in photos for me to sign and I was still conscious of being watched all the time, and that may have gone on for the whole year if I hadn't been given the opportunity to deal with all the unspoken curiosity once and for all.

I couldn't resist the open goal laid on for me by the teacher when we were all asked to give a talk about a special day in our lives. I strolled to the front of the class, sat down on the large desk in front of the blackboard to face everyone and said, 'A special day? OK, let's talk about the FA Cup final.' For weeks I had turned up to each of my classes with a sort of dread about the constant scrutiny I was placed under, which turned every mundane thing into an object for comment: 'Look, he's sharpening his pencil now.' That day, like so many before it, I turned to football to break down the barriers. As ever, it did not let me down.

CHAPTER TWO

BELFAST CHILD

When you tell people you come from the Shankill Road, it doesn't take long before you have to correct some pretty ingrained and usually false preconceived ideas. The first, that your home was on the actual street, is harmless enough and easily explained – the Shankill encompasses the road itself and the scores of tight back streets and housing developments that have sprouted around it over the last century and a half.

Those who have never visited it tend to think of it in *News at Ten* terms: that it's the loyalist capital, somehow separate from the rest of Belfast. But geographically (at least) it is not remote

— only a few minutes' brisk walk from the city centre and bordered on both sides by the Catholic communities that live on the estates and streets that have gathered around the Falls and Crumlin Roads. The layout of the three areas is very characteristic of West Belfast; the heart of the communities are the main thoroughfares which give them their names and a lot of residents, such as my parents, never feel entirely comfortable away from them and stick close by in those roads' arterial offshoots.

When I was growing up, the Shankill was home to 75,000 people, a figure that has fallen by two-thirds in the years since I left. Industrial decline and the economic deprivation that came in its wake, twenty-five years of the Troubles and the last five years, with the murderous turf war between the Ulster Volunteer Force and the Ulster Freedom Fighters, have left my birthplace a shadow of its former self.

Back then, though, there was virtually full employment, with the men going off to work at those great Belfast enterprises — Harland & Wolff shipyards, Mackies Metal Works, Shorts, the aircraft manufacturer, and Gallahers' cigarette factory in York Street. It was a vibrant, hardworking, proud, solid, loyal workforce that left the Shankill each morning, and though, of course, it was not at all culturally or religiously integrated, it was wholly integrated socially. There was a communal element to everything the residents did: everyone knew each other because they travelled together, worked together, ate together, drank together in the numerous bars and clubs and trooped off to watch Linfield together after their Saturday morning shifts. It felt very much like a village.

However, when I go back now and talk to people, I cannot help but notice the effects of thirty-five years of turmoil. There is a sense that they are an entrenched, embattled people who have been let down by everybody. You have long-term unemployment, thirty-year-old grandparents and a couple of generations that have lived their whole lives in the presence of terrorism, violence and drugs. As Baroness Blood, who has lived all her life there, says, 'From my experience on the ground, there is a growing lawlessness. Young people are growing up thinking they can do whatever they want.' I am often told that I was lucky to 'escape' when I did. But I have never thought that. The Shankill of the late seventies was not the place it later became. In fact, I think I was only lucky in being born when I was and not twenty years later and that my parents and their values gave me and my two brothers the foundations to be successful; opportunities many kids there today may cruelly never have.

My parents, Norman and Aileen, met at a dance in 1960, were married two years later and had me, their second son, in 1965, two years after the birth of my brother Ken. It was far more usual in Protestant working-class families for the first-born to get the honour of being given his father's Christian name and my mother had wanted to abide by that tradition with Ken, but my dad overruled her and gave him instead his own brother's name. He had been concerned that his son would be stuck in the supporting role of the double act of 'Big Norman' and 'Wee Norman', but by the time I came along my mum was adamant and marched off down to the registrar to award me Da's name.

I've always liked it, but the fact that it was so uncommon,

even then, used to distress me on a daily basis when tormented by the otherwise saintly Miss Adrienne of Ulster TV's *Romper Room*. That programme was a pre-school childhood ritual for most kids in Northern Ireland and had a similar format to the BBC's *Play School*. In one section of the show the host would hold up a mirror and say some names – for example, 'Today I can see Tom and Mary and Annie and Gerry.' I'd have my dinner, then race to sit in front of the set every afternoon, confident that today would be the day she would see me, but in all the years I watched it she never once said 'Norman'.

It didn't take long for disappointment to turn into frustration and eventually rage. Years later, when I was ten, I vowed to stop swearing and cursing, but back then I was as foul-mouthed a child as you could wish to meet and I would stomp around the room, creating and carrying on like Rumpelstiltskin in a right paddy, screaming, 'Can't you effing see Norman?' That would earn me a slap from my mother and I'd run off and hide behind the chair, with tears of indignation at the injustice of stupid, effing *Romper Room* streaming down my cheeks. The next day I'd be back in my spot, full of hope. My poor ma told me she used to feel so sorry for me that each morning she would pray for Adrienne to say it, but her magic mirror remained a Norman-free zone and I was left to pound the floorboards and slam doors like a rowdy, tiny troll until I was old enough to go to school, which I'm sure couldn't come quick enough for my mum. There is no doubt I was stubborn, wilful and quite difficult to handle which caused my mum no end of trouble. I remember when we lived on the Glencairn estate on the Upper Shankill and my ma, with the identically dressed Ken and me in tow, caught a bus to visit my granny. When the conductor came round and my mother asked for 'one and a half' she must have been mortified when I was pointed at and she was asked, 'What about him?' Given that I was hooked on a tapeworm-friendly diet of sugar butties and jam fritters and resembled a short Billy Bunter, my size probably gave me away, but my mum said, 'Ach, no. He's not three yet.'

We spend the whole of our adult lives being flattered if thought younger than we actually are, but as children we take grave offence for some reason and I was no different. The slur of being thought two years old set me off. 'I am!' I yelled. 'I'm effing four.' My mum must have been terribly embarrassed, as she had to get another coin from her purse then walk us home from my grandmother's as my crude outburst meant we couldn't afford the bus fare back. I can only say that my reaction, like the *Romper Room* episodes, stemmed from some notion of unfairness. I didn't think it right that the conductor might think I, a big boy, was only a baby.

God knows why it mattered, but when I heard that my next-door neighbour, Charles, who had been born two months before me in March 1965, would be going to school in September 1969, but those born in May were to be held back until 1970, it provoked the same extreme response. I stormed straight over to confront him. 'I'm bigger than you,' I said with a four-year-old's logic. 'How can you go to school and not me? It's not fair.' To emphasise the point, I whacked him with a stone, but as soon as I did it I knew I'd gone too far so I decided to run away from home. Unfortunately, my ma was too quick for me and she chased me all over the Glencairn until she caught me and gave me the hiding of my life.

By the time I made it to school we had moved south to Danube Street, to a house opposite my granny's. They say the middle child of three often has a very close relationship with his grandparents and it must have been around this time, when the baby of the family, Hughie, was born, that I started to spend some nights keeping my grandmother company. I was aware that she must be lonely living alone and I would tend to sleep there so she wouldn't have to wake up in an empty house. We grew very close, Granny and I, and she would back me up in whatever I did and fought my corner when my ma had grown exasperated with my behaviour.

There is a stream that runs behind my old primary school, Edenbrooke, and one of our gang's regular dares ordered you to try to leap over it. Time and again I tried to jump it and usually ended up sprawled short of the far bank and wet through. I knew my ma would have given me a telling off for being so careless, so I used to hole up at my granny's, with my clothes wrung out and steaming in front of the fire while I munched my way through a packet of crisps or the bag of broken biscuits she used to like as a cut-price treat. She never once let on to my parents that I'd been so stupid, just patched me up and smothered me in affection.

It was a dreadful shock then, when, aged nine, following my normal routine, I went into her room one morning to say, 'Goodbye, Granny, I'm going over the road now to get ready for school' and she made no response. I thought it odd but was not particularly concerned. When I went to fetch my mother, however, she went over and found Gran had died during the night. It was a terrible blow to me, the grandchild she had doted on, and even back then at such a young age I remember feeling not so much grief but a sense of injustice about it. She was fifty-four, frighteningly young, but not outrageously so for Belfast in the early seventies, where life expectancy because of the diet and working and living conditions was alarmingly low. Indeed, her husband had died just after he turned fifty and I know it's one of my ma's biggest regrets that her father, who used to call me 'Second-hand Rose' because I was normally dressed in Our Ken's hand-me-downs, did not live to see how 'Rose' bloomed.

Our place at 10 Danube Street was typical of the thousands of dilapidated terrace houses that endured on the Shankill until finally they were subject to compulsory purchase orders, condemned and demolished in the late 1970s. By that time, they had been left largely untouched by landlords since the thirties and most, like ours, were damp, cold and overrun by mice. They had been built in the late Victorian age on the classic two-up, two-down model, with a kitchen and 'parlour' down-stairs, two bedrooms upstairs and an outside toilet in the small yard where my dad sometimes used to hide in the alleyway by the coalhole to jump out and terrify us if we had to use the bog when it was dark.

Long before stories about footballers' three-in-a-bed adven-tures hit the headlines I had spent much of my childhood in that night-time formation, sharing a double bed with my two brothers, always hopeful of bagging the shallow end to escape a soaking from the phantom bed-wetter. In the mornings when we got up to get ready for school we would have to shake our shoes out by knocking them on the bed-posts, to make sure there weren't any rodents nesting there before we put them on.

When I finally got to primary school, a year late in my view, my major disappointment was that there was no football other than the kickabouts we would have before the morning bell, at break time and again at 4 o'clock. My form teacher, Heather Mulligan, specialised in PE and took a keen interest in this ball-mad lump and she remembers me constantly edging towards the door at the end of lessons, itching to get outside and play again. When I went back to college at the age of twenty-six to resume my education, it dawned on me how little attention I'd paid during lessons. I had been so obsessed with the game from such an early age that I didn't have time for much else.

Mind you, one of the teachers at primary school, Mrs Caters, handed out such strange punishments that I am surprised she didn't petrify me into taking more heed of what she was trying to make us learn. If you were caught talking or daydreaming or even making mistakes, she had three ways of disciplining you. The first and most severe was a stick like a sergeant-major's baton that she called 'Sam Stinger' and which she used to whack your behind with. The second was a sort of strap with a hook on the end called 'Willy Wobbler', with which you'd have your knuckles rapped. The third, the gentlest but oddest of all, was the instruction to sit beneath her desk and play 'Mousey, Mousey', which entailed running your fingers up and down her stockinged legs from ankle to mid-thigh for several minutes while she continued with the class. If you refused the 'Mousey, Mousey' option then 'Willy' and 'Sam' would come into play. It took us some years to realise how dodgy this was, an old lady getting small children to tickle her. Perhaps it is small wonder that after this 'education' I ended up all these years on with a career specialising in feet and legs!

Ironically, although it has become a more dangerous place, there are far more leisure facilities available for the children of the Shankill now than when I was a boy. The back streets were our playgrounds where, of course, we'd play football most of the time, but apart from that we would get up to all sorts of mischief, usually the result of dares. Lead would be pilfered from roofs, then we'd carefully wrap bricks in the proceeds of our crimes and try to con the scrapyard men to pay us according to its enhanced weight, but they were never fooled. The other big thing was the painstaking preparation of enormous pyres for bonfire night, which in Northern Ireland falls not on 5 November but on 11 July, the day before the public holiday to commemorate the Battle of the Boyne that marks the opening of the marching season.

In the days leading up to bonfire night there would be a scramble for wood, as the kids from each street attempted to build the most impressive bonfire. The tradition was that the hardest kid in the street would be leader and he would deploy the rest of us: some would go off to find original pieces of 'bony wood', others sent to steal odd bits of old furniture from neighbouring streets' fires and the remainder left to guard our stock.

In Danube Street, the leader was Michael York and when he and Our Ken had a falling out, he ended up knocking lumps out of my older brother. When I heard about it I tracked him down and, despite the age gap, kicked seven bells out of him in my hobnailed boots. In the dog-eat-dog system, that made me the boss and from then on I gave out the orders. The night before we lit the fire the custom was that the boys would sit up outside in dens all night, nattering and acting as watchmen. My parents never let us out after dark, yet for once they relented after hours of nagging. I later learned that my ma spent the whole night keeping her eyes trained on us from the parlour window so we didn't come to any harm.

And in that story lies the answer to a question I'm frequently asked: how come my parents managed to raise three boys on the Shankill at the height of the Troubles and not one of us got involved in or touched by criminal or paramilitary activities like so many of our contemporaries? Mum and Dad were not overtly religious, not political and shielded us from it entirely. We lived in the Shankill and stayed in our enclave almost exclusively as we felt safe there. We never crossed boundaries to venture into other parts of the city until we were much older and even then the warnings drilled into us about how careful we had to be were ringing in our ears until the moment we got home.

Though not even involved in legitimate institutions such as the Presbyterian Church, Unionist parties, the Orange Order or Apprentice Boys, Ma and Da are, nonetheless, Protestant to their bootstraps. That is certainly how they identify themselves and they know just about everyone of a certain age that lives on the Shankill. They have a great deal of solidarity with and loyalty to their neighbours. You could see that communal strength during the 1974 strike, called by the Ulster Workers' Council in protest at the Sunningdale Agreement, when the whole of the Shankill stayed out for a fortnight. Adults who went through both say it had the same atmosphere as what they had experienced during the Second World War, when Belfast suffered repeated air-raids. I was only nine and remember the strike mostly for having to go to the church halls to pick up tinned food and cooking our hand-outs on open fires in the backyard as the power had been cut off.

The paramilitary groups that enforced that strike and the organisation that became known as 'the enemy beyond', the Provisional IRA, however, were never mentioned in our house. Yes, we were aware they existed and later we occasionally had to abandon school when we'd hear an explosion and rush home to lock ourselves in. It was frightening, but there was a strange normality to these occurrences. When it's all you've ever known from such a young age you don't find it particularly unusual, so long as it does not impact on your family directly. Our view was it had nothing to do with us and whatever happened was not done in our name. We didn't know what the paramilitaries were up to and we did not want to know.

The one time it came close to the family was when my father was working at painting and decorating on the night shift, and he came home in the early morning, woke my ma and told her that he had been held up. She thought he meant that he had been delayed by traffic and told him to be quiet and get into bed, but he soon corrected her. He had been held up at gunpoint by an armed gang robbing the premises and he had genuinely thought he would be shot and that he would never see his family again. It shook him badly and we sometimes wonder if his nerves ever properly recovered.

Some English people I know have the idea that what happened in Northern Ireland when I was a boy happened to all the people equally and we were all used to it. But it was not like that at all, so when your family was affected it was just as horrifying as it would have been for any family in other parts of Britain. Despite the shorter odds of it happening to us, there was still a deep sense of shock. All the news bulletins in the world cannot prepare a child for something like that.

Consequently, we were kept close to home and were never allowed to go out and roam about at night like many other kids. The summer schools and Boys' Brigade battalion we enrolled in, therefore, must have been a godsend to my parents, as they helped to keep us occupied during the evenings and holidays. The Boys' Brigade, in particular, was to play a pivotal role in my life, as it was during my time in the 72nd Battalion that I was first introduced to organised football. When I was seven, I simply walked across the yard from our house to the church which backed on to it and joined Our Ken as an 'anchor' in the first section of the Brigade.

I would go there, proudly dressed in my Thunderbirds hat and uniform, on Thursdays to drill and sing our anthem, 'Will Your Anchor Hold', on Saturdays for football and on Sundays for religious classes. At first, I only went to the Sunday school because I needed to be there to get my stamp for attendance, but later I enjoyed a brief devout phase when I joined our neighbours, what my ma would call 'good-living people', who held regular prayer sessions in their home. It was there that I vowed to stop cursing and in the thirty-odd years since I have stuck to that pledge. I was so determined to live the right way that I even forsook the 'bony wood' hunt one year and spent it at my neighbours' house reading the bible. Sometimes, in the summer, our little group would go down to the beach at Helen's

Bay, near Bangor, have a barbecue, pray and sing gospel songs. My interest in religion didn't last all that long, but I think it did change me for the better by teaching me self-discipline and curbing those childhood rude tirades.

But it was football that changed me even more profoundly. Because all you really need is a ball, the game was the cheapest way to enjoy yourself on the back streets of Belfast and I became obsessed with it as soon as Our Ken let me join in. My elder brother had exceptional talent as a kid and there are those on the Shankill who will still tell you that he had what it took to make it as a professional. But his choice of secondary school, the Boys Model, while benefiting him academically, played rugby and he gradually drifted away from the game.

I played all the time in the streets, from pre-breakfast games of three-and-in with my brothers to full-scale twilit matches with hordes of kids. I've never really been one for tricks and to this day when I'm coaching kids I'm forever telling them to concentrate on becoming the best passer rather than a prodigy who can juggle the ball from shoulder to shoulder, but back then I was so competitive that if a neighbour could do 300 keepy-uppies I'd practise relentlessly until I could set a record no one could better.

As I've said it wasn't until I joined the Boys' Brigade that I discovered the joys of grass, pitch-markings, goals and nets. Organised football was such a rarity that the knowledge that it was available at the Brigade was, I think, the most persuasive piece of advertising ever inflicted upon me. I couldn't wait to sign up and within days I was turning out for the C team in my first proper match. It took only a few weeks of regular goal-scoring to become a first-team regular at the age of seven playing alongside the eleven-year-olds.

By the time I was ten, I had scored countless goals, each one of them giving me that familiar adrenaline rush that led to a perfect sense of pleasure and fulfilment. I don't mean to sound boastful, but they used to just give me the ball from the kick-off and I could dribble it up the pitch and, often as not, score. As soon as I'd racked up ten goals in a game, Eddie Cooke, our coach, would say, 'That's enough now, Norman,' and make me go and play in defence, to save him from embarrassment. Eddie was reluctant to take me to a Brigade tournament in Lancashire in 1975 because they felt I was too young – not for the matches, but for the trip itself. He changed his mind when he saw how upset I was, though. I rewarded him with a hat-trick in the first five minutes of our opening match, which made him substitute me to spare a rout and not disgrace his opposite number.

In the next game, I scored six against a Manchester battalion. If you have a picture of me at seventeen in your head, what the press called the 'man-boy', I can imagine how you would think my size gave me a huge advantage throughout junior football. Yes, I was big for my age, stronger, taller and broader than my class-mates, but I was always playing with and against older boys so it wasn't as beneficial as it might seem. What gave me an edge was that, in addition to a decent technique honed in the Danube Street Theatre of Dreams, I was searingly quick. It might amuse some of you who have heard managers bemoaning my lack of speed or read journalists who have portrayed me as 'lumbering' into tackles, but before the age of fourteen I was a sprint champion and could not be caught by any schoolboy defender from a standing start. I also had the quality which allowed me to flourish when speed had long since abandoned me: the instinctive ability to read the game and know at any given point where players were, our side's and the opposition's, and what they were likely to do. It was these attributes that led Eddie Cooke to start telling people of my potential and it wasn't long before I was being seduced by a number of secondary schools who wanted to recruit the 100-goals-a-season kid.

When I went to the World Cup in 1982, it was said that it must have been very hard for me to cope with all the scrutiny that arose from my instantaneous fame, particularly so for a seventeen-year-old. And they were right, to a certain extent, but only in terms of scale because, and I don't want to sound like Billy Big Time, 'Smiley Whiteside', as they called me, had been 'famous' from the age of eleven, at least within my own community. Daft though it may seem, when you're eleven, if the Shankill's your world, you are world famous if you are famous on the Shankill. And by the time I came to leave Edenbrooke I had the pick of the Protestant schools in Belfast. As exams were hardly the priority, I chose the nearest one to home with a decent football team, opting for Cairnmartin, while my brothers decided on the better education but a misshaped ball.

It wasn't a bad school, but I did get away with doing very little work. Other kids used to turn up with a bag full of books, but by the end of my time there I would simply stuff a jotter in my blazer pocket every morning and bash one of my classmates over the head with it to get them to do my homework.

Because of the goals I scored and the progress I had begun to make in football, they still wanted me to be head boy, but I didn't fancy the idea of the responsibility nor, ironically given how I make my living today, the prospect of having to make speeches.

My first year was marked by a century of goals for Cairnmartin alone in our after-school matches which clinched the school's first ever Belfast double of League and Cup, and I couldn't tell you how many on top of that I scored for the Brigade on Saturday mornings or my other team, Clara Boys, on Saturday afternoons. Three full matches a week, and two in one day, for an eleven-year-old would seem like madness now, but my appetite for the game carried me through that heavy schedule until I left the Boys' Brigade. In my last years with Clara Boys, who were based in Templemore Avenue, the club changed its name and affiliation to East Belfast Liverpool Supporters' Club. If only they'd known at Anfield, when booing my every touch, that once I had been one of them, although in name alone. Well, anything for a game in those days!

We went one better than our usual city dominance when I led the school to the treble in my last year there – Belfast League and Cup and Irish Cup. We won the latter Cup final 7–2, but, by scoring six goals, I enraged a member of the opposition, who belted me. Knowing that I'd get sent off if I retaliated, Our Ken, a touchline spectator, ran on to the pitch and chinned my assailant. In the newspaper report of the game they mentioned that 'a thug ran on the pitch'. That thug, my brother, spent almost twenty years as a police officer! Punch-ups, though, weren't all that rare. We only ever met Catholic schools in cup competitions and almost always there would be someone on either side who would want to start something during those games. Sometimes Cairnmartin would turn up looking like the toe-rags some of our number were – no boots, borrowed shorts, odd socks. I remember one lad, who was wearing Doc Martens boots, sizing up the opposition before kick-off and shouting, 'We can't play football, but we can fight.' That was the attitude.

I started playing for the Northern Ireland schoolboy side while I was in my second year at school and the national team's training sessions, on Monday evenings and Wednesday afternoons, forced me to regularly leave the safety of the Shankill for the first time. I had to get a bus into town from school, change at City Hall and get another one out to East Belfast to meet up with the other boys in the gym. But on the way back there were more buses that went up the Crumlin Road, adjacent to the Shankill, so I usually ended up going that way, as the stops there were actually closer to our house.

Protestants and Catholics on the Shankill, Crumlin and Falls lived totally apart from one another, even though all three are linked by interconnecting streets. Because of the segregation, you could tell the religion of a person on that bus journey by which stop he got off at. This could cause problems. If you were to avoid a kicking after the first few stops on the (Catholic) start of the road by a Catholic youth who was staying on the bus as it went on to Ardoyne, you had to be very canny about how you got the bus to stop at any of the three stops which led towards the Shankill. The last thing you would do is stand up a good distance before your stop, pressing the bell and thereby announcing your religion. The best you could hope for then would be a kick up the backside to help you towards the pavement. The preferred option was to wait for someone else to press it then nip off in their slipstream, but if you were the only one needing to use your stop you had to wait until the last minute, whistling and trying to look cool, before hitting the buzzer and racing off.

That was the closest I ever came as a child to sectarian violence: the odd nutter on the pitch and a weekly bus journey that had me playing Russian roulette with the bell. It's happened since, most notably in Dublin when I was sitting at a bar and was attacked by an idiot with a chair. There was verbal abuse, too, in Belfast and, just after the 1982 World Cup, in the Republic again, at Dalymount Park in a 'friendly' for United against Bohemians, when I was pelted with oranges and repeatedly called an 'Orange bastard' while I warmed up as a substitute. I took it all with a pinch of salt. You have to be bigger and better than loudmouths with minute brains.

I have never been bigoted about religion and, as you will see, married a Catholic girl, but there have been times when the very place I come from, and I am a proud Shankill man, has led people to believe I epitomise a certain kind of Protestant Ulsterman. And never more so than the time my friends and team-mates Paul McGrath and Kevin Moran, both Catholics, talked me into going to see the staunchly republican band, the Wolfe Tones, at a concert in Manchester with them. Paul paints a cosy picture of that night in his book, but it was far from the evening of respectful banter he remembers. Of course it was all rebel songs and the room was full of republicans, as I'd expected, but as the drink went down I became more and more aware that, for some of the band's fans, I was about as welcome as, well, a Shankill Road Protestant at a Wolfe Tones gig. When I went to the toilet, a few of the punters tried to rough me up, jostling around me and telling me they 'knew where I came from and where I lived'. A word from Kevin and it was all sorted and I had bouncers protecting me for the rest of the night, but it was a bleak reminder that for some people the quickest way over the religious divide is head first with a threat and an outstretched fist.

I suppose it was no different to the Crumlin Road bus journey: make the wrong move at the wrong time and you could be in real trouble. Bombings and shootings could be quite random and nothing could protect you from them, but I do think those of us who grew up in Belfast in the seventies developed an acute awareness of the lower-level risks that helped to keep us safe. Fortunately, I always made it off the bus unscathed, and only a few months after my debut for Northern Ireland schoolboys I was swapping the double-decker for an aeroplane to England in the care of a seventy-eight-year-old toothless man in a battered hat who had recently knocked on my ma's front door.

CHAPTER THREE

BOY WONDER

Seventeen years after Manchester United's Northern Ireland scout had first sat drinking tea with Dick and Anne Best in their kitchen on the Cregagh estate in East Belfast, Bob Bishop rapped on the door of our house at 10 Danube Street. I sincerely doubt he worded his telegram to Dave Sexton in 1978 in identical fashion to the famous one that he had sent to Matt Busby in 1961, 'Chief scout stop I think I have found a genius,' but he did seem genuinely gutted to find that he wasn't my first and only suitor.

That had been Jim Rogers from Ipswich Town, who had beaten Bob by a year. Town's boss, Bobby Robson, had felt that

a twelve-year-old was too young to be worth flying over to
Suffolk and had told the scout to bide his time for a year. In
one phone call to Rogers, the future England manager's reti-
cence ended an unlikely career path which may have made me
both a Tractor Boy and, who knows, a Canarybuster. So, though
Bob had been worried that he hadn't been as quick on his feet
as he had with the likes of Bestie, Sammy McIlroy, Jimmy
Nicholl and Dave McCreery, he was still pretty nimble for a
man pushing eighty and he was the first of the scores of scouts
who had been watching me play to offer something concrete.

I was understandably thrilled to be given the opportunity to
go on trial at United, but it was not the culmination of my
long-held boyhood dreams, as it has normally been described.
I often say to myself now that I always wanted to play for the
club from a very early age, but in truth my ambitions then were
more practical. The first thing I wanted to do was play in a
proper match. Once I'd done that I wanted to score a goal,
then progress to the next team, then score a hat-trick, then play
for my school, be top goal-scorer, win a cup, then play for
Northern Ireland, get a schoolboy international goal, captain
the team and, finally, be a professional footballer. At every stage
when I was developing, my only focus was on the next thing I
had to achieve, not on the ultimate goal. And I had tunnel
vision – no girlfriend, no hobbies, no recreations such as discos
or the cinema. It was football, football, football.

Much to the surprise of supporters, most of us who end up
playing the game professionally do not share their experience
of being diehard fans of a particular club from a young age.
And it's not because you're a mercenary who wants to keep his

options open, you're just too busy playing, training and learning to passionately follow one team exclusively. So while my father and brothers were Manchester United through and through, they would probably tell you that my allegiance was a constantly moving thing and that I was a glory-seeking fan of anyone who was top of the League at any given point.

All that changed after my first trip to Old Trafford with Mr Bishop and I became as fanatical about the club as my family was, but as a kid it was not the romantic and sentimental standing of United in Northern Ireland that made me want to join them. If Ipswich had been bold enough to take the plunge, or Arsenal, or, whisper it, Liverpool, or if any First Division club, for that matter, had beaten Bob to the punch, flown me over and made a good impression, then I would probably have signed for them. All I wanted was to make it as a professional footballer. That I reached my target with United turned out to be a wonderful bonus but was not in itself my ambition.

Not that I was uninterested in watching live football, I was simply too busy playing. I always tried to catch *Match of the Day* on a Saturday night, but I never had posters or photographs of players torn out of *Match* or *Shoot!* on our bedroom wall. When I watched players I would look to see if there was anything I could pick up from their play, but I didn't really take notice in terms of looking up to them. It might sound cocky, but from about the time I got into the international schoolboys set-up I was so convinced that I wanted to play the game for a living and I was working so hard in making progress towards that end that I had already identified myself as being on the professionals' level. I had no aspirations or daydreams to be anyone other than myself.

When we filled in forms, part of the latest anti-terrorist drive, at Belfast International Airport before my first trip to Manchester in August 1978, I have never forgotten that Bob entered his year of birth as 1899. Never mind my granddad, he was old enough to be my great-grandfather, but he had such a sparkle and a gift for communicating with young footballers that it never felt as if you were dealing with an old man. His own story is remarkable. He was a riveter in the shipyards for over thirty years, and it was through running the works team and Boyland Youth Club that he first came to United's attention after the war. He joined the club's payroll, at Jimmy Murphy's invitation, when he was already fifty and stayed on it until he was in his nineties. If all he had done was spot George it would have been more than enough to justify forty years' employment, but he had such an eye for talent and such an extensive knowledge of the relatively small Northern Ireland pool that he came up trumps time and again.

Sitting next to him on the plane that took us to what the locals still called Ringway Airport, I remember how much of an improbable adventure it all seemed. It was my first flight and when I felt the thrust of the engines as we started down the runway I could have easily believed that I was bound for Mars. When we arrived and I met up with the other trialists at the Cliff, United's much-loved former training complex, Bob came into his own. He was like the Pied Piper of the place and all the kids from different parts of the United Kingdom would congregate around him in the evenings and first thing in the mornings and he would regale us with tales of 'Georgie', 'Sammy Mac' and 'Wee Dee McCreery'.

When the trials themselves got underway, conducted under the eye of my fellow Northern Irishman, the Munich hero Harry Gregg, who was a member of Dave Sexton's staff, Bob patrolled the touchline, a Woodbine permanently gripped between his lips, shouting out his own brand of encouragement. If you got kicked, he'd bark at you to get up: 'If your leg's broken, you'll soon fall down again.'

My first game took place on the Monday and by the time I left, a day early, on the Thursday, I had been pitted against better, older and stronger centre-halves as each day passed. Looking back, it was pretty obvious I'd done well. Every time the coaches tested me I came through it and scored goals and Harry subsequently told me that he and Sexton had liked what they had seen right from the start: the confidence, attitude and competitiveness which supported the ability that had earned me the opportunity. They even liked my skinhead haircut, as it gave the impression that I was no-nonsense and serious. In reality, it was the result of a part-time holiday job I'd taken back home on a coal delivery lorry. I had got my da to get his scissors out when I'd grown sick of trying to shift the coal dust out of my hair.

I suppose if I had been able to stay the full week they might have told me I had succeeded to my face. But, having only taken my first flight earlier that week, I had to leave the Cliff before everyone else to fly to Dublin to meet up with my class-mates and catch a jumbo jet to the United States. We were fortunate to be the beneficiaries of an American scheme to help deprived kids from Northern Ireland. It was an extraordinary experience and we were in awe of the place even before we landed. As the aircraft made its descent into Boston, I had the experience of something that's turned into a bit of an old chestnut for first-time visitors to America: being gobsmacked by the number of houses with swimming pools. There definitely weren't too many of those on the Shankill!

We were farmed out to host families for the duration of our month's stay in Boston and though I had little spending money, and it had been explicitly forbidden by our teachers, I just had to ring home to see if United had been in touch. I remember it was one of those old telephones where you had to repeatedly click the buttons on the transmitter to get through to the operator to make a reverse-charges call. Because of the cost, I only spoke long enough to learn that I had passed the trial and the club would be offering me associated schoolboy forms as soon as I reached the minimum age of fourteen. Even though it was likely to cost me a punishment for breaking the rule, I had to tell my friends and teachers. They seemed as excited as I was, the teachers probably more so, and I was let off my little misdemeanour.

The highlight of the trip was an invitation to Washington DC and a special presentation at the White House, where a group of us met the peanut farmer President, Jimmy Carter, in the Oval Office. I can't remember too much about what happened, apart from being relieved to wriggle out of having to make a speech of thanks on the school's behalf, but I do recall his bright-white smile. Football opens up a hell of a lot of doors for you and many players can become jaded by the places they visit and the people they meet. Not me, though. I loved all that and there can't be many better ways to start than to meet the President of the United States of America in his actual office.

On a more serious note, however, that holiday was the perfect preparation for what lay ahead. Being away from my family, essentially living in digs and having to cope in a foreign but familiar country for a month, made me realise that this is how my future would unfold: I'd be living away from home and I was confident that I would be OK. Homesickness never came into it. A few days previously I had won a chance of a professional career and here I was now with a practice run at the personal sacrifices I would have to make if it was to work out. That was when the life I have today really started.

From the moment we got home for the start of term in September until my fourteenth birthday in May 1979 most of my holidays were spent at the Cliff. I did give the club a wee scare days before I was eligible to sign forms when my ma rang them to say I had been contacted by Liverpool through the Saturday team I played for and that I was interested in going there on trial. I hadn't just said it to get United to commit to me, I *had* been approached, but it had that effect just the same and Joe Brown, the chief scout, flew straight over and dashed to our house from the airport in a taxi with the forms for my parents to sign.

I sometimes joke in my after-dinner speeches that when Joe left Danube Street we had a new cooker, telly and dishwasher, but it isn't true. In fact, my parents never sought a penny from the club, quite the opposite. Later, before I turned sixteen, when they were invited to accompany me over and had to take time off work, they never asked for the full compensation from United for lost pay, unlike certain other parents who would have the club believe they averaged six hours of double-rate overtime every day. No fortunes were made that day and, apart from the delight at signing the agreement, the most memorable thing was my sense of mischief when Joe Brown asked to go for a pee and I had to strongly resist the urge to point him to the grate in the yard, which was closer than the toilet.

It probably seems strange, given all I have said about my determination to become a professional and how I didn't really have any concerns about making the break from home, that I turned down United's offer to move to Manchester for the last couple of years of my education. But there didn't seem to be any point. There were a couple of other Northern Ireland schoolboy internationals in the same predicament: Dave Jeffrey, who now manages Linfield, and Alan McFaul, both of whom were a year older than me. Dave chose to fly in when needed, while Alan accepted the club's proposal and moved to a Manchester school. My ma would never have left the Shankill. In fact, when asked to do so by United and subsequently by me, she always said she wanted to stay at home, even though my brothers and father were fairly keen to try it. So I chose to carry on living in Danube Street and going to Cairnmartin, and the club, still mindful that they had almost had their fingers burnt when George Best bolted after only a week when he first went over, were happy enough to agree. Thirty-odd return air tickets a year and fifty or so nights in £10 digs was, it must be said, a small price for them to pay for my decision.

The arrangement worked very smoothly. Just before the end of each term, United would call me to confirm when I wanted to go over and, Christmas apart, I would be in Manchester from the first day of the holidays until the day before I had to go back to school. In addition, I went over there every weekend during the season: it was a simple routine of getting a taxi to the airport after the final lesson on Fridays, taking the thirty-minute flight, then being picked up in Manchester, sometimes by that great club servant, Jimmy Curran, who has been at United for decades as B-team manager, assistant physio, minibus driver and fixer in general. My lift would drop me at the digs and the following morning I'd play a match at the Cliff in the Lancashire League or away at Bellefield or Melwood or Bolton, watch the first team at Old Trafford in the afternoon or the reserves at the Cliff if the boys were away, and either sleep over in the city on Saturday night and fly home Sunday morning or fly back after fish and chips on the Saturday evening.

It was probably more fun doing it that way than moving over full time, as it turned every weekend into an adventure. It definitely gave me something to talk about at school on Mondays, even if the kids, by that age, were largely more interested in trying to appear cool than asking me for details. Some teachers were United crazy, however, and would overlook my failure to do any homework and badger me for all the insider gossip. In the end, I became such a regular face on the weekly flight that the pin-striped brigade eventually stopped giving funny looks to the skinhead in Dr Martens brogues and a duffel coat who unsettled them by walking on to the plane with his boots slung over his shoulder.

Those boots, by the way, were an example of how far my parents would go to back their children. With three boys to provide for, my ma and da lived pretty much hand to mouth and would buy expensive items, like footwear, on credit. My ma ran the local shoe club, which would collect the payments, a few pence a week to set against the fiver it cost in the early seventies to get all five of us shod. But when I needed proper boots to go to United for my trial she took me to the shop, where I chose a pair of Puma Kings. They were £25, a king's ransom in 1979, but even though they were five times the price of my previous pair, my ma just asked me if I was sure, then bought them without wincing once. Mind you, she often cracks that she's still paying the debt off now.

It wasn't only sacrifices for my ma and da, there were some treats too. When Northern Ireland qualified for the European Schoolboys Championship finals, which were held in Manchester in May 1979, my parents came over to support me and ended up being royally entertained in the hotel by Bob Bishop. One night he went out to dinner with my ma and da and ordered the steak, despite the fact that he had about as many teeth in his head as Albert Steptoe. Perhaps he intended to suck his way through it, but his gums made little headway and he had to admit defeat. Then his face lit up, as if he had been struck by a stroke of genius. He wrapped the meat in a napkin and put it in his pocket. Outside the restaurant he told my parents of his plan: it was too good to waste and his sister, back in Northern Ireland, would appreciate it. So he popped it in the postbox with the napkin as a makeshift envelope. The following morning, from our window in the hotel next door, we were in hysterics over the sight of the postman unlocking the box. A look of supreme disgust came over his face as he started kicking a greasy piece of meat down the gutter while swearing his head off. Bob found it as funny as well. He was such amusing company because he never acted his age and was always happy to play the joker.

We won the tournament, beating Wales 2–1 in the final, with me scoring the first and setting up the second goal. I know I played pretty well, but even I was surprised to see the following headline in the *Daily Mail* the day after the final and only a few weeks after my fourteenth birthday: 'Have United found the new Best at last?' I suppose it's a reflection of the long shadow cast over United by George's retirement five years before and the fans' prevailing sense of loss that the journalist, Derick Allsop, could get away with talking about a boy being the possible reincarnation of a man who was not only still very much alive but, at thirty-three years old, was at an age when other players were still in their prime. Looking back, that level of scrutiny should have unnerved me but while I do remember thinking that likening me to Best was absurd, I did not really feel any additional pressure. I wasn't even particularly flattered; all I wanted to do was show them the original Norman Whiteside, not an imitation of anyone else, no matter how legendary their gifts might have been. At fourteen my reaction would have been: 'Me? Georgie Best? Really? What's for breakfast?'

In a couple of years, Allsop's question had become a cliché and everything I did was compared to George, so much so that I had a Homer Simpson moment on television trying to play it down. 'The only thing I have in common with George Best,' I said, 'is that we come from the same place, play for the same club and were discovered by the same man.' I wasn't far short of a full house, but I had my reasoning: by then I understood that what the press and certain fans wanted was a saviour in George's mould, rather than just a hero. Fortunately, I was not alone: earlier Sammy McIlroy had endured the 'Best Mk II' label and later Ryan Giggs, David Beckham and Wayne Rooney have at some point in their careers been reduced to failures when measured up against George. It's a pointless pursuit with no winners, but one that seems to fascinate the press all the same. At fourteen, I was flippant about it, but had plenty of opportunities to have it sussed as a mug's game by the time it had become journalists' shorthand for 'promising Manchester United forward'.

On one of my holiday stints in England I was called up to play for the Northern Ireland Under-18 side in Scotland. Even before the match kicked off I was in a bad way with painful stomach cramps and resorted to guzzling Rennies from the physio's bag to calm it down. I don't know how I got through the game because at times I was bent double in agony and afterwards spent the whole night staring at the ceiling in our lodgings as I couldn't get to sleep. When I reported back to the Cliff the following morning, after an excruciating train journey south from Glasgow, I was fortunate that the club doctor, Francis McHugh, was on the premises and he promptly sped me off to the consulting rooms of his good friend and Manchester City director Sidney Rose, who had me admitted to hospital within forty-five minutes. He whipped my appendix out that afternoon. That was one of the major perks of being part of such a big club – any problem, medical, financial or even personal, would be sorted out very quickly and with no fuss.

I was stuck in hospital for a few days, recovering from what was a very painful operation and I was bowled over when Harry Gregg came to see me. The only problem with that was that he decided that laughter was the best medicine and he kept up this hilarious patter of jokes and insults all morning. Every time I chuckled it made me crease up in eye-watering torment and the drainage tube that was sticking out of my tummy would overflow with streams of poison from my gut. One afternoon I had a visit from the manager, Dave Sexton. He didn't really know me from Adam, but still took the trouble to come and sit at the end of my bed for a chat and bring me a gift of football magazines and annuals. I wasn't even an apprentice, just some schoolboy, but that shows the class of the man. It wasn't a PR stunt, he came out of kindness and, while I know it's something that Sir Alex Ferguson would do and does do, it wasn't normal behaviour in those days.

It was symptomatic of how friendly most people at the club were to me. If I ever saw Sir Matt Busby or his former assistant, Jimmy Murphy, around Old Trafford, they were wonderfully encouraging and complimentary. I wouldn't have thought they would have bothered giving someone potentially so insignificant the time of day, but whenever I bumped into them they would say, 'I hear you're doing well' and 'keep going', building me up all the time. Bob Bishop's other three graduates, Sammy, Dave McCreery and Jimmy Nicholl, also welcomed me wholeheartedly and invited me to join them for tea or for a chat if I felt lonely or had any problems they could help me with. Sammy gave me his Admiral United tracksuit during my first summer there and later, turning doctor, diagnosed the spots on my face one morning as impetigo. Instead of sending me off

to see the physio or Dr McHugh, the captain of Northern
Ireland popped down to the chemist himself to get a fourteen-
year-old boy some lotion.

Mickey Thomas was extremely generous too. He once collared
me after training and said, 'Go out to the car park and fetch
the fruit on the back seat of my motor and I'll give you a pair
of boots.' So I walked ten yards, climbed five steps, retrieved
an apple and an orange from his car and was rewarded with a
pair of brand-new boots. He's never let me forget that he was
my benefactor, but, then again, I never let him forget that I
have long been glad that he didn't offer me one of his 'special'
still wet bank notes as payment!

Some of the established players were more frosty, particularly the captain, Martin Buchan. He took his responsibilities
very seriously and could be quite dour and protective about his
players' status. For example, if he saw anyone leaning on a car
parked in a first-team player's designated space, he would be
straight over to give them an ear-bashing: 'That's a player's car.
What do you think you're playing at? Step away!' He was a
classic 'know your place, stay behind the rope' kind of guy. It
must have been summer 1979 when I was first invited into the
senior dressing room at the Cliff by Dave McCreery. I couldn't
have been any older than fourteen when I had a run-in with
the skipper because I know McCreery was transferred to QPR
before the start of the next season. I opened the door and
walked in to have a chat with Dave, but before I'd got over the
threshold Buchan, who was shaving at a sink by the door, turned
to me with his face still covered in foam and barked, 'You're
supposed to knock before you come in here. Get out!'

Whenever I tell that story, my pals say, 'You must have crapped yourself,' but I didn't. It never crossed my mind to be intimidated. I thought he was rude so I gave him a dose of his own medicine, told him to get stuffed and slammed the door in his face. It wasn't pre-planned at all; it was sheer instinct that made me stand up to him. In a way, perhaps, it's what set me apart as a young player – I was confident and secure in myself when dealing with grown men at a far earlier age than my contemporaries.

The last time I saw our goalkeeper, Gary Bailey, he reminded me of another incident in the dressing room that occurred around the same time. They had this lame tradition that a first-team player would point to the corner and order a kid who came into the inner sanctum for the first time to 'go and ask the broom for a dance'. They'd keep going on at him until he gave in, walked over and talked to the broom. When he'd stuttered out the embarrassing invitation, the whole dressing room would chorus, 'No, f*** off, you ugly b*******.' It was Gary's turn to ask when I wandered in and I was dismissive of him, just wouldn't do it. He says he tried to pressurise me and I still refused. In fact, I told him to do exactly the same thing as I'd told Buchan to do: stick some Paxo up his jacksie, but more politely. He says he saw something in my eyes that made him back down and when he later asked me why I'd behaved like I did, I told him, 'I grew up on the Shankill Road. I saw people get drills through their kneecaps. Why would I be frightened of you?'

I doubt I said the kneecaps thing, or if I did I must have been playing with his head because it isn't true. Shaking them up was not my real motivation for standing up to either of them, though. It's not that I lacked respect for Buchan and Bailey, but that the captain and goalkeeper of Manchester United, or Wales's Under-18 centre-half, or Lytham St Annes Boys' Brigade Battalion's full-back were genuinely all the same to me – they were obstacles in my way. If I let them hinder me then I wouldn't get to where I wanted to go. I was not naïve enough to seek confrontation with first-team players, but if they came looking for it what was the point of running away? What could they do? Fight me? I was willing to take my chances. The fact that I was named as a substitute for Manchester United's reserve team that summer in a match at Colwyn Bay when I was still fourteen – not the A or B teams but the reserves, with full internationals in the team – surely proved that my attitude was right.

Over the course of the following two years, I flew backwards and forwards to Manchester probably a hundred times. That's why I don't have close friends from my schooldays. I was hardly ever there for the last two years and even when I was I tended to be only ever a couple of days away from my next match with United, school or the national side. Most of the teachers just let me get on with it. I suppose that, with unemployment such an issue in the early eighties, they weren't going to stand in the way of someone with the prospect of a job, any job.

Towards the end of my last year at school, I was clocking up more miles than Freddie Laker and could recite the air safety procedure in my sleep as a result of the club whisking me over for midweek FA Youth Cup fixtures as well. My mate John

Armfield, son of the former England captain and Leeds manager, Jimmy, was the other schoolboy in the youth team and was chauffeured back to his Blackpool home after Tuesday night games. If we were at home, I'd stay in digs before getting the red-eye flight to Belfast and school on Wednesday morning, or, as when we played Spurs at White Hart Lane in the semi-final in 1981, caught the last flight from Heathrow and (this is what I thought mind-blowing at fifteen) then nudged my snoring brothers aside and lay in my own bed, hundreds of miles from what had taken place only hours before, sleeplessly spooling the match over in my mind.

As my sixteenth birthday approached, I was pretty confident that Dave Sexton was going to offer me an apprenticeship deal. You can never be sure, but I'd spent my last year at school largely playing for United's A team, in effect the third team. The way I rationalised it was that, at fifteen, I was already part of the club's regular third-choice centre-forward partnership and, if you stretched that idea, possibly only four injuries away from the first team. Moreover, I had already made my debut at Old Trafford and scored in a 'final', albeit at a pre-season open day, when I was co-opted into the winning Northern Ireland six-a-side team alongside Jimmy Nicholl, Sammy Mac and Chris McGrath in the club's international competition. Things were looking good and the people who counted seemed to have faith in me. I'm sure Bob Bishop told me that the feedback he was getting was extremely positive, probably on one of the weekend trips he arranged for 'his boys' to his tiny house on the beach at Helen's Bay. Barring any unforeseen hiccoughs, my future seemed bright. Yet ironically it was Bob, to whom I owe so much, who was to play a part in an incident that nearly wrecked my career before it began.

What started as a groin strain in 1980, possibly general wear and tear due to the amount of games I was playing, quickly deteriorated into something far more serious. And it was not the ailment that almost did for me, it was the 'cure'. The injury was still bugging me a few days after my return from Manchester and, desperate to be fit enough to play again at the weekend, I asked Bob for his advice. He used his connections with Linfield's fierce rivals Glentoran to get me an appointment with their physio, Bobby McGregor. Off we went to wait hours at Glens's ground, while queues of players went through his treatment rooms. Bob recommended him highly and told me all about his reputation as not only what was still known in those days as a 'trainer', but also as a miracle or faith healer who had even restored sick dogs to health. He sounded like a cross between Sam the Spongeman, Eileen Drewery and James Herriot.

McGregor was an old-school manual therapist who believed the only tools he needed to treat me with were his two hands, and he set about me as I lay on that table like Giant Haystacks kneading sausage meat. First off, he put his hands on the front of my hips and wrenched so hard I could barely draw breath. Then he moved them to my groin, digging his thumbs in on both sides, probing and manipulating so deep I felt my pelvis move. Finally, he had me roll on to my front and he pummelled my kidneys for a few minutes and said, 'That's it, you're fine.' I left that session in such a state I felt as though I had been beaten up. And, in essence, I had been. Perhaps if I had been a Labrador I would have been OK, but I was never the same athlete again.

From that day onwards, I lost all my pace and when I next had a medical at United they noted that I had lost the ability to rotate my hips. Not only that, but they made a popping noise. For the first few months after it happened it was like a scab that you can't help but pick at and I used to sit in my ma's front room watching television and move my legs to the position where they would start to make audible clunks and clicks. When I began running again, first my hips would catch and then my back. On my return to Old Trafford a week later, I found myself totally outclassed in sprints by kids from my age group whom I had once left for dead.

It's the only significant moan I have about my career. I went to see a highly experienced physiotherapist who was affiliated to a semi-professional football club and the Northern Ireland national team. I walked into his surgery with a normal foot-ballers' occupational hazard-type groin strain and, basically, he done me in. Bobby McGregor moved my pelvis so drastically that my hips have never worked properly again. He knackered the player I should have been. I know it sounds harsh, but it's true. Five years later I was stood next to Ron Atkinson at the Cliff watching our new Danish full-back, Johnny Sivebaek, in his first training session and he was like a wasp in a bottle. Ron turned to me and said ruefully, 'Kid, if you had his pace . . .' Gordon Strachan also made much of the fact that an 'extra half-yard' would have made me 'the complete player' and Sir Alex, in his autobiography, wrote, 'The addition of pace would have meant that Norman had absolutely everything. I honestly believe he would have been world-class, one of the finest players we have seen.' Well, I had it and lost it.

McGregor had left me months before crunch time, the deadline for an offer of an apprenticeship, as a wannabe professional footballer who had lost his speed and could no longer lift his knees properly when he ran. That's why I started to run in that singular fashion that was likened to a robot. Yes, I still had the other stuff that had first caught Bob Bishop's eye and it helped me to salvage my dream, but sometimes I can't help thinking back to that day and speculating about the toll an essentially well-meaning person took on me. I've always believed that 'what ifs' are pointless — I'm a firm advocate of the old saying, 'If your auntie had balls, she'd be your uncle' — but I am still annoyed about it. When McGregor died of a heart attack during the 1981–2 season while running on to the field to treat a player in a European Cup tie, I had every sympathy for his family. I can assure you that I am not heartless enough to dredge the issue up if it hadn't made such a crucial difference to my life.

Everything else I can take: the other injuries, the time out and even prematurely packing the game in. These sorts of setbacks happen to players all the time. But once done over by the healing hands of Bobby McGregor, old King Midas in reverse, the original Norman Whiteside, the one I alone can still see in my head, faded away and was replaced by the one you recognise shortly before the club offered me a deal on my sixteenth birthday. Pace or no pace, at least I had a professional career to look forward to and, having had my dose of bad luck, I hoped I could look forward to a long spell when fortune favoured me once again.

CHAPTER FOUR

APPRENTICE DEVIL

Almost all United's trainees signed a two-year apprenticeship on their sixteenth birthdays and spent the next two years working on their games in what was effectively a prolonged trial. Those who flourished were taken on, but the majority usually didn't and were ushered away with as much compassion as the club's employees could muster. It's a brutal world – the club feeds on fresh blood, but only that of the requisite quality – and that is one of the reasons why I've never sought a career in coaching, despite having all the FA badges. I admire the many people I have seen who act sensitively and with genuine concern about the young players' futures, but I've seen too many heart-broken kids ever to contemplate having to make those decisions part of my life.

As for myself at sixteen, I was fortunate not to have to go down that traditional route. The invitations sent to my parents to give permission to release me into United's care over the holidays had long been appended with notes from the chief scout, Joe Brown. 'Norman gets better each time I see him,' he wrote one Easter. 'I am delighted with his progress.' I think the fact that over the course of a fortnight I had gone from being the quickest forward at the club to the slowest was something they thought could be remedied by conditioning work. It had not made me damaged goods in their eyes, I was relieved to discover. I was determined to fight back after my brush with Bobby McGregor, but I still felt vulnerable. I could not have had a greater confidence boost, then, than when United offered not the normal two-year traineeship, but the security of a one-year apprenticeship, to run until my seventeenth birthday, which was to be followed by a guaranteed three-year professional contract.

My ma and da, having again turned down United's offer to follow the parents of Jimmy Nicholl and Sammy McIlroy and relocate to Manchester to a house owned by the club, flew over with me on my birthday to give their consent to the offer. As soon as they had co-signed my contract with the club secretary, Les Olive, they were given the grand tour of the stadium and my da fulfilled a lifelong ambition by walking on the Old Trafford pitch. It was a weekday, there was no game on or anything and no manager to meet either, with Dave Sexton having been sacked and the search on for his replacement, but it didn't matter – Big Norman was made up. The club was excellent at recognising its prestige and how much it meant to the families of young players (it still is) and was very classy in the way it treated my folks that day. I suppose it helped them to say goodbye to me and reassured them how seriously United took its duty towards their son. I felt no sadness at our parting that evening, it was everything I had hoped and worked for. As they got in a taxi to go to the airport, I loaded my bags into the club minibus and was ferried to my new lodgings in Chorlton-cum-Hardy, home of the Wheelies. My two years of being the flying schoolboy, never in one place for more than a few days, were finally over. The day had come – it was time to clock on as a professional.

I was given a place in Bet and Tom Fannon's three-storey south Manchester house, which was something of an Irish enclave. Ashley Grimes and the trainee goalkeeper, Phil Hughes, were my fellow lodgers and Kevin Moran, whose purchase of a house had created the vacancy I filled, was still living there. I was worried that there might be some Dublin–Belfast sensitivity between Kevin and me because he is very proud of his roots in the south, but we quickly became good friends. He used to pop back to the digs after training, probably to get his washing and ironing done, and then take me off in his car back to his place to spend the rest of the day with him. Kevin had already made his name as a Gaelic footballer before joining United, and one afternoon he sat me down in his living room to watch a video of the two All-Ireland finals he had helped win for Dublin in 1976 and 1977. I remember sitting on his settee, laughing at the thoughts running through my head, and saying to him, 'If they could see me now on the Shankill. Here I am in the house of a Catholic, a Republic of Ireland international, watching a game of Gaelic – no one would ever believe it.' Almost every day at the beginning my horizons were broadening in subtle ways like that.

Which is more than could be said for my diet! Bet and Tom were excellent hosts. He worked for British Airways and would give me lifts to and from the airport whenever I used one of the six return tickets a year to Belfast that were part of my contract. But if there was one small gripe it was that Bet had fallen hook, line and sinker for that advertising jingle, 'Go to work on an egg.' Each night there would be some variation: scrambled, fried, poached, boiled with soldiers or omelettes. We would often have to resort to a Chinese takeaway in the evenings to supplement our rations. And as for the odour in the bedrooms after four young players had wolfed down their nightly egg quotas, it was sometimes so strong you would have sworn your eyes were about to start bleeding.

We were joined in Chorlton that season by Peter Bodak, who never made it with us but went on to play for City. He had an obsession with the number seven: if he was buying six drinks in a round he would always buy a seventh 'for luck' and was adamant about wearing that shirt in every game. One night the following season, Peter, Paul McGrath, who had moved in at Easter 1982, and I were playing cards and in that brutal bantering way professionals adopt with each other, when Paul, who had recently made his first-team debut, threw down two sevens on the table with the cry, 'What have I got here? Two Peter Bodaks in the reserves!'

I shared the attic room with fellow Belfast boy Phil Hughes, who never made the first team at United, but had a decent career with Scarborough, Leeds, Bury and Wigan. We entertained ourselves up there with a massive stereo given to me by the club's sponsors, Sharp, and with the ritual clack-clack-clack-oh-sod-it of my Rubik's Cube, the number one craze of the early eighties. It was in that room one Sunday morning, as Phil dozed in the bed opposite, that I got out of bed and lurched head first on to the floor when my right leg gave way beneath me. I had played for the A team at Preston North End the day before, but had not been the victim of a bad challenge and certainly had not felt injured on Saturday night. I managed to struggle back into bed and when I next got up all seemed well with it so I was happy to kid myself that it must have been a one-off. The rest of the day, however, was littered with incidents when the knee would lock vertically, catch me by surprise like a man breaking in a false leg and topple me sideways or simply collapse under my weight. I was barely six weeks into my career when I reported to the physio for the first time the next morning. That consultation, like that first symptom of knee trouble, alas proved not to be a one-off either.

I think it was the late Jimmy Hedridge who sent me to see Dr McHugh, though having subsequently studied anatomy myself I now know it must have been pretty obvious to them that my knee was functioning with the classic clinical signs of medial cartilage damage. It was definitely one of the quickest examinations I ever had to endure and I was told within ten minutes that I needed an immediate operation. I spent the day before surgery in the Highfield Hospital in Rochdale watching

John McEnroe defeat Björn Borg in the 1981 Wimbledon final, but even that enthralling match didn't distract me enough from the fear of the consequences if the operation went wrong. This wasn't like the appendicitis I'd suffered the year before; that had been straightforward, though at times excruciating. But it wasn't the prospect of further pain that worried me, it was that they were going to cut open my knee, basically the tool of my trade, and remove part of it. I may have been a sixteen-year-old kid who only a few weeks previously had been blunting chisels in double woodwork, but even I knew the ominous equation: knee surgery equalled potential end to career. No wonder, then, that I vomited the evening before the operation and spent much of the morning before they administered the general anaesthetic making repeated trips to the toilet.

It was unfortunate that I had to have such a major operation so early in my career, and it was even more unfortunate that I missed out on the rapid emergence of arthroscopy, or keyhole surgery, over the next few years. My timing was particularly poor – if I'd had the injury at eighteen they would have used the new and less invasive techniques which had just been perfected. The surgeon would have simply put a needle-sized blade into my knee, trimmed the damaged part of the cartilage and left the rest of the medial meniscus in place to leave me with something to provide a cushion and prevent friction between my femur (thigh bone) and tibia (shin bone). That procedure was still a pipe dream in 1981 and I was stuck with the old-school remedy. My surgeon, Alan Glass, cut open the joint, removed the cartilage and stuck it in a jar beside my bed to greet me when the general wore off.

It wasn't a bespoke treatment for footballers; such specialist solutions simply did not exist back then. I got the same orthopaedic surgery that would have been given to anyone displaying the same symptoms. There's no blame whatsoever attached to Mr Glass, who followed the best possible course at the time. It is a pity, however, that the methods available to the famous American knee specialist Richard Steadman which were later used to help the likes of Henrik Larsson, Alan Shearer, Ruud van Nistelrooy and Roy Keane recover from far more serious injuries had not yet arrived in Britain. Without a cartilage, I have been left bone-on-bone in my right knee ever since and, twenty-five years on, the point where my femur rubs the tibia has gouged out a hole the size of a 2p piece, while the top of the tibia sports a cavity the size of a 5p piece. When the edges of the holes catch each other the knee gives way. The other effect has been severe stomach upsets from a quarter of a century spent taking anti-inflammatories to stop the constant grating of the two bones making the knee swell up. All that was still in the future when I was discharged from hospital, but in retrospect I can recognise the day of the operation, 17 July 1981, as the day the countdown to my retirement from football began.

Jimmy Curran came and picked me up from Rochdale to take me back to digs, but he made a detour to Old Trafford to take me in to see Ron Atkinson, who had been appointed as manager the previous month and had started work that morning. I hopped into his office on my crutches when summoned, but, seeing him on the phone gesturing and talking about a transfer, turned to leave. He wouldn't let me go, though, pointed me to a chair and carried on. I know now that Ron was behaving as he would always do – he was performing and, if the situation merited it, was delighted to have an audience. I sat there for ten minutes as the new boss, in his shirt-sleeves and tinted specs, continued with his telephone negotiations. I quickly gathered that he was selling our centre-forward, Joe Jordan, to AC Milan and, when the clauses and terms had been argued through and agreed, he did the deal right there in front of me, hung up, shuffled some papers and turned to address me. 'I've heard good things about you, son,' he said. 'Now, you just concentrate on getting fit. Go back to your mum and dad for a bit and we'll have you back here playing in no time at all.'

It wasn't the first time Ron proved somewhat optimistic, but it was unique in that he actually bothered to utter more than his habitually curt 'How long, then?' to an injured player. Perhaps he exempted me on the grounds of my age or maybe he just got carried away on his first day, because it didn't last. In common with most managers then, Ron focused on the short term: if you were injured you were no good to him and therefore you rarely registered on his radar until you were fit and became useful again. By his reckoning, I was to prove pretty useless for the next six months.

My rehabilitation programme seemed to go on for ever and bore few positive results. I was first put under the supervision of the physio appointed by Ron, Jimmy Hedridge, but he died at the tragically young age of forty-two, shortly after joining the club. His death was traumatic for the staff and many players at the Cliff who witnessed his collapse from a massive heart attack while he was out on the training pitch. His replacement, Jim McGregor, joined us from Everton and soon became a hugely influential figure to me, but at the beginning he had to put up with my groans at the laborious exercises and how slowly progress was being made.

After surgery, the prescribed exercise involved straight-leg raises to strengthen my thigh muscles to compensate for the knee's fragility. I would report for training every morning as usual, but instead of going through the glass doors into the fresh air, I would go to Jim's treatment room, haul myself on to a table and begin the following routine: bend my knee so my right leg was horizontal, hold it for ten seconds, release. I did that another 199 times then had a break for a coffee and a read of the paper and went to the boot room. Two hundred more were done before I went off to the canteen for lunch, then another 200 before a mid-afternoon break set me up for the last 200 of the day. If it felt OK after a couple of weeks (and this was before the advent of ergonomic and durable modern gym machines, so we were stuck with antiquated stuff like old dumb-bells and medicine balls) I would get the added excitement of attaching a weight to my foot with an improvised harness. All this was undertaken in front of large windows through which I could see my fellow trainees bounding around. Even when it was freezing outside, I was so envious of them, despite their dragons' breath, chapped faces and that crestfallen look they adopted whenever they were on the receiving end of a bollocking.

Yet however strong my right quads had become, even they could not compensate for the lack of flexion in my knee. I couldn't extend it properly, nor go down on my haunches and at times it would crunch and stick like a faulty gearbox. In general, I wasn't a bad patient over the course of my career — as long as

I felt that Jim was leading me in the right direction I could put up with the treatment, even if it was ball-achingly boring. If I was confident that I was going to recover, I could cope because that knowledge was more important than a timetable. My problem in December 1981, however, was that I had done a hundred thousand straight-leg raises and, despite one tentative outing, it seemed I was no nearer to kicking a ball without pain than I had been when Alan Glass turned to his assistant and first said 'scalpel' five months earlier.

One of the few moments of relief during that frustrating period came in the gym with an also-injured Martin Buchan. Both of us were fed up with the rehab exercises we had monotonously adhered to and improvised something a bit more interesting. Pulling two benches to face each other a couple of yards apart, we started a game to build up our shoulder and neck strength. With me sitting opposite him, he lobbed the ball for me to power-head back at him. The object was to head it past him to earn a point while he tried to save it goalie-style. Then it was my turn to throw it back to him. We must have looked like a couple of distressed racehorses with pulsating neck muscles after a couple of hours of this, but we were still locked in a stalemate.

Both of us were so competitive that we threw ourselves around to make sure the other could not score. And then it dawned on me. In our haste to get started we had only cobbled together the simplest of rules for the game and a loophole suddenly occurred to me. Neither of us had mentioned that we had to head it straight back, so the next time he pitched the ball to me I fired it off the adjacent wall and it ricocheted past him at an angle. I had won and he gave me a look, sizing me up, half in admiration I think, which said, 'So that's your game, then.' I might have had only one functioning leg, but that display of ruthlessness or canniness showed the club captain, a great player, but one who was very particular and had mastered the use of the cruel, sarcastic put-down to defend his high standards, that I was deadly serious and not just some cocky, rude kid.

Because I only did a one-year traineeship, those that had the longer ones must have felt that I was on easy street when it came to the traditional apprentice's tasks. But thanks to the injury I did as much during those six months I spent out of football as the others endured in two years. We each had six players to look after and had to make sure all their training kit and boots were clean, laid out and stored properly. A couple of hours each morning at the Cliff were spent blacking boots and I would always be first on hand to haul the first-team's kit about in skips and load them on to the coach to help the kit man, Norman Davies, prepare for away matches because I was always there, in the treatment room, when the others had long since departed.

Since I couldn't play on Saturdays, I would report to Old Trafford if we were at home, watch the match, then go into the dressing room with the other injured lads, working in pairs, and while the boys were having their baths we would pick up the boots, take the laces out and hang them on pegs in the boot room to dry. On Sunday mornings we'd be back at the club to polish them and paint on the manufacturers' stripes. And I loved it. Yes, it was my job and good discipline for me, but I also felt enormously privileged to be stuck down a corridor at Old Trafford, where few people ever got to tread. It made me feel like I belonged, an insider, and one that was happy during such a long layoff to be contributing something to the cause.

For six months I had my hands in as many boots as Imelda Marcos's cobbler, but I had still to get a pair on my feet. Every six weeks I would be sent to see a specialist and given a new exercise regime to follow, adding hamstring stretches and joint mobilisation to my quad schedule. At times I think the medics thought my problem was psychological, that I perceived a weakness in the knee that wasn't there and I simply had to learn to trust it. By Christmas I was in danger of having a right leg like Arnold Schwarzenegger's, but improved muscle power could not help me when the knee crunched or locked. Finally, it was agreed that I would go back in and on 31 January 1982, seven full months since I had last played a match, I was put under general anaesthetic again, my knee vigorously manipulated and the tissue broken down, the intra-articular adhesions that made my knee scrape like a poorly hung door and had caused the lack of flexion and pain when I tried to run were at last defeated. Three days later I went to the Cliff, got changed, walked out of the doors into the open and launched myself into full training. Just addressing a ball, pivoting on my right leg and belting it with my left, gave me the biggest rush I'd had all year, a mixture of relief, satisfaction and sheer joy. Man and ball reunited at last.

Even the best of us sometimes don't fancy training in February, when it's cold, gloomy and depressing, but I couldn't get enough of it and rejoining my colleagues in the youth team was just the tonic I needed to banish my autumn frustration for good. We had a decent side, five of whom went on to graduate to first-team duty with me: the centre-halves Billy Garton and Graeme Hogg; Nicky Wood, whose career was wrecked by injury; and two Welsh lads whom I had faced in schoolboy internationals – Clayton Blackmore and Mark Hughes. Three other lads went on to have good careers at other clubs: my room-mate Phil Hughes; the right-back Andy Hill, who finally made it to the top flight with Manchester City just as my career was coming to an end; and the midfielder Mark Dempsey, who ended up at Sheffield United. I was the youngest, apart from schoolboy Nicky, but made the first team eighteen months before anyone else. For that I had to thank a remarkable man, Eric Harrison, who would emerge under Sir Alex as the head of the most fertile youth system of the past twenty-five years.

Eric will tell you that when he was youth coach at Everton he always felt that United's kids were a bit soft. On his appointment, when Ron joined the club in the summer of 1981, he vowed to change the culture of the youth set-up and he set about his task with such zeal that he pushed several of my team-mates to the limits of their physical and mental capabilities with his intensity and enthusiasm. I was still running about very gingerly during the first few days of my return, but Eric, who had read the reports about me dating back to 1978 and had heard his staff talk about me, was gagging to see me play. I was lying in the bath after training on Friday and he came over and said with a smile, 'You'll be all right for tomorrow, won't you? Give it a go, even if you're on one leg.' I wasn't at all confident that the knee would stand up to it, but I had been out so long that I agreed to it. The match was against Everton at Bellefield and Eric was desperate to beat his former employers to prove that he had made the right move. We won 3–1 and I scored twice, so I got off to the perfect start with the coach. There I was finally getting myself back to fitness by beating Eric's old club. The lads said I was the golden boy from then on, the gaffer's best mate, but I doubt his great happiness at me coming through the game could have matched mine.

At the back of my mind during that game, however, was the knowledge that the knee was not the same as before. Without the cartilage it would always feel like I was carrying my right leg to some extent and, though I had a fair way to go before the bones started to erode, I knew that it was impaired and could never be cured. I tried to be positive and blank out my fears, but my knee kept reminding me that all was not well. It became an inescapable worry and by its weakness compared to my left let me know too often that my body was not functioning properly for me to be in a state of denial about it.

To adapt I had to change my running style again. As I said earlier, I had adopted a robotic method, with shorter, shallower strides, after the pelvic manipulation stopped me lifting my knees. Now it became more mechanical still, with me dragging my right leg. My days of running like an athlete had gone and with them the way I had played before the operation. From that point on hitting the ball over the top for me to run on to was out, as was giving it to me and letting me set off on a fifty-yard dribble to goal. I had to become a centre-forward who weighed options as much as he relied on instinct, used his body more, one that worked on the strengths I retained — shooting, heading, positioning, passing — and developed the art of holding the ball up and turning with it to compensate for the fact that from 1982 onwards I was, as Eric had suggested as merely a stop-gap solution, basically playing on one leg.

I found Eric to be an ideal mentor. I know Clayton Blackmore and Billy Garton have since likened him to a slave-driver because of the way he was constantly at their throats, but even they acknowledge that it forced them to toughen up, the essential personality change that gave them their careers. By the time players are sixteen, their ability is taken for granted. All apprentices can play, but what they lack are awareness, the speed of thought necessary for professional football, self-assurance when under intense pressure and an appetite to take responsibility, no matter the situation. Eric was a very shrewd judge of a player, but his best quality was that he had a driven mentality focused on winning, very much like Bryan Robson and Roy Keane. Of course he wanted his players to show their skills on the pitch, but he liked you to be able to withstand the opposition's bullying, get your foot in and dish it out. He didn't like 'fancy Dans' or those that went pussy-footing into tackles like Billy and Clayton did in their early days.

He took to me in particular, I think, because I was not one for bouts of self-doubt. I was hyper-determined, wholly committed and the one best equipped to handle myself. There was a second-year apprentice called, improbably, Grant Mitchell, cock of the youth dressing room. He tried to taunt me one afternoon after a training session and, having warned him to pack it in, I brained him with a steel orange-squash jug when he carried on abusing me. I can't say I'm proud of it, but I'm not that ashamed either. I only include it to show what I was like back then: I stood up for myself if I had to. Later that season, we had a game where the trainees took on the trialists and one lad was really putting himself and his studs about. It's not at all the done thing in practice matches to go about clogging players, so I decided to deal with him and absolutely cleared him out when he tried to challenge me for the ball. In doing so, I injured myself and my ankle quickly ballooned. After the game Eric called me into his office and said, 'You can do without this. You've got to tailor your aggression more and wait for the right opportunities.' He was disappointed I'd been reckless enough to hurt myself, but I could sense his satisfaction that I'd had the balls to do something about that kid.

The first coach you have as you take the first step to becoming a professional naturally has a profound influence on you, but because of their power to make or break your dreams they can be extremely intimidating figures. I don't doubt that Eric frightened the life out of some of the lads, but I knew from that first game for him at Bellefield that he liked me and, more importantly, rated me, so I wasn't cowed by his aggressive manner. I loved the way that he always let you know where you stood and offered constructive criticism, pulling you in for a chat to say you hadn't done well that week, but only because you had stopped doing x, y and z. He could put up with bad individual performances and his only concern was that your effort never waned. Responsibilities were not shirked, even if you were having the proverbial nightmare, and you didn't hide from a battle. He would update you on your progress month by month, praise you fulsomely or sternly steer you back on course. Whether it was a kick up the backside, an arm around the shoulder or a pat on the back, they were all delivered with passion and a hunger to see you make the most of your talent. You would hear horror stories from other clubs about kids who were no nearer to knowing if they were going to make it a month before the end of their two years than they had been during their first weeks at their club because there was never any feedback. With Eric you always knew.

Having only played a couple of Lancashire League games for the A team and a fourth-round FA Youth Cup replay against Leeds, it came as a huge surprise to earn a call-up to the reserves a month into my comeback. It was around then that those early comparisons with Best were replaced for a while, with talk about similarities with the Babes, and Duncan Edwards in particular. I'm on guard here against another Homer moment, but little links me with the immortal Edwards other than my age and size when I made my breakthrough. At sixteen, both of us could match up physically to a man of twenty-five.

Another player who gets this treatment is Wayne Rooney. Go to Old Trafford today and if you only usually watch football on television, which is full of close-ups that distort what you see, you would be shocked at how small, wiry and lean most of the players are. Rooney got the 'new Norman Whiteside' tag when he started and still has to take the 'who ate all the pies?' stick, but he only gets them because of his youth, physique and power. Duncan Edwards and I, like Rooney, were well built, tough and so much more developed physically than others in our age group. That's why Sir Matt was not afraid to throw Duncan into the first team at sixteen. Neither, later, was David Moyes afraid to do the same with Wayne. As for Ron Atkinson and me, I didn't think it possible, given that no sixteen-year-old had played for United since Edwards in 1953, and, what's more, I had only had two months of football. Even that short spell had been interrupted by the swollen ankle from sorting out the hard nut in the trial game.

I was happy following the established path, tracked by where you got changed at the Cliff: youth-team dressing room for one to two years, then reserve-team dressing room and, finally, not having to knock to enter Martin Buchan's domain. In early March the first team were scheduled to go to Belfast to play my boyhood favourites, Linfield, in a testimonial and the manager had initially included me in the squad. It would have been the dream start for me and I think he thought there would be no better place for me to sample the demands of first-team football than in my home environment, with spectators wishing me well and with none of the UK-wide media spotlight that is always drawn by a teenage United debutant. Unfortunately, my ankle was too sore and I accepted that an injury-ravaged season would be played out gaining experience against established professionals in the reserves. 'Don't be too greedy,' I thought. 'Next year will be soon enough.' That was until Ron strolled over to me before training one Friday morning and enquired whether I owned a suit.

CHAPTER FIVE

IF YOU'RE GOOD
ENOUGH . . .

I was almost too shocked to answer the manager's question,
but I managed to bluff my way through by nodding my head
and jogging off towards a club taxi which Ron had ordered
to take me to fetch my only suit from my digs across town. I
wonder now if it would have been a deal-breaker had I not
possessed one or whether I would have been dispatched towards
the Arndale Centre or Market Street with a loan from petty
cash to grab something from Burton, Hepworth or Fosters.
Sitting in the back of the minicab, I was simply grateful that
my ma was the kind of parent with old-fashioned views about

smartness and had equipped me with the Sunday best which hung, barely worn, at the back of my wardrobe in Chorlton.

I hastily packed my bag, shouted to Bet that I wouldn't be home until late Saturday night, climbed into the waiting taxi which crawled back through the city centre and into Salford, just as the Friday lunchtime traffic jams began to snarl up the route. On my return to the Cliff, I bolted down fish and chips in the canteen before boarding a coach with a white sign propped up in the front window, its red letters spelling out Manchester United AFC. I knew I was only going for the ride, to soak up the match-day atmosphere and learn how the professionals handled the pressure. But who cared? I was now a member of the first-team squad and my earlier nerves had long since evaporated. Brighton and the big time, I thought, bring it on.

I was made to feel very welcome on the long journey down the M6, but I had no inkling that the next day was going to bring my debut. Back in Manchester, speculation was growing. Local radio and the *Evening News* said that my exploits in the eight reserve matches I'd played in February, March and April had earned me the call-up and that I had a decent chance of joining Jeff Whitefoot and Duncan Edwards in what the *MEN* correspondent, David Meek, called a special club within the club – United's sixteen-year-old debutants, the 'Super 16s'. But given that Martin Buchan and Remi Moses were also in the squad after injury lay-offs, I took Ron's invitation to 'come down for the experience' at face value.

Atkinson's promising start as manager had floundered a little in the spring and the team had yet to find its typical Big Ron-style swagger. You can tell by the transfer targets he failed to get that year – Trevor Francis, Frank Worthington and Glenn Hoddle – that he felt his side lacked the flair of the gung-ho West Brom team he had moulded over three seasons. Though Garry Birtles finally broke his duck under Ron after twenty-eight League games without scoring for poor Dave Sexton and had, like his partner upfront, Frank Stapleton, passed double figures, neither looked remotely capable of becoming the club's first twenty-goals-a-season man since George Best in 1968. Moreover, they shared only three goals between them in February, March and April. Even Bryan Robson, whose £1.5m transfer in October had galvanised the club, stuttered in front of goal during his bedding-in season and was outscored by a centre-half, Kevin Moran. Looking at the situation objectively – United were ten points behind Liverpool with seven games to play and had little to lose by experimenting – my involvement should not have been as surprising as it seemed. Had I known Ron better back then, I would have recognised it as the type of gut-instinct gamble that he loved to take. But that night, in the Metropole hotel, as we paired off and were allocated our rooms, I was still very much in the dark.

I was fortunate to have Steve Coppell as my first room-mate and I suspect it must have been planned that the model professional was given the youngster to set me the perfect example. I know he comes across as being fairly dour since starting his managerial career, but Stevie was a great guy: bright, unselfish and genuinely interested in players and their development. He also had a nice, dry wit and, though I've forgiven him for banging on in his autobiography about how I shared a face with Russ Abbott, I'm still not sure if his regular pre-match night-time prescription for me, which began in that Brighton hotel room, was a wind-up or part of his mission as chairman of the Professional Footballers' Association to show concern for my welfare. After we'd had our evening meal and gone back to our room to lie on the twin beds and watch telly, Steve fished something out of his bag and threw it to me. It was an energy bar, which, back in 1982, was not the sort you find in Tesco these days, but had come out of a chemist's shop and was made of pure glucose. He must have got the idea because he was an excellent athlete and had seen me struggle on distance runs. 'Go on, have it,' he said. 'It'll give you strength.' So the night before the Brighton match and every subsequent away game for the next year, I tucked into the ideal snack to help me get a restful night's sleep: an energy bar and a cup of coffee!

My room-mate had already picked up the injury that would end his career eighteen months later and although he battled on through the World Cup and a last season with United, it was difficult to watch his athleticism ebb away as he bravely struggled through matches with a patched-up knee. His influence on me persisted long after he retired, and not just through the good habits he passed on. It was a sad coincidence that we both succumbed to chronic knee damage and what happened to him was always at the back of my mind, and those of the consultant and medical staff, whenever my knee seized up over the next few years. I always tried to be positive when the familiar stiffness and pain returned, but the added psychological burden of knowing that Steve had not recovered was ever present and gnawed away at everyone's confidence.

Still, all that was in the future on the morning of Saturday,

24 April 1982, as I joined the first-team squad in a morning stroll along Brighton beach. We would have been mobbed ten years later, but at the time it was quite easy for fourteen track-suited players to walk around, not exactly unrecognised, but certainly not pestered. At the hotel we tucked into the sort of pre-match meal that would have modern nutritional experts spitting out their pasta – fillet steak, mash and baked beans – before trooping off into the lounge to flick through the news-papers and see what was happening in the Falklands, watch a bit of *On the Ball* or *Football Focus* and wait for the manager to read out his team. It was there, in a private room of the great beachfront Brighton hotel, that I learned I had pipped Buchan and Moses to the No. 12 shirt and twenty minutes later I was in my suit and boarding the coach to the Goldstone Ground feeling elated but bemused.

It was a pretty dull game, if truth be told. Brighton were a dour but efficient side that season and, given our strikers' poor form, we were reduced to pinging in long shots to try to break the deadlock. I got the call to get stripped from the assistant manager, Mick Brown, with a quarter of an hour to go and was sent on for the final twelve minutes at the age of sixteen years 352 days to become the third-youngest player in United's history. I took the place of Mick Duxbury, a full-back who had been moonlighting in midfield, to make a re-jigged three-man forward line alongside Stapleton and Scott McGarvey. Once out on the field, I felt an odd paradox: the game flew by and yet it seemed an age before I touched the ball. A few minutes from time, I got my second touch when a pass from Ray Wilkins found me out on the right and I hit a simple ball to Stapleton's feet. Frank, on the half-turn, took one touch to lay it back to Wilkins, who whacked a thirty-yard shot into the bottom corner. If that was unexpected – Ray played all forty-two games that season and it was his only goal – an even bigger surprise awaited me on the bus, after much ritual hair-ruffling and shoulder-slapping had marked the end of my debut.

Norman Davies, the kit man, doubled up as chef on the trip home, and it was while he was taking orders and blitzing soggy pasties in the luxury coach's microwave oven, which was the size of Wilmslow, that I overheard a conversation between the captain, Wilkins, and Bryan Robson. 'What's the win bonus today?' Robbo asked. '£800?' Having agreed the sum was correct, Ray turned to me and explained how the figure was based on our League position and said, 'You'll be getting it too.' Well, I was on £16 a week, so I was picturing myself as a rich man as I daydreamed on the coach back to Manchester. By the time we pulled into town, I'd already decided which sheepskin jacket, which shoes and which records I was buying as soon as my wages came through. Of course they didn't actually give me the money – I'm not sure if they were allowed to – until the salary payment due after I had officially turned professional on my seventeenth birthday. By then, I had appeared as a non-playing substitute in two further victories so, in the space of three weeks, I had earned £48 in wages and £2,400 in bonuses!

Before that happy windfall had a chance to fatten my anorexic pay packet, April brought another pivotal moment in my life when we were joined in the Fannons' house by a new lodger, a player whose name has become inextricably linked to mine: Paul McGrath. When he first walked through the living-room door to introduce himself, I was lounging on the sofa watching television and I turned to take in his 6ft 4in frame. I'd heard a little bit about him from Bet and I said, to break the ice, 'Big man, it's bad enough being a Catholic, but being a black one is bang out of order!' It looks stark in print, but it was only said to make him laugh, to play up to the Shankill stereotype in an over-the-top way, and from the moment a broad smile spread across his face we clicked and became inseparable buddies for the next seven years.

Although he is five and a half years older than me, I played the elder brother in our relationship, partly because I'd had maturity thrust upon me prematurely by joining the club at fourteen, while he'd been a late developer and was extremely naïve about the customs of professional football and what lay in store for him. It was also, of course, because I was self-assured despite the injuries, while he was riddled with insecurity. Everyone likes praise, but no one needed to tell me that I was good enough. I knew. But Paul would have men of the calibre of Sir Matt Busby, Bobby and Jack Charlton, Bryan Robson and Arnold Muhren on at him about how outstanding a talent he was and it never made the slightest difference deep down. Yes, there were times when he could accept their opinion and occasionally even recognise the esteem in which we held him as deserved. But it was usually short-lived. Logic went out of the window with Paul when it came to himself and no kind words could lift the gloom when he descended into a downer about his worth and prospects.

Of course, as his friend and best man at his wedding, I knew about some of the problems he so movingly talks about in his autobiography, if not their extent, but it would be unfair to define him in those terms during the time we spent living in each other's pockets. He had his bleak moments and at times he drank way too much when injured, as I did, but he was also a joy to be around – full of warmth, fun and mischief. Take the time he bought his first car, a shocking-yellow, boxy, ancient BMW 2000 for £250. Neither of us had licences – me because I was sixteen, Paul because he hadn't taken a test nor, as I learnt later, bothered with little things like tax and insurance – but that didn't stop us spinning around Manchester during those long afternoons after training, playing at Big Time Charlies. It was a truly horrible car, with a slack gear-stick like a wooden spoon in a pan of porridge, which hopped away from traffic lights until it finally reached 30mph as if Paul had filled it with a mixture of 4 star and kangaroo juice. One afternoon we had stopped to give way at the Ardwick Green roundabout by the Apollo Theatre when Paul started fiddling with the radio. Getting a beep from behind to tell us to start moving, Paul said, 'Slap it into first, Norm.' So I did, and Paul floored it as usual. But this time the Bananamobile screamed off the line like we were Bodie and Doyle in *The Professionals*. That was the first time under its new owner that the car had ever been in first gear – Paul had been slamming it into third all the time – and the surprise almost caused us to crash. We had to pull over to the side of the road in fits of giggles. Looking back, I can't believe we were so reckless and obviously I am relieved we never hurt anyone. It was stupid, but as young professionals so preoccupied were we with adventure and the craic that responsible behaviour was way down the agenda.

When I passed my driving test later that year, I did a deal with my landlords to let me drive Tom's clapped-out Datsun Cherry. I paid them £20 a month as a contribution to the insurance and became the house's driver. Instead of having to take three buses to get to the Cliff, I'd charge my passengers petrol money and ferry everyone around in the Fannons' car. It even looked like a minicab, but it was a godsend as it put an end to those freezing mornings spent shivering at the bus stop. Paul, who usually travelled upfront with me, took a couple of years to establish himself in the first team and was too old to play in the first final of my United career. Shortly after his arrival, and two days on from my Goldstone Ground bow, I ran out at Old Trafford in the first leg of the FA Youth Cup final, determined to win the club's first Youth Cup since Best & Co. had lifted the trophy in 1964.

The first match against Watford did not go to script and we found ourselves 3–1 down with five minutes to play when I raked a long pass which split Watford's centre-halves and found Clayton Blackmore who scored. Earlier, I'd had a pretty decent chance saved by the Hornets' excellent goalkeeper, Neil Price, after a lovely one-two with Mark Hughes allowed me to hit a strong shot with my left foot which sadly fell within the keeper's reach. A week later we were confident that we would turn it on at Vicarage Road in the second leg, but they proved a very resilient side, full of good headers and powerful runners, as you would expect of a Graham Taylor team. We ended up drawing 4–4 after extra-time and were unfortunate in that we conceded two deflected own goals – from Billy Garton and Andy Hill – but my partnership with Hughesie really gelled that night at the exceptionally high tempo we were forced to play in. I put us 4–3 up with a cute header with eighteen minutes of the added period to go, but despite our greater flair, we couldn't hang on and, by drawing 4–4, we lost the final 7–6 on aggregate. We were all shattered by the defeat and, when you realise how many of our side went on to play in the First Division and that no Watford player did, it does seem strange that we fell short. It would take another decade and a team with David Beckham, the Nevilles, Nicky Butt, Paul Scholes and Ryan Giggs in it for the club to again win the Cup which it had felt was its birthright when the Babes won five on the trot in the 1950s.

To add to the runners-up medal, I got a far more attractive reward the morning after our return from Hertfordshire, 7 May, my seventeenth birthday, when I signed the three-year professional contract that had been promised the summer before. David Meek had written after my Brighton outing, 'No time for the Irish youngster to make his mark, but his record in the juniors and reserves suggests that if his peers don't buck up their ideas in front of goal he might be appearing on a more regular basis.' It was nice to read, but I thought my season had probably ended with the reserves' last game and my original plan was to go home for the long holiday. After a couple of weeks spent watching the World Cup on the big telly I was going to buy my ma and da with my win bonuses, Ron had lined me up to work with the Olympic gold medal-winning pentathlete Mary Peters, who, as instructed by the boss, would pull apart my running stride and teach me how to sprint again from scratch.

Instead, I found myself back in the first-team squad for the last two games of the season — away at West Brom on the Wednesday and at home to Stoke City three days later. The Hawthorns offered only the chance to jog up the touchline as the home supporters gave their former manager Ron dog's abuse for abandoning them for United. Now there's an art to substitution and if you are stuck on the bench you would expect to get on, but back then, with only one at their disposal, managers were far more reluctant to use the sub tactically in case of a late injury. If you look at the statistics before two subs were allowed in 1987–8, in more than half the League games during a season the starting XI finished the game. Therefore, even for someone who should have been happy to be part of the set-up, it was an irritating role, especially if you had a thirst to play like I did. On the few occasions I got lumbered with it, I would often find myself sitting there as time ran out and, with no outlet at all for the desire and adrenaline that made my body twitch with energy, going barmy with frustration.

I thought it would be another frustrating experience on the Saturday too, and it probably would have been if Frank Stapleton had not picked up an injury at the Albion. I think Ron weighed his options, knew we could not be caught in third place and deprived of our UEFA Cup spot, reasoned that he'd had plenty of chances to look at Scott McGarvey and threw me the No. 9 shirt for my first start. It was the usual end of season affair, with famous old boys like Best, Charlton and Crerand on the pitch at half-time, and we ran out carrying a banner to thank the fans for their support. It's such a long time ago, but parts of it remain vivid. Although there are names and faces that elude me as I get older, I only have to be watching a match today and little incidents may happen that happened to me — a player gets into a specific position as he approaches the Stretford End goal, say — and the memories come flooding back.

I scored in that Stoke game, a far-post header from a looping Stevie Coppell right-wing cross, to put us 2–0 up a minute before half-time, which, and forgive me if I'm starting to sound like Roy Castle and Norris McWhirter here, makes me the youngest Manchester United goal-scorer in history at 17 years and 8 days. But it's a miss that still haunts me and is the first thing retrieved from the recesses of my brain whenever I see someone fail when one-on-one with the goalkeeper. The ball fell free about twenty-five yards from goal and I outran Stoke's veteran captain, Dennis Smith, with only Peter Fox, who had advanced to the edge of the eighteen-yard box, to beat. Clipping it over his head into an open goal would have been the easiest option and one I would have gone for ninety-nine times out of a hundred. What possessed me to hit it low and go for power I'll never definitively know — the way the ball sat up probably — but he pulled off a good ground save to my shot and palmed the ball away for a corner. I remember I wouldn't let myself resort to any excuses about my age or take any comfort from my team-mates' encouragement, stuff like 'at least you worked the keeper'. I was gutted, livid with myself, and twenty-five years on it still bugs me. I also recall a few better moments: a couple of firmly hit volleys, holding the ball up several times with the burly Smith heaving at my back and my simple goal celebration — a 'Smiley Whiteside' grin and a modest leap in

One of the greatest European nights at Old Trafford.

Taking on and beating Maradona's Barcelona in March 1983.

'Jimmy, before my injury I used to be able to raise my knee this high ...'

I certainly wasn't the 'new George Best', but I could sometimes run rings around him. Look, I'm doing it here.

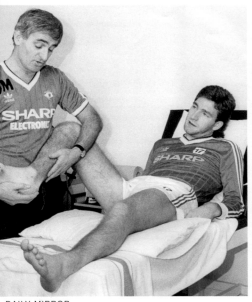

the air. That was pretty much it, 'the debut of delight' as *The Pink* called it, and I suppose I should be happy at performing and scoring. And I am really, until the old reel starts to spool in my head and I see the yawning goal behind a stranded Peter Fox and every time it makes me want to kick myself.

Perhaps because George was at the game, my goal started the newspapers off on the Best trail again, even though our assistant manager had asked them not to. 'The first time he disappoints,' Mick Brown said, 'people are going to jump in and say he's not as good as Best. Football's hard enough without having to live in the shadow of a great player like George.' It was good of him to stand my corner, but our protestations made little difference. A letter written to *MEN* pointed out how clumsy the comparison was. 'Whiteside is nothing like Best,' wrote Mr Williams on the Monday after the match. 'To older fans it would be clear he is a larger version of 1948 era forward Jack Rowley.' In a nice twist, my ma's granddad Tanner, who had played in goal for Distillery in the twenties and became Linfield's trainer in the thirties, was Rowley's physio of choice when he had a long-standing injury and he would make a trip to Belfast for treatment. Still, I could appreciate that 'the new Rowley' does not make for as sexy a headline as 'the next Best', but little did I know that the reports on my full debut were only a baptism for what followed that summer.

Immediately after the match, I got a tap on my shoulder from Ron to confirm that I was to join the boys on the post-season tour of Canada and America, and I crossed the Atlantic the next day. It was an old-fashioned end of season jolly to thank the players for European qualification and we didn't take the three matches against Vancouver Whitecaps, Seattle Sounders and Hajduk Split very seriously. The game against Split was very tough, but the most memorable moment of the tour was the impact made by a tiny Peter Beardsley, playing for the Whitecaps. He must have impressed Ron, as he was brought over on a three-month loan the following season. He was sent back at the end of it, however, having played just one first-team game in the League Cup, when Vancouver quoted £500,000 as a transfer fee.

We had four days off in San Diego and Palm Springs at the end of the fortnight and it was there that I was initiated into the 'social' activities of the boys on tour. They took the mickey out of me all the time; whenever a round was to be fetched, I, the youngest, was sent off to get it. Even though I was seventeen and the legal age for drinking in the US was twenty-one, I passed for twenty-five and was never refused. We spent much of our free time hanging around the pool, drinking from big quart bottles of beer that I lugged over from the neighbourhood liquor store. If this was what life in the first team was like – play hard and party hard – I thought it would suit me right down to the ground. My first experience on the pints with the boys probably set the tone for the rest of my career, but I'm sure I would have developed a fondness for a drink whether I'd been a footballer or, like my da, a painter and decorator. It was in my bones. But it wasn't the beer but another telephone call I received in America, like the first in Boston four years earlier, that changed my life more profoundly.

The first inkling I had that my planned summer at home in Mary Peters' mobility boot camp might have to be abandoned came quite quickly after my comeback. I was the only passenger in Eric Harrison's car, getting a lift from the Cliff to Old Trafford in early April, when he turned to me and said, 'If you keep going you could get in the Northern Ireland World Cup squad.' As I hadn't even played a minute of first-team football by that stage, my first instinct was to question my coach's sanity, but I was too respectful to say that out loud so I just shot him a puzzled look. He went on to tell me that the national team's manager, Billy Bingham, a friend of his since their Everton days, was getting regular updates on my progress from Eric and the Northern Ireland and United physio, Jim McGregor, another Goodison Park refugee, and that he was monitoring me.

A few days later Jim confirmed that I was in contention, so it did not come as an enormous surprise when I was named in the preliminary forty-man squad on 9 May. My international experience was largely limited to those twelve goals in fourteen games for the schoolboy side and a few Saturday afternoons spent at Windsor Park as a ball-boy during Home Championship games as part of our national schoolboy team duties. Yes, I had played for the Under-18s when stricken with appendicitis the previous year, but we didn't have an Under-21 team at the time so I couldn't get experience at that level. I felt sure that I, along with most of the nine part-time Irish League players, had been included only as a precaution against injuries to the boys who had achieved qualification. Maybe the ninety minutes against Stoke had tipped the balance, I don't know, but I certainly didn't spend my time in America in a state of limbo, worrying whether I'd make it or not because I'd all but ruled the faint possibility out.

It was probably for the best that Jim McGregor tipped me off while we were on tour that I was more than likely to make the cut because one afternoon I got back to my room in San Diego and was told by my room-mate, Gordon McQueen, that the manager had been on the phone and was pleased to inform me that I had been selected in the twenty-two. Big Gordon was the joker in the pack at the club, the wind-up merchant supreme, and I'm sure that if I hadn't had the whisper from Jim I would have taken it as a typical McQueen prank. The official confirmation from the Irish FA summoning me to a training camp in Brighton put the lid on my doubts. It was a nice piece of symmetry: my association with United had started in the States and put me on the road to Brighton, and now my international career was following the exact same path.

When Sven-Goran Eriksson picked Theo Walcott for England's 2006 World Cup squad I was contacted by journalists for my opinion and I said, as was said about me, 'If he's good enough, he's old enough.' The controversy which greeted his selection surprised me because my own, in 1982, caused few ripples until we got to Spain. Of course, that's a reflection of the size of expectations – England always generate far more coverage than Northern Ireland – and the hype that has grown around the game over the past twenty-five years. Many people noted the similarities between us – our age and experience – but few pointed out one essential difference. Walcott had not played in the top flight, but had turned out twenty-odd times for Southampton before his transfer to Arsenal and had featured in one of England's warm-up games. Me, I had 102 minutes of action, a fragile knee and had never even met the manager or the majority of the squad. OK, I had the build of a man, but in truth never has a greener player than me been selected for the tournament. I should have felt nervous, daunted even, but all I could think was something eminently practical. Because of the injury, I had missed so much football that year and now here was Billy Bingham handing me the opportunity to carry on playing. It was the prospect of games as much as the prestige of the World Cup that excited me. For that reason, and to postpone the dull reality of a football-free summer for as long as I could, I couldn't get to Brighton quick enough.

CHAPTER SIX

RECORD-BREAKER

By the time I checked back in at the Metropole on the last day of May, the team affectionately known as Norn Iron had got its World Cup underway without me. I was far too late and obscure to get my face on to one of the Panini stickers that were furiously being swapped by kids only a couple of years younger than me, and, mercifully, our song, 'When Yer Man Gets the Ball', a diddly-dee collaboration between Dana and the squad, had long since been put in the can. Sadly, the devout Eurovision winner missed out on all kinds of everything by being deprived of a once-in-a-lifetime opportunity to duet with the Shankill Skinhead. The Top 40's loss was certainly everyone else's gain!

The contrast between the media coverage then and only four years later was amazing. In 1982, we hadn't reached the saturation point of today, when entire television channels are devoted to discussions about metatarsals in the run-up to the tournament, but I can't help but be struck by how relatively untroubled and low-key our stay in Brighton was. In fact, the major talking point was not who would be in the team or how we would fare, but whether we should pull out altogether.

That frustrating prospect wasn't to do with the doommongers back home, chief among them Jimmy McIlroy, the deft inside-forward who had played such a major part in taking 'our wee country' to the quarter-finals in 1958, Northern Ireland's only previous appearance at the finals. Indeed, his type of pessimism was rife in Belfast because of poor results in the Home Championships, which culminated in a fourth winless game in succession, a 3–0 hammering by Wales at Wrexham two days before we met up. It was the possibility of having to face Argentina in the second round, while the Falklands War was ongoing, that raised the question of our participation, along with that of England and Scotland.

Argentina's surrender on 14 June, the day after the opening game, ended the argument that British teams should not be playing while troops were dying and enabled us to go ahead. The strength of the campaign to prevent us from going has largely been forgotten over the past twenty-five years. At one point, I recall it seemed very touch and go. Happily, we were saved from having to make any decision by the Irish FA's sensible determination not to do anything rash, despite the criticisms, and we were spared from football's ultimate sacrifice by events in Port Stanley.

The other European teams jetted off to training camps in relatively glamorous locations such as Portugal, Malta and Cyprus, to try to replicate the extreme heat they would face in Spain, while we were bussed daily from the hotel out to the University of Sussex sports ground. Ironically, we had a fortnight of the hottest weather in Europe and even the most pasty-faced members of our squad took on a tan. We thought we scrubbed up pretty well, yet while we don't all fit the stereotype of chalk-white complexions and freckles, Northern Ireland people in general tend not to have sun-lovers' skin. This became most obvious when we strutted back to the Metropole and compared ourselves with our fellow top-of-the-bill guests, the contestants in 1982's World's Strongest Man competition, a breed of bronzed, beefy, long-haired Scandinavians who had upper arms bigger than my thighs. By contrast we looked like the Milky Bar kids.

I don't think I've ever been fitter than I was that month. The training programme was intensive and I managed to get a lot of running under my belt without the soreness that later hampered me whenever I did distance work. It was almost like another pre-season, which was manna for me as I hadn't played a lot of games and had been injured during the orthodox one the summer before. Billy arranged for one of the university athletes to come in every day to act as a pacemaker and we spent whole mornings doing laps and interval sprints to improve our stamina and sharpness.

There was great camaraderie too in the camp and with two weeks' pure, tropical-like sunshine it was as though everything came together to give us the best possible chance in Spain, almost as if what we went out and did when we got there was somehow meant to be. We started out as a squad that had little hope, but by the end were so confident you could sense the bubbliness was more than simply excitement at taking part. We flew from Heathrow with genuine optimism and belief in our capabilities, as our captain, Martin O'Neill, speaking for us all, explained: 'I honestly feel we have the spirit to do something special in Spain.' It is astonishing the effects that strenuous training can have. Physically we were more than ready, but it also gave us a bedrock of belief in each other which grew every day as we witnessed our team-mates getting tougher and stronger. Even the *Belfast Telegraph*, our cheerleader in chief, had called us 'minnows'. By the time we arrived in Valencia and were greeted with news of a ceasefire in the South Atlantic, we felt more like sharks than their quarry.

If we thought we'd reached a peak in Brighton and only needed a few days of ticking-over exercises to keep us fresh for our opening match against Yugoslavia, we were mistaken. The level of professionalism Billy Bingham displayed, by the standards of 1982, was truly remarkable. He had booked the ground of the city's second club, Levante, as our headquarters, but when we got there on the 14th he discovered that the then Third Division club was on the verge of bankruptcy so he had to hurriedly arrange for the IFA to step in and pay some bills to restore the electricity supply that had been cut off and get the ankle-high grass cut. It only took an hour or two to arrange and then we were straight into the manager's programme, which he said he had drawn up after consulting his medical staff about the body's biorhythms. For three days no one was allowed to deviate from the schedule: we took the coach across town to the Estadio Ciudad de Valencia each morning for a light session of jogging, shadow-playing and walking through set pieces; back at the hotel we would do a routine of physical jerks in the grounds before lunch; a lengthy, compulsory afternoon siesta was followed by another meal at 5.30 p.m. and then we were herded back on to the bus to Levante, where we'd do a properly vigorous training session at 9 p.m., the kick-off time of our three group matches. If you ask any of my colleagues what Billy's chief strength was I am sure they would plump for his motivational skills. In Spain, however, he showed he was everyone's measure in his thoroughness of preparation and attention to detail.

His methods certainly worked for me and, looking back, I consider myself to have been at my physical peak at the tournament, quite a premature height to hit when you're only seventeen. I am often asked whether I felt surprised to be picked for the opening game and I can only tell the truth. I genuinely wasn't because it's part of my make-up to have belief in my ability. Of course, I'd also had the opportunity to suss out who I was playing alongside in practice matches and I knew I was doing all right. And although they were all ostensibly my squad-mates, I was also competing against them for a place in the side. If you asked me my opinion on whether team interest comes before self-interest I'd have to say yes, as long as I am in the team. Later, when someone took my place at United and

I was substitute, I wasn't so mercenary that I'd pray for them to get injured, but I definitely wanted my replacement to have a shocker. So, comparing my performances in training to those of the other fringe forwards in the squad – John Jameson of Glentoran and Bradford's Bobby Campbell – I knew I had a far better shout than they did.

Until the team is actually named, however, you're surviving on hope, which can be mentally exhausting. I know the uncertainty took its toll on a couple of squad members who expected to play: the goalkeeper, Jim Platt, my room-mate, and the midfielder, Tommy Cassidy. Both were experienced players who knew it was their last shot at the World Cup and you could tell that sometimes their desire to play turned into desperation. There was never any rift among us, but our successes glossed over the personal disappointments that were never allowed to fester but were real enough nonetheless.

When we have one of our regular get-togethers, Billy always tells the story that a goal I scored on the college sports ground at Falmer in East Sussex made his mind up about my inclusion in the starting XI. Funnily enough, it was the spit of the goal I scored at Wembley in 1985, a powerful, curling shot from a similar position wide of the penalty area that eluded Pat Jennings's snow-shovel hands by millimetres. If I could beat Big Pat from that angle, he thought, I was ready for a place on the team-sheet. Not that he told me then, and he even gave me the No. 16 shirt, while the players that had contributed to our qualification were numbered 1 to 11. I don't know if he did that to throw reporters off the scent, but he always maintains that he knew I would line up against Yugoslavia after only a couple of days in Brighton. But he carried on the illusion that I was more of a possible than a probable, looking to protect me by informing the press that their interest in me was 'unfair on the boy. [You] are putting too much pressure on him and I have not even said he will be playing in the side.' I think he knew the firestorm would come, but for now he instructed television crews to steer clear of me and stop going on about 'the new George Best'.

Ron Atkinson, however, was obviously out of the loop when it came to this particular media mind game. As the *Belfast Telegraph* pointed out, it was very much open house at our hotel for the press, and they quaintly described Billy's attitude as 'come into the parlour, there is a welcome here for you'. Big Ron, who was working for ITV, was one of 200 journalists staying with us in Valencia and he let the cat out of the bag by saying I was not even a probable, more of a definite. 'I wouldn't have dreamt of him playing for Ireland a month ago,' he declared, 'but since our American tour he has matured so much it is amazing. Out here in Spain he has it within his grasp to save me a lot of sweat in the transfer market. I have listened to the Irish players talking about him. They are all very excited and impressed. If it was up to them he would be in already.' It was nice to read, but I doubt it would have endeared him to Billy Bingham, who was trying to throw a smokescreen over the issue, just as he usually did to everyone around him each night in the café with his pipe.

The day before the game we stuck to our schedule, except we moved to a venue 30 km away in Sueca to escape the press. After training the others went up to their rooms, but I stayed downstairs and shared a pot of tea with Pat Jennings. He played the role of father figure to the squad to a T and at twenty years older than me could indeed have been my dad. He was a legend, even to us who knew him, the best goalkeeper in the world, who had first pulled on the Northern Ireland yellow No. 1 jersey the year before my birth, but he was just as thrilled at the thought of playing his first World Cup match as I was. Later that evening, when Billy tipped me the wink I was in, after we had gathered around the TV in the team room to watch Spain draw with Honduras in our group's first game, it was Pat, who was about to win his ninety-second cap, who was the first to congratulate me on my first. I came over a bit Barry McGuigan as I received all the pats on the back from my team-mates, except I said 'Thanks a million' repeatedly instead of his famous, high-pitched 'Thank you very much' catchphrase. I think it was probably more difficult for my parents to handle than it was for me. They were delighted when I rang to tell them the following morning when it had been confirmed, but they were definitely more nervous than I was. I had even slept well that night, apart from the usual side effects from Billy's order that we drink ten pints of water every day.

I've never really enjoyed being the centre of attention in any group, so imagine my unease in the morning when the announcement of my selection was greeted by all hell being let loose as the world's press scrambled for an interview. Again, I think it was worse for my ma and da, as they suddenly became the focus of colour stories about me. Eamonn Holmes, then of Ulster TV, was straight round to Danube Street to interview my mum and the back page of that day's *Belfast Telegraph* had a large picture of my parents and a piece underneath where they spoke about their anxiety and expressed their relief at having rented a video recorder a month earlier so now they could tape my debut! I knew that being selected at such a young age was a decent story, but I hadn't had the faintest idea until that morning that it would make the biggest splash of the World Cup so far. If Billy hadn't been told at one of his press conferences and then passed it on to me, it would have taken the three-inch-high headline on the back of the *Telegraph* to spell out what all the fuss was about. As introductions to the world stage go, small wonder that BELFAST BOY BEATS PELE caused quite a commotion.

Who the hell else in the world remembers what they did when they were precisely seventeen years and forty-one days old? My day, the one when I broke Pele's fourteen-year-old record as the youngest player ever to play in the World Cup finals, a record I still hold, began with a chartered flight to Zaragoza, where we were due to play Yugoslavia in the evening. The cabin crew made us feel very welcome on the thirty-minute journey and had taken the trouble to pipe Irish music through the PA system. We all joined in the singsong as 'When Yer Man Gets the Ball' began. When we got to the hotel, Billy was adamant that I wouldn't be available to talk to the media until after the match, but as I stood outside the door of my room on the second floor I could see down the stairwell into the lobby, which was mobbed with hundreds of journalists. For an hour or so I felt more like a prisoner than a pop star, but I kept hidden away in the team room until the time to go to the stadium arrived.

It was then that I got my first taste of how the next couple of weeks would unfold. There were so many photographers crowding around me as I walked through the foyer that Billy summoned a security guard – a policeman who was armed with a sub-machine gun to protect us from ETA, the Basque separatists – and he pushed my head down and bustled me through the throng and on to the coach. Home-town fame was one thing, instant world celebrity was quite another and I must have had a bemused look on my face as I sat in my aisle seat on the coach, facing inwards to avoid the cameras pressed up against the windows. I wasn't nervous; it just felt so intrusive and weird to be in the spotlight. But as soon as the bus pulled away I became more relaxed, safe in the certainty that I had breathing space, with my team-mates around me, and the press couldn't get a piece of me for several more hours.

Northern Ireland had qualified for the tournament playing a pretty basic 4-4-2, with Gerry Armstrong and Billy Hamilton in the two forward positions. I don't know whether the tactical change was made solely to accommodate me or if Billy Bingham had accepted that he needed to try something fresh to succeed at the highest stage. John McClelland had replaced John O'Neill as centre-half in the previous game and he remained in this position. Poor Noel Brotherston, who died at the age of thirty-eight in 1995, now made way for me. Billy lined us up in a 4-3-3, with a midfield of Martin O'Neill and Sammy McIlroy slightly upfield from Dave McCreery, our Nobby Stiles. Gerry was to hug the right touchline and me the left, while Billy Hamilton stayed in the traditional centre-forward's slot. It's a fashionable formation now because 4-3-3 can quickly retreat to become 4-5-1 when the opposition has the ball, but our twist on it was the energy the front three put in to make sure we were compact when under attack. The aim was to make life difficult for the other side by pushing back to the halfway line: when we were on the back foot 4-3-3 turned into 4-6-0 as we flooded midfield and said, 'If you're so good, get through that.' It wasn't wholly negative, though, the idea being that mine and Billy's ability to hold the ball up and Gerry's formidable running power drew Martin and Sammy into attacking positions whenever we had the ball.

It was here where the benefits of all that running in Brighton paid off. Eventually we would come up against a team that outplayed us, but we were never outfought or outrun. We had spent hours working on ways to overcome the worst problems 100°F temperatures would wreak and were drilled to maintain our shape. This meant that every team member had to be aware all the time of his responsibility to fill in when something off-the-cuff happened. For example, if Jimmy Nicholl went on an overlapping run up the right wing, David McCreery had to cover for him at right-back, Martin took the holding role and Gerry moved infield. Now, of course, a player like Gabriel Heinze in his pomp goes on a storming run up the left and still sprints back to cover. In the heat of Spain in 1982, without the superior fitness of the modern footballer, even given our two weeks' intensive training, we had to be conscious of our limitations. It made far more sense to take a breather after a lung-bursting dash and have someone else temporarily discharge your duties. A Billy Bingham team, therefore, was one engaged in a continuous cycle of organisation and reorganisation, like a defensive version of total football.

I've never been one for pre-match superstitions and routines. I tended to get stripped and sit there quite calmly waiting for the referee to come and get us. Later on, the vogue in the dressing room was to try to wind you up, perhaps inventing a lie that Vinnie Jones, say, had said something derogatory about you to fire your anger. I thought that was all rubbish. I never gave a stuff for those crude attempts to boost my aggression and gave whoever tried it the old bored face. But if anyone ever did reach me in the hour before kick-off and gave me an extra stimulus to play, it was Billy Bingham. It's hard to specify exactly how he did it – I don't think you could put his team talks together and sell them as general motivational guides for businessmen on those strange satellite TV channels, for instance. They were tailored for the Northern Ireland football team, and were about our country, its people, what they'd gone through over the past decade and what our being out there meant to them. People talk about the hairs on their neck standing up during Billy's speech and I had goose bumps. Being the youngest player and making my international debut did not matter to me, but I felt so inspired to play that I could have kicked down the door for the honour of putting on a green shirt in the company of these ten fine men. The coaches, Martin Harvey and Bertie Peacock, went from player to player emphasising small details of the tactical plan and then Billy simply wished us well and the eleven players and five substitutes gave a fullthroated, rousing 'C'mon!' as we were summoned into the tunnel.

When we walked out at La Romareda from the air-conditioned dressing room, the heat, even at 9 p.m., hit us like a violent slap to the face. I remember singing the national anthem and as the camera panned down the line and focused on my face, one of my mates later said that I seemed to be on the verge of tears. I was proud to be there, but I think the moisture he said was in my eyes was more likely to have been sweat. Yugoslavia had a big, physical team in those days, but I didn't feel in the least overawed as we paused to shake hands with them. It was a relief, however, to spin away from the dignitaries and get the feel of the ball at my feet for a few moments while we waited for Martin to swap pennants and the referee to blow his whistle.

There had been a bit of a row over money before the tournament began, when the IFA proposed a sliding scale of bonuses, with the highest match fees, £600, going to the starting XI, £400 to the five subs and a £200 token payment to the six who were left out. We thought that was too divisive and decided at a squad meeting to pool all the money and split it into twenty-two equal shares. It was an excellent move for morale, but I remember thinking about it as I bounced up and down on the left touchline and caught a glimpse in the stand of Bobby Campbell clutching a burger in one hand and lifting a beer to his mouth with the other. It made me smile to think that he was on the same money as me, but, hey, where would I rather have been? He was a rum turkey, Bobby, a folk hero at Bradford City but always in Billy's bad books because he bent every rule. He didn't play in Spain and never added to his two caps. If you are wondering why Billy turned his back on such a prolific goal-scorer it probably had something to do with Campbell's parting shot as the plane hit the tarmac at Heathrow when we got back. 'Hey, Billy,' he shouted as we taxied off the runway, 'You can't effing send me home now!'

When we eventually kicked off, we discovered Yugoslavia were every bit as good as Billy had warned. Technically, they were masterly, a team full of ball-players which included someone I'd watched many times at the Cliff, the centre-half Nikola Jovanovic, who had left Old Trafford the previous summer. I knew all about the excellence of his distribution and we'd all heard about the class of their play-maker Vladimir Petrovic, who joined Arsenal the following season. Their tendency, however, to play a flashy keep-ball game at a cautiously slow tempo meant that they found it hard to break our new system down. There were a few scares in the opening minutes, when Safet Susic made some headway down the right-hand side of our defence and got a couple of shots away, one of which Big Pat scurried down to save. But on the whole we contained them quite well.

Because they chose to attack down our right side, our comfort ball out of defence was hit to me on the left and quite early on I managed to fool their right-back, Ivan Gudelj, who threw himself into a challenge. At the moment he sold himself, I dinked the ball over him, hurdled his leg, got to the byline and spun in a cross which I still think Martin O'Neill should have met on the full. Instead, he barely connected with it. From then on Gudelj resorted to kicking me every time I was one-on-one with him and he conceded a free-kick right on the edge of the box which Sammy, unfortunately, floated straight into the wall. Some players go into their shells when repeatedly booted across the shin, but it never bothered me. I'm not saying I had a high pain threshold, far from it, but it sort of lets you know you've won your personal battle. If you can look your opponent in the eye after he's kicked you and show you're not intimidated, it gives you the upper hand, as if you're saying, 'That was your best shot and you haven't left a mark.' Moreover, if you're built like me a menacing smile can also carry the implied threat that while they've done their worst, you haven't even started yet.

All in all, the match went well for the team and for me individually. Yes, we were wary when Susic and Edhem Sljivo had the ball around our eighteen-yard box, but we had a dominant period just after half-time, when Billy Hamilton might have scored from Gerry's right-wing cross with an ambitious scissor-kick, and we broke impressively several times, having successfully stifled their creative players in midfield by constantly pressing them and crowding them out until they were forced to lay the ball off. In terms of what I had put into every game I'd played to date, the major difference against Yugoslavia was the amount of concentration required. At United even the youth team under Eric Harrison was always expected to win and our game plan was to dominate from the outset. In Spain, however, each thing you did had to be measured and when the heat began to sap my strength in the second half I really had to screw the nut, as we say in football, to focus on my task. I coped until the sixty-first minute, when my touch let me down and the ball squirted too far ahead of me as I tried to dribble forward. As Nenad Stojkovic, a rugged centre-back who had leant too heavily on me a couple of times and whacked me more than once, collected it, I launched myself at the ball and hit him with all my weight. Even by the standards of 1982 it probably deserved a yellow card and I had no complaints. Back then, my age gave me some leeway and the reports the following morning said it was a result of my 'over-exuberance'. When I caught David

O'Leary in a similar fashion six years later, he said I 'went in like some sort of fruitcake'.

The match petered out after that, though we did have a goal disallowed when the referee blew up for a foul on Billy Hamilton, who had ridden the challenge and hit the ball into the net. I don't know how I managed to survive the last twenty minutes; I was so done in and dehydrated that I had enough on my plate trying to breathe let alone make much impact. On those occasions you go into automatic mode, relying on your instincts to get you through, playing simple short passes and keeping a tight line in defence. I can't remember how much weight I lost during the match, but it wasn't as much as the 10-12lbs some of the lads had shed. I still staggered rather than skipped off at the final whistle and my throat was so dry I couldn't even speak. Even so, we were pleased enough with the point we'd won for the 0–0 draw against a fine team whose outstanding talent has largely been forgotten over the past twenty-five years.

I was absolutely spent after the game, almost in a trance as I sat on the bus waiting for the two poor souls who were necking gallons of water to allow them to dribble out urine samples for the drugs testers. I passively watched the antics of our fans as they were making their way back to their campsites and hotels; the most I could manage in response to their shouts of encouragement was a weak smile and a frail thumbs-up. Martin Harvey took the seat next to me for the journey back to the airport and asked me how I felt. When I replied that I had never been so exhausted in my life, he patted me on the shoulder and said, 'Right enough. That's how you're supposed to feel when you've given your all.' I couldn't really argue with that.

My first public utterance to the press after the game, before the avalanche that came the morning after, was the rather muted 'I'm glad to have played my part in a superb team performance. I thought we all did brilliantly. I'm knackered.' I must have croaked the words out because it wasn't until I'd guzzled pints of fluid over the next few hours and had a long sleep back at the hotel in Valencia that I started to recover and my voice returned. Attending my first press conference was a nerve-shredding experience. In the past I'd had the odd word with the *Belfast Telegraph* and the *Manchester Evening News*, but facing the world's press was something I was ill-prepared for. Billy did his best to shelter me, sitting alongside me and my interpreter while trying to field a lot of the questions himself. But he couldn't answer any of the ones about my private life, like whether I had a girlfriend or the nature of my emotions as I surpassed Pele's feat. Mind you, by the time the question had been translated into very formal English I was totally daunted and confused. They got very few words out of me. I gave nothing away and stuck to repeating the words 'pleased' and 'proud', probably earning another world record that day for the most uses of 'unbelievable honour' in a press conference to date.

I wanted only to train, play and hang out with my mates, but instead I was plastered all over the papers as the writers made the most of the few things I said and turned them into feature articles padded out with quotes from the lads. Don't get me wrong, it was nice to read the praise, but I had only played one game, had been out on my feet at the end of it and would have preferred to be preparing for my second cap rather than dwelling on my first. I must concede, though, that it gave my family immense pride to open the local newspaper and flick past the photographs of themselves sat in front of the television and see that Malcolm Brodie had written: 'The world's press now realise what we at home have known for two years, that properly developed he could be a legendary forward.' So, I was faced with mixed emotions: I resented the invasion of my privacy, but I was not wholly immune to the flattery the media directed towards me. Yet it would all be a pointless flash in the pan if we didn't beat Honduras in our next match. Back in Brighton, we had targeted it as the banker win in our group. Fail to get both points, we agreed, and we were out.

Spain's 2–1 victory over Yugoslavia the night before our second game made it imperative that we win so that we could go into our last game with the hosts needing only a point or, if results went our way, a narrow defeat to go through. Honduras, however, failed to read the script. Billy had obviously had them watched, but in those days before coverage of the game went global, some teams remained a mystery. We were unchanged from our opening game and took the lead after nine minutes when I got the ball inside their half by the left touchline, darted towards the eighteen-yard box and shimmied to go past the full-back, Efrain Gutierrez, who chopped me down from behind. It should have been a penalty. I landed comfortably inside the area, but the referee from Hong Kong pointed to a spot inches outside. Sammy McIlroy curled the free-kick over the wall and it skimmed the underside of the crossbar and bounced off the deck towards four advancing players. Chris Nicholl got there before Gerry, Billy and me and should have buried it, but the keeper recovered to nudge his header back on to the bar. Again, I was a split-second away from the rebound as Gerry beat me to it and nodded it from right on the goal-line into the open net, thus depriving me of a second record as the youngest ever scorer!

We had the upper hand throughout the rest of the first half, enjoyed twice as much possession and were confident that a second goal would soon come. We seemed to be getting closer with the chances we created – Billy narrowly missed, then Gerry hit the bar – but after half-time we were mugged by our opponents, whose skill and durability had been undervalued by our scouts. We tried to steamroller them with powerful running and crosses into the box, but they undid us with dainty footwork and short, rhythmic passing, which made us chase shadows as we grew more and more frustrated and tired. Their equaliser was a bullet-header from a corner and we had to endure several heart-stopping moments as the lads visibly wilted under the heat and pressure. By that time I was a spectator, Billy having resorted to Plan A by putting on Noel Brotherston in my place, and I had to endure far more tension watching the last twenty minutes as the boys clung on for a draw than I would have felt if I'd stayed out there.

The common consensus was that we had missed our chance and we only had pride to play for in the last group game, one reporter going so far as to point out the positive to our fans, that while we lacked finesse at least 'the side so far has not proved the embarrassment we expected'. That verdict encapsulates why footballers tend not to care what journalists write. On 17 June the *Telegraph* said of me that 'few have ever made a debut of such elegance, class and impact' yet four days later the same man had come to the conclusion that 'at seventeen he is much too immature for such a heavy burden to be placed on his shoulders'. Of course you expect people to be fickle, but you'd think a consistent line could be maintained for a bit longer. I had heard the cliché about building you up to knock you down, but at times you want to say, 'Make your mind up!' How could I go from superstar to child in such a short space of time?

It would have been all too easy to turn up against Spain and go out to save our faces by adopting a conservative strategy. In fact, the draw against Honduras did us a favour. As we reflected on our performance on the flight back to Valencia, we knew we had to do something we had found difficult so far: score goals. Therefore, for the two days of full training between the games, we worked on perfecting the counter-attack and the forward trident springing out of our own half in fast, fluid moves. If it was to be our last match we must play without fear because we knew we had nothing to lose. As the game approached and we read more and more comments about us being 'no-hopers', our defiance grew. Hadn't North Korea beaten Italy in 1966 and East Germany defeated West Germany in 1974? I looked around the practice field and could sense the boys were up for ramming the critics' words back down their throats. No-hopers? 'This is the World Cup, for God's sake,' Billy said. 'There's no such thing as an unbeatable team.' I know my professional career was barely four games old, but I hadn't been defeated yet. Why should I start now?

CHAPTER SEVEN

OUR '66 AND ALL THAT

Before the World Cup began the IFA freighted crates of Guinness over to our hotel in Valencia, no doubt more with the blazers in mind than the tracksuits. Even so, in the eleven days we were there before the match against Spain, the players, Bobby Campbell before the Yugoslavia match apart, didn't get so much as a whiff of a Rioja cork by way of a spot of relaxation. That didn't stop the Spanish press, however, from portraying us as a bunch of party-daft reprobates like our supporters and José Santamaria, the national team's manager, joined in on the eve of the game. Pointing out that he was puzzled by our high spirits, he said, 'It seems as if they are on vacation.' I realise you can interpret that in two ways: that he was being dismissive of our preparation, or that he was envious of our carefree approach. We chose to read it as an insult, to provide a little extra motivation, but I recognise now that he was probably feeling the dreadful weight of expectation faced by the host team. With all the scrutiny he was under and the importance of keeping a serious face on to show the Spanish people he meant business, I'm sure he cast a jealous eye at us. Three of the past four finals had been won by the hosts, a thought that must have been laying heavily on his players' minds. It was some contrast, therefore, between his own squad, who had a haunted look about them when you saw them on television, and ours — a bunch of lads who stuck together in a social unit, lounging around the foyer of our hotel instead of hiding ourselves away in ones or twos in our rooms, playfully messing about and laughing our way through an endless procession of pots of tea.

We knew the result we required against Spain before we kicked off, as this was the last tournament where the final group games were played on successive dates. On the afternoon of our match West Germany beat their neighbours Austria 1–0 in a fishy and farcical game which put both teams through at Algeria's expense, who had played their last group match the day before, and caused such an outcry at what looked like a stitch-up that from 1986 onwards the third round of group games always kicked off simultaneously. Anyway, because Yugoslavia had defeated Honduras 1–0, we knew we needed a victory or a 2–2 draw in Valencia to go through. On ITV Brian Clough and Lawrie McMenemy said we hadn't a hope in hell. We, on the other hand, knew

Cloughie was often as wrong as a pundit as he was usually right as a manager and were determined to upset the odds and leave the experts in the studio with egg all over their faces again.

Billy named an unchanged side for the third match in a row and sat us down in the team room at the hotel a couple of hours before the game to run through his instructions one last time. He acknowledged how difficult we had found it to score so far, but emphasised that a gung-ho approach would be a disaster. Stick to our guns, he said, swamp midfield to stop Spain passing the ball through us and make them go over the top instead because they didn't have the strength in the air or pace to stretch our back four. Above all, he insisted we keep a high defensive line because their players would go to ground at any excuse in and around the box and he was worried the referee may not be able to remain clear-headed under the pressure of the occasion and 45,000 partisan home fans.

There was a reason Spain had chosen to play all their group games at the Estadio Luis Casanova, and it hit us as we ran out. Madrid would have been the more obvious choice, but they were probably tentative about playing before a crowd of 90,000 at the Bernabéu before they had found their feet, and Seville, where their most hardcore following is based, would have been suicide, like playing in an oven — even if they had survived three games there they would never have had the legs for the next stages. Valencia was a happy compromise: a respectable size rather than a vast concrete coliseum, exuberant fans and, if we were fortunate, the small chance of a coastal breeze. But, just our luck, it was as furnace-like as inland Zaragoza that night. The huge difference was the support and the atmosphere the fans created — a raucous, ear-piercing mix of horns and screams. Also present was Manolo 'El del Bombo', Spain's so-called twelfth man and probably the world's most famous supporter. You could easily spot him in the crowd, wearing his Basque beret, arcing a spray of wine into his mouth from a *bota* and incessantly banging on 'the drum of Spain'. Over in one corner were the Norn Iron fans, many of whom had come on thirty-six-hour coach rides via the Liverpool ferry and, though they were outnumbered ten to one, it gave us a hell of a lift to be greeted by their barnstorming cheers and songs when we walked out of the tunnel.

It was clear from the kick-off that Spain thought they could intimidate us, and their two centre-halves, Tendillo and Alexanco, tried it on with us throughout the whole game. I doubt they could have picked two forwards who would have been less frightened by their tactics than Billy Hamilton and me. Kick us and we couldn't care less, we were big, brawny Belfast guys who knew precisely what their game was. By ignoring it we turned the tables on them. When we didn't shy away we sowed doubt in their minds, making them ask, 'Who are these lunatics and what are they capable of?' However, the entire match was littered with their attempts to provoke us into retaliation. In the tackle they persistently went over the ball and their style of marking at set pieces involved nipping my upper arms, hanging on to my shirt or shorts and stamping down with their two heel studs on the top of my feet. It simply riled me into wanting to win even more. Of course I was very tempted to give either one of them a smack, but I knew I couldn't give an excuse to a referee who was itching to send off anyone wearing green and white.

Amazingly FIFA saw fit to appoint a Latin American, Hector Ortiz of Paraguay, to referee Spain's decisive match. Let's be charitable and say he must have found it difficult to handle the pressure, the non-stop hectoring by the Spanish players in his native tongue and the near hysteria of the crowd. We felt we got no protection at all and later, after a score of cynical fouls committed by the hosts, we started even to question the very laws of the game when Mal Donaghy became the victim of an extremely rash decision.

They had the better of the first few minutes and Pat had to make a great save to stop López Ufarte putting Spain 1–0 up. Most of my work in the two previous games had been devoted to maintaining our shape and taking the responsibility that went with being the only naturally left-footed player in the team to be the creative force from that side of the park. Yet early on against Spain, I had a rare foray into a more central area when Martin O'Neill broke from midfield, played me in and from a couple of yards inside the touchline went on a run and dragged their right-back, Camacho, twenty yards infield. I threw my body to the left to make some space and saw my right-foot shot saved by Luis Arconada. It was from then on that the hacking began in earnest, when Alexanco and Tendillo were joined in their crusade by the midfielder Periko Alonso, who is, incidentally, the father of Liverpool's Xabi Alonso.

During the rest of the half I must have been fouled six or seven times and though I'm not saying the referee didn't award free-kicks to us, he kept his cards firmly in his breast pocket except for Juanito's early booking for a filthy tackle from behind and a yellow each for Billy Hamilton and Sammy McIlroy for

retaliation after earning free-kicks. It was a cowardly performance from Spain, not only the dirty play but also the fact that
they didn't seem to have the courage to complement their skill
and attack us. Instead, they tried to nick a win on the counter-
attack and quickly pulled their midfield back to shield the
defence as soon as we had the ball. You may remember that I
described us doing the same thing, but the difference between
the two systems is that our forwards also retreated when we
were playing a counter-attacking style, strangling the space in
which the opposition could play. But Spain's attackers, Quini
and Juanito, were more sluggish coming back and it left a huge
gap, almost half the pitch, between their attack and midfield.
It was in that space, Billy had said before the match and re-
iterated at half-time, that we could determine whether we stayed
in Spain or went home.

He was spot on. With only two minutes of the second half
gone, Spain's left-back, Gordillo, went on a run inside our half,
played a short one-two with López Ufarte, cut inside, dithered
and tried to set his winger free with a too-cute pass about thirty
yards from our goal. Gerry Armstrong, who had gone back to
help Jimmy Nicholl, as he did throughout the tournament,
launched himself off his left foot into a semi-splits lunge to
intercept with his right, stole possession and was off. I was in
a mirror position to Gerry, between our penalty area and the
centre-circle out on our left, and held my line, keeping pace
with his run, which was easier for me because I was going
straight.

Gerry's dart was anything but straight. First, he moved diag-
onally infield, crossed the halfway line and then switched his

run to bear right again. It was hardly a Cristiano Ronaldo-type dribble, with the ball constantly on the end of his toe, more an old-fashioned muscular charge, knocking the ball a yard or so ahead of him with every kick. On he went, despite Sanchez's wild hack at his heels, and I stayed with him, knowing the left-back's mistake had started our move and he was struggling to get back. I realised that if I could keep Camacho occupied marking my run down the outside-left channel, there would be plenty of gaps in the penalty area. So I stayed left, but as soon as Gerry went past halfway, Billy Hamilton peeled away from the centre of the park into the hole where Gordillo should have been. Gerry looked up and flicked the ball to him and Billy took on Tendillo, who had come out of central defence to cover. My Spanish friend attempted to body-check Billy, but our centre-forward straightened his left arm with quite a bit of force to shrug him off, ran on for about five yards and crossed it with his right foot.

I was still out on the left when the ball went into the area, ready to make a far-post run if Billy had shaped to lob the ball above the goalkeeper. Instead, he sent a tempting, thigh-high, out-curling chip across the six-yard box. That was the moment Spain's goalkeeper and captain, Luis Arconada, came to our assistance and ensured his name was inextricably linked to Gerry's in Northern Ireland's eyes for all eternity, thanks to John Motson's oft-replayed commentary: 'And Arconada . . . Armstrong! . . . Northern Ireland have scored!' I don't know what the keeper was trying to do, as Gerry had at the point the ball came in advanced no further than the penalty spot. I was only just in the picture, on the left angle of the box, when

Arconada decided not to leave the ball for the two defenders behind him to deal with but came to catch it one-handed, found it was just out of his grasp, parried it with the fingertips of his right hand and couldn't have teed Gerry up more if he was deliberately trying to pick our No. 9 out.

I can't confirm that the finish deserves to be remembered as the best goal in Northern Ireland's history, as I haven't seen any of the five Peter McParland scored in Sweden in 1958, but Gerry's finish was certainly the most famous, even if it was relatively straightforward. The ball bounced a couple of times as it bobbled to him off Arconada's gloves and Gerry hit a simple, straight shot under the goalkeeper's legs and beyond Camacho and Alexanco, who were trying to cover. I was thrilled, but if you watch the match now you'll get a sense of how exhausted we must have been because we were only forty-seven minutes into the match and none of us had the energy to sprint towards the hero. There is a nice picture of Gerry, Billy and I embracing when we eventually made it to him and although we are smiling, we are plastered in sweat and blowing hard. Oddly, it was the first time in the match that we could hear one another, as our goal was greeted by outraged silence apart from our couple of thousand fans going deranged in the corner. Indeed, at first Gerry thought the goal would not stand. 'When I hit it into the back of the net,' he says, 'all I could hear was a sudden silence. I thought something had gone wrong and the referee had disallowed it. He hadn't been giving us anything much. But then I heard Norman yelling, "Gerry, Gerry, it's a goal!" and he jumped on my back. Then it sank in.' If the match up to then had been the most physically and mentally demanding of my career, the remaining forty-three minutes were more like the Alamo than a game of football.

If it had been more like the West Germany v Austria 'match', perhaps the game would have petered out into a 1–0 Northern Ireland victory, as it would have meant both teams qualified for the second round. But the only controversial thing about our game was the referee's reluctance to punish the Spanish properly for persistent fouls, gamesmanship and diving. They became less cautious once we had scored, since they were terrified of conceding another goal. A 2–0 defeat would put them out, while we were desperate to hang on to our lead as a 1–1 draw would eliminate us. It was a classic knife-edge, as we were forced to retreat for almost all the fifteen minutes after we had scored and though Pat Jennings saved from López Ufarte, he could not save Mal Donaghy from Mr Ortiz. After an over-hit cross into our box from our right, Mal shepherded the ball out of play on the left, holding off Camacho by leaning into him. Their momentum took the two into an advertising hoarding and when they stood up, Mal pushed Camacho away. The referee was over there like a gazelle and gave Donaghy a straight red. So harsh and unjustified was it, not only when compared to the brutal tackles that had gone before but even by the way modern refs apply the laws nitpick-style, that I did a double-take, looking up a second time to make sure the card really was red. Mal stood there with his hands on his hips, shook his head in disbelief, looked at the floor and trooped off, leaving us half an hour to play with ten men.

I lasted just ten minutes longer before Billy decided to bolster our make-do-and-mend back four with an orthodox left-back and replaced me with Sammy Nelson. I sat next to Billy on the bench for the last twenty minutes, utterly shattered, constantly staring up at the clock. It seemed to take a day for each minute to pass. We were put under so much pressure by Spain and were frightened to death because in each of their two previous games they had been awarded highly questionable penalties so you never knew quite what could happen. But every one of our ten men put in a remarkable performance, keeping Spain's attackers away from the box and throwing themselves three at a time to block shots. Inevitably, Pat was key to it, pinching the ball off Juanito's head when it seemed he was going to bury it, constantly marshalling his team-mates into a stonewall defence. The crowd, whipped up by Manolo's drum, went berserk in the dying seconds of the game and with every minute in that heat a form of torture, no wonder we all felt light-headed on the bench. Relief and the whistle finally came in the ninety-second minute, after Gallego hit a hopeful forty-yard ball into the box which was belted clear by Jimmy Nicholl. Full-time had the same effect on me as spinach had on Popeye and I bolted on to the pitch to hug the lads. But even though I enjoyed a thirty-four-year age advantage over Billy Bingham, our manager still beat me to Gerry. The picture of the two of them hugging became the definitive image of the win, a victory which Norn Iron fans cherish as our greatest achievement, 'our '66'.

Having made sure I slapped every one of the lads on the back and received my fair share in return, we trudged down to the corner where our fans were. Manolo's drum was finally silent and had been replaced by raucous and deliriously happy chants. All we could see was a sea of green and white, peppered with scores of red-and-white Ulster flags. For some time we stood there clapping them as they applauded us in return until Billy managed to quieten them slightly and shouted, 'You know where we are. Come and join us.' With that we were back in the dressing room and I sat there in my shorts, revelling in the air conditioning, gradually restoring my strength with blasts of cold air and sips of champagne.

I doubt the five-star Sidi Saler hotel had ever hosted a party quite like the one put on that night. Billy was as good as his word and when we got off the coach, just before midnight, he went over to speak to the police. As I said before, they all had mini-machine guns and were supposedly there to protect us from ETA or anyone with an axe to grind over the Falklands or indeed Gibraltar. The last thing they wanted was an open-house, all-night party, but Billy was insistent and opened up the gates to the hotel complex himself to let our supporters in. Meanwhile, we were ditching our kit in our rooms and phoning home. My ma told me there were people dancing up and down the Shankill. It was only then that the scale of our achievement hit me. Of course I'd expected my ma, da and brother to be jumping up and down in front of the television, maybe their neighbours in Danube Street too, but when we pieced together all the reports the lads had received from their families we all became aware that the whole of Belfast was having a massive party that night, Protestant and Catholic. It went down well in the Republic too, I understand, and Simon and Garfunkel were actually cheered at their Dublin reunion concert when, maybe not knowing which side of the border they were on, they dedicated 'The Boxer' to Yer Men.

I never slept well after evening matches and later, at United, would often head into town with Remi Moses to play snooker until 7 a.m. at one of the twenty-four-hour clubs after midweek games. I didn't sleep that night in Valencia either. I went from the ITV reception – where I met up with Big Ron, who thrust a beer in my hand and told me to forget his order to head back to the Cliff at the end of the tournament to work on my speed – to the downstairs bar. Felix Healy led the singsong downstairs and we must have reprised 'When Irish Eyes Are Smiling' at least ten times. My brother Ken had come out to Spain with a group of his pals and they joined us to down a few Guinnesses. This was a few years before he joined the RUC and he was still working as a decorator alongside our da but had already had his holidays for the year so had to ring in sick to come to Valencia. The next day Ulster TV broadcast an interview with me and cut away to show footage of him and me walking down the beach. It blew the lid off the tale he had told his bosses when they saw the sick man skipping around in the sun with his brother in Spain!

I remember looking over at Martin O'Neill, the skipper, as he held court in the bar. The man you see on the BBC these days hasn't changed at all – he was as bright, acidic, wordy and hilarious then as he is now. Most of all it was his tremendous enthusiasm that shone through and though you wouldn't think it, he never allowed his intelligence to isolate him from the boys. There was a special bond between all of us for the next few years and it became the norm after internationals at

Windsor Park for us to sit in the hotel bar in Belfast after games, having a singsong all night. Martin was very much part of that scene, one of the lads, and many were the times we would look at our watches at 5 a.m. and decide it wasn't worth going to bed. I often boarded the flight back to Manchester two hours later, with my international kit in a black bin liner, after a night spent unwinding after a European Championship or World Cup qualifier with the boys of '82.

But it is Gerry I remember most vividly as he laughed and joked through the night that made him famous. He was so talkative and deservedly proud of what he'd done and he gabbled away so much to anyone in earshot that Sammy Nelson ended up calling him 'Don Quick Quote'. He hadn't even been a regular at Watford the previous season, but here he was, the architect of the biggest upset in the World Cup. It earned him a move to Mallorca and when he came back to play for us he was full of improbably funny stories about how he'd played Barcelona and been man of the match in the Nou Camp, while Maradona and Bernd Schuster weren't even in the picture. He went from Vicarage Road reserve to the Bernabéu in two years and no one could have deserved it more than him for his sheer determination, application and wit. We got on really well and six days after his finest hour our two mothers were also brought together. A TV company thought it would make for a symbolic show of the country's unity if they watched our next match in each other's company. So my ma obliged and, taking the day off work, went from the Shankill across the Falls to Gerry's house in Mica Drive for an unlikely Protestant–Catholic summit which taught neither, I think, anything that they didn't already know — namely that the tiny cultural differences were insignificant when compared to the things they had in common.

The singing and drinking continued until we broke for tea and toast just before dawn and when I finally got my head down I could still hear the excited chatter of a few of the diehards out on their balconies amid the chirping of the birds. It was a fantastic feeling to lie there knowing that we'd beaten the hosts, won the group and were heading for the second round, only four games away from winning the World Cup. The praise for us all was fulsome the following morning. It was amusing to note that Malcolm Brodie, who had said I 'was too immature for such a heavy burden' against Honduras, now felt I showed 'the flush of youth, the brain of maturity, the strength of a budding Atlas. He shielded the ball brilliantly, was never knocked off it, never overawed by the passion of the fans.' It's true what they say: if you believe everything that is written about you over the course of your career, you'd probably end up in the nuthouse!

To some of our fans the remainder of the tournament must have seemed like an anticlimax. Understandably, that night in Valencia was a pinnacle that we failed to reach again, even though we gave it our best shot. The truth is that underdogs always have a puncher's chance in a one-off game, but I'm a firm believer that cream always rises to the top in football and it was almost impossible for a team like ours to sustain a giant-killing run game after game. Eventually you're going to come up against a side that is simply too good, like we did when we faced France. But that was still far off in the distance when we woke with hangovers after the Spain game, hastily packed and headed off to Madrid for our first second-round group game against Austria.

It was obvious that the IFA had not expected us to go through and officials spent the night alternately celebrating, cancelling flights home and hurriedly contacting FIFA about accommodation for the next phase. They also had to call adidas and get them to make and send out a green home kit, as they had only ordered the white away strip required for the three group games. It was obvious that Yugoslavia had also felt that Spain would comfortably beat us because when we arrived at the Hotel Alameda on the outskirts of Madrid they were being turfed out of the rooms they had occupied in anticipation of our defeat. We literally passed them on the stairs.

After the delights of our digs in Valencia — sea, sand, swimming pool and beautiful grounds — the Alameda was a massive comedown. I'm not complaining, it was still a luxurious hotel, but it was right out by the airport, had no gardens and we soon felt stir-crazy confined there day after day. The West Germany squad were in a similar predicament in the hotel opposite us, but our only real contact with them came when some of the lads broke Billy's order that no more than one hour a day could be spent sunbathing, found a fire escape, clambered on to the roof and found the Germans had done the same thing on their roof and exchanged waves and a bit of banter twenty storeys up. That brief association was cut short when Billy discovered what was going on, climbed up to their perch and ushered them back down again. I'm not much of a sun-worshipper so I wasn't busted with the others. Billy was very reasonable about it. He knew it was only done

127

to relieve the boredom, but he was extremely concerned that the games against Austria and France would be played during the afternoon and sunbathing would sap the players' strength. Good job he didn't try to restrict his friend and fellow hotel guest Big Ron's time in his Speedos, though. He would have got short shrift from the sun king!

We had six days to prepare for the Austria game and changed our schedule so we trained at the Vicente Calderón at 5.15 p.m., to coincide with kick-off time. The mood in the camp, which had been buoyant on our arrival in the capital, took a bit of a knock when we learned that Pat Jennings was going to have to miss the game with a groin injury. The hotel also played its part in dampening our sparkle – the noise of the airport was only kept at bay by the thick double-glazed windows which made the place like a sauna. It was also the custom that curtains would be drawn and the lights not put on to combat the heat, so at times during the middle of the day it was so sticky and gloomy it became quite depressing.

I will not use that as an excuse for my performance against Austria, however, which was my least effective of the tournament. I was so desperate to play against France in the second game that, for once, the thought of picking up a second yellow card against Austria, which would have ruled me out, had played on my mind before kick-off. But as soon as the match started I forgot about that and tried to get stuck into my normal game. We took an early lead through Billy Hamilton, after Gerry Armstrong had surged from our half to their dead-ball line and cut back a wonderful cross on to Billy's head. I had made the pass to Sammy McIlroy to set Gerry free and had earlier linked up with Sammy to put him clear, but that was the sum of my attacking contribution really, as I spent most of the game, in 108°F temperatures, as a left-sided midfielder to counter their sweeper system, which pushed both full-backs forward.

I took a knock on the calf after about twenty minutes, which stiffened up after half-time. We knew that Austria would be dangerous after the break, but recognised that if we could get a second goal to better France's 1–0 victory over them, then we could go into the France game needing only a draw to get through to the semis. It was Roy of the Rovers material, and for the entire squad not just for me. Austria, however, had other plans and made two substitutions which changed the game. Having nothing to lose, they threw on Reinhold Hintermaier and Kurt Weizl and shifted to a 4-3-3. They absolutely flew at us and deserved their equaliser on fifty minutes, even though it came from a fluky deflection. By the time I hobbled off, when they were awarded a free-kick seventeen minutes later, we had been under the cosh since the restart. Unfortunately, my replacement, Noel Brotherston, did not even get a touch before they went 2–1 up through Hintermaier's shot from the free-kick. Given the pressure we had been under, it seemed that defeat was inevitable, but Gerry once again came to our rescue with another forty-yard run and shot which was blocked and fell to Jimmy Nicholl out on the right. He was at full stretch, but got his toe to the ball and looped it into the area and Billy Hamilton dived to make it 2–2 with a brilliantly precise and powerful header. In that heat it was natural that dominance should ebb and flow between the two sides and we ended the game with the upper hand. We were realistic enough not to be disappointed: we finished as we started, knowing that if we could beat France we would be through.

Although Gerry and I became the media darlings of our World Cup campaign, I'd like to pay tribute to the unsung hero, David McCreery. He was magnificent in every game, an unobtrusive workhorse who tirelessly made us tick by winning tackles and playing short, rhythmic passes from his position in front of the back four. I was delighted he went on to become something of a legend at Newcastle because he had a difficult time at United. The Old Trafford crowd is exceptionally demanding and probably looked at him and thought, 'He's no Bobby Charlton.' But sometimes it's as much about not making mistakes as it is about anything else, and every team needs players who can stick to their role, execute their orders professionally and give the players who can shine a platform. Without his consistency and commitment and his quiet, honest contribution we would never have got as far as we did.

The build-up to the France game back home was incredible. Even for Austria on the Thursday, Harland & Wolff and Sirocco had to have overtime shifts on the Wednesday to allow the workforce home early the next day to catch the game. Our final group game, however, was on a Sunday and though there was some dissent from the Revd Ian Paisley about us playing on 'the Lord's day', as there had been from other sources in 1958, the news we were getting from our families told us that almost the whole population of 1.5m was planning to tune in. Apparently, more video recorders were hired in Belfast that week than at the time of the royal wedding a year earlier. If you look at the *Belfast Telegraph* on the day before the match, you get a flavour of the fervour back home: 'On July 1, 1916, a glorious chapter was written in the history of Northern Ireland at the battle of the Somme. Perhaps here in Madrid sixty-six years later the sons of Ulster will bring even further honour to the Province.' Only a game? It was one hell of a tall order we were looking at.

It was France who had knocked Northern Ireland out in 1958 and my colleagues had been on the end of a 4–0 thrashing by them only a few weeks before we departed for Spain, so it is understandable that many saw the game as a chance for revenge. In truth, however, they were too good for us. Billy went back to his first-choice XI and reinstated Mal Donaghy after suspension and Pat after injury, but their return made little difference to the 4–1 scoreline. The outcome could only have been changed if luck and the referee had been with us because at 0–0 we scored a perfectly good goal that was disallowed. I remember the move began with me getting the ball out on the left, beating Bernard Genghini and Manuel Amoros, then stopping and back-heeling a flick to Martin O'Neill. The captain hit a quick one-two with Gerry, shot and scored a goal which the television replays showed was onside. It wasn't given. Anything might have happened had it stood and I'm not being facetious when I say we could have just kicked the ball out of play every time we got it during the remaining sixty-odd minutes to cling on to victory. I know it never works out that way, but it would have been nice to have had a lead to defend.

Instead, being let off the hook provoked the French into turning on one of the most captivating displays I've ever seen. Their midfield – Genghini, Alain Giresse, Jean Tigana and

Michel Platini, their captain – was so fluid and skilful and it was almost a privilege to watch how graceful yet devastating Platini's movement, passing and shooting could be. He was the greatest player I ever faced, absolutely supreme. They also had the pace of Dominique Rocheteau and the defensive class of Marius Trésor. They were 3–0 up by the time we knew what had hit us – the first from Giresse, after Platini had sailed past three of our players to cross, and two more from Rocheteau, a powerful shot after a forty-yard run and a bullet-header.

Strangely, after my ordinary showing against Austria, I played much better against France, even though we were getting tonked, and set up our goal when I beat Amoros and sent in a back-post cross which Gerry put past Jean-Luc Ettori. They scored again five minutes later to confirm how significantly they had outplayed us, but although we were soundly beaten, I'm proud that we gave it a go against such a formidable team. They went on to lose the semi-final on penalties to West Germany, after Toni Schumacher's dreadful foul almost decapitated Patrick Battiston, and I admit to watching it with envy from the sofa back in Belfast, thinking it could have been us. Looking back from the perspective of twenty-five years, I am not at all jealous. I'm full of respect for our achievement in getting to a spot where we were two victories away from the World Cup final.

We had done our utmost to get to the semi-final, but I think the sadness we all felt at falling short was tinged with relief at the thought of going home. For six weeks we had put up with motorcycle outriders escorting the coach, armed police and heli-copter patrols when we went training, which made us all feel claustrophobic. That was exacerbated by Billy's insistence that we conserve our energy at the hotel, so there were few outings and only the one party. We did go to the Lladro factory in Valencia, and at the end of the tournament Granada TV presented me with one of the glassmaker's limited edition replicas of the World Cup trophy as a souvenir, which I cherish. So, if I'm being honest, I have to admit that you can get sick of being cloistered away together, focusing solely on training and football, what the Italians call *ritiro*, no matter how well you get on. We'd been constantly monitored and were subject to a schedule — eating and drinking by the clock — 12 p.m.: salt tablets; 12.15 p.m.: two pints of water; 12.30 p.m.: a lunch of grilled chicken or fish, etc. I hope I'm not sounding ungrateful because I can't tell you how much pleasure I got from being out there and the honour I felt to be in the service of my country. Still, I was looking forward to replacing the gallons of water with something more nutritious!

There was a huge press presence at Heathrow when we landed as a team and, indeed, at Manchester when I arrived there on my own a couple of hours later and at Belfast the following morning. Because of the holidays and the sense of surprise at our achievement, no civic reception had been arranged and we didn't do the traditional open-top bus ride through Belfast until 15 November. My memories of walking through three airport arrival halls in succession over the course of twenty-four hours are dominated by flash-bulbs and reporters thrusting micro-phones and small tape recorders into my face, particularly when I flew into Belfast. It's amazing when you think about the protection a club like United gives to its players now, even when on international duty, but I walked alone into a media storm.

I tried to be as polite and short as possible and wasn't particularly worried whether it made a story or not. I was more concerned with avoiding the spotlight, but for the next few years that proved impossible.

It was the same five years later in 1987, when I flew into my home town on a Saturday night after a United game. On that occasion, I had kidded my ma that the club had refused to let me attend her silver-wedding party, but the interest in me was so great that my cover was blown. As Ken and Hughie put my parents into a taxi to go to the venue they were surprised to hear over the radio that 'Norman Whiteside has come to Belfast tonight to be the mystery surprise guest at his parents' twenty-fifth wedding anniversary celebrations.' At that stage of my life I would have made a useless spy! It was rarely as intrusive as that and, of course, brought many benefits, but my crash course at the World Cup fame academy had repercussions that pursued me for the next decade.

CHAPTER EIGHT

MAGIC CIRCLE

Writing off Ron Atkinson's achievements as Manchester United's manager has become the norm in recent years. Even before he seemed to destroy his second career with what has been described as the 'moment of madness', when he made his apparently racist comment about Marcel Desailly in 2004, critics portrayed his period in charge of the club as a wasted opportunity, a triumph of style over substance. Of course, I have a vested interest in defending his record – his time in charge coincided with my peak years as a player – but I think any comparison between Ron's reign and the trophy-filled empire built by Sir Alex Ferguson has to be taken in context. There were different circumstances and a different culture and ignoring those factors does him, and by association us, an injustice. I don't only mean the recreational indulgences, the boozing sessions that were once common practice in English football, which are said to tarnish our reputation and are supposed to have been a 'cancer' excised by Sir Alex's disciplinary zeal. You also have to take into account the ruthless consistency of Liverpool's excellence during those years and the inability of any team to match their relentless pursuit of titles. To be fair, you have to assess Ron's team in the light of those factors rather than using his failure to win the championship as an invitation to kick the man when he's down.

That's not to say the contrast with Sir Alex's methods necessarily does him a disservice. Ron was an old-school motivator, full of enthusiasm and encouragement, but not one who would endlessly drill us on set-plays or put on a coaching master class to outline his defensive theory. His team talks reflected this — there was no essential difference in their content and tone whether our opponents were Barcelona, Juventus, Arsenal, Liverpool or Bury. His whole philosophy was: 'We are Manchester United. Let's not worry about what they're going to do. Let them worry about us.' When Fergie came in he would have the opposition watched three or four times and would come out with all sorts of intricate instructions, for example: 'In three successive games between the sixty-fifth and seventieth minutes, their left-back began to tire because he had made too many runs. I want you to start hitting that channel in the seventieth minute.' His level of preparation was such that anyone would look bad when measured up against him. Ron never gave a hoot about anything like that. Perhaps he bought into the status of the club more than anyone, I don't know, but for him it was all about us. He sincerely believed that if we all played our best then we would triumph and his attitude was that we should play attacking football, go out and win every game.

Ron's other misfortune when appraised alongside his successor is that he wasn't what you would call a manager of the whole club in the same vein that Sir Alex is, or indeed Sir Matt, Bill Shankly, Jock Stein and Don Revie were. All that mattered to Ron was his first-team squad. If you look at it objectively, I suppose you could say that his job depended on those players alone, so it was understandable that he focused on us. We were what he called his 'magic circle', and if you were one of his chosen sixteen you were made – he backed us to the hilt, lavished us with praise, played five-a-sides with us, made us all eligible for win bonuses and even, occasionally, socialised with us. If you were in, you were part of Ron's gang, but if you were outside this charmed set for whatever reason – dropped, injured, too young or not good enough – then he wouldn't give you the time of day. Sir Alex is obsessed with detail and runs the club from top to bottom, but Ron geared all his energy to the first team and everything else was left to the staff. I went to Spain on the periphery of the manager's elite group, but when I reported back to the Cliff after two weeks' break I doubt Ali Bongo himself would have had better credentials for entry into Big Ron's magic circle.

I may have been a household name, but I had still played only seven games in my professional career, so when the rumours started going round that one of the previous season's first-choice forwards, Garry Birtles, would be sold back to Nottingham Forest, I suspected Ron would buy an established replacement to play with Frank Stapleton. I backed myself, whoever the new signing should be, to displace either him or Frank given an opportunity, but feared I might have to waste some time between the bench and the reserves if the manager reached for his familiar comfort blanket of a high-profile purchase. In the end, I was saved the wait by three factors: Ron had already shown bottle in giving me my debut and now I'd done enough at the World Cup to convince him that I had the maturity to cope; the boss was sufficiently PR-savvy to know that giving the home-grown kid a run would be a popular, crowd-friendly move; and finally, incredible as it may now seem, United were skint. Ron may have wanted to sign Andy Gray but, fortunately for me, the club could not afford him.

For pre-season training in the Atkinson era we used to go out to Heaton Park, to the north of the city. Now the programme is meticulously planned, follows a strict timetable and takes place far from the public gaze, but then we used to go to the municipal park. Every day sixty Manchester United professionals and trainees would be bussed from the Cliff, limber up for a few minutes and then Ron, with his bobble hat on, would point to a landmark somewhere in the distance, which could be anything from a tree or, as I remember on some occasions, a woman pushing a pram, and shout, 'Round there and back to me.' It must have been like a scene from *Zulu* for that one poor mother taking her baby out for a morning stroll as a horde of men steamed towards her. You should have seen the look she gave us: at first anxious, then quizzical as we approached and she could make out our faces, as if she was relieved but puzzled as she tried to work out why the England captain, Bryan Robson, was at the head of a pack making a beeline for her. For the first few days before the first pre-season friendlies we were like the Boys' Brigade at summer camp doing these oddball fitness routines that came straight off the top of the boss's head.

The first clue I had that I was going to get an early chance came when I returned to the Cliff on my first day of pre-season training and was bumped straight from the youth-team dressing room to the first team's. Traditionally, you could log your progress on the park at United in geographical terms – the room in which you took your pants off before training told you where you were in the structure. Your passage was mapped out through the respective changing rooms occupied by the trainees, reserves and the 'magic circle'. The World Cup allowed me to skip the middle step and bypass the reserves' dressing room altogether. My mates in the youth team accepted this and seemed happy for me, but there was a lot of envy from those professionals too old for the youth team who hadn't been invited to join Ron's inner sanctum. I understand that mentality: most footballers can't accept that a colleague is being fast-tracked because he is better than them. They can't afford to have that sort of perspective – to get even a reserve-team dressing room peg at United they have to believe in themselves totally and banish all doubt. So they look for another reason – favouritism perhaps, or luck – to justify their lack of progress compared to another's.

Reserve teams full of twenty-two-year-olds on three-year contracts don't exist any more; they're more like finishing schools for the youth team, rather than a parking spot for players in whom the club lacks faith. In the early eighties, however, the reserve team at United was mostly a no-man's land for those whose careers had stalled, and as such there was a lot of bitterness about. I didn't even get on well with the reserve-team coach, Brian Whitehouse. It is possible that the reason we never had a rapport was because I was terrible at running and he was a fitness nut, but I always suspected, rightly or wrongly, that his coldness towards me had more to do with me leapfrogging his level, failing to follow the established path and proving that you could beat the system the staff had carefully put in place.

The oddest thing about pre-season that year was that I finally met the man to whom I'd been compared for so long, another apprentice who at the age of seventeen had given the stiffs a miss and was propelled into the first team. George Best was going through that last phase of his career when he was jetting around picking up pin money as the crowd-boosting guest star in exhibition games. Within the space of a week I faced him twice, first when he was playing for Valur in Iceland and then, appropriately enough, in Belfast, when he turned out for Glentoran. I scored two in Reykjavik and discovered that he was a self-effacing guy, quick to downplay the aura around him. He knew that being dubbed his heir would destroy anyone, told me I was potentially a great player in my own right and endorsed my view that it was better to be the 'first Norman Whiteside' than the 'second George Best'. We were never buddies, but our paths crossed hundreds of times over the next twenty years and we always got on very well. He was too superb a player for his talent on the park ever to be forgotten, but I think his problems have been so well documented that they tend to obscure his merits as a man. OK, he was unreliable — all alcoholics are — yet I won't forget how gently modest he was, how generous, kind and sharply funny. Being in his company, most of the time, was a delight.

My friend Scott McGarvey was our top scorer in pre-season, but two goals in our last warm-up match, a testimonial for Jimmy Hedridge, convinced Ron to start the season with me as Frank Stapleton's partner. Frank was an extremely thoughtful player and he taught me a lot in those early days. Before hooking up with him, I'd instinctively bomb into space when the ball went wide or was about to be delivered from a dead ball. But one day in training he told me to make a run and when I tried to go for the obvious gap he grabbed my shirt and told me I was telegraphing my intentions. If I made a dummy run or gave a little shimmy before going to the place where my instinct took me I would find that the defender would be wrong-footed and wouldn't have the time to make amends. It worked a treat.

As a pair neither of us were out-and-out prolific centre-forwards in the mould of Jimmy Greaves or Gary Lineker and we were very similar in style. Our movement, though, benefited the team and if neither of us would become the twenty-goal-a-season man that the club had lacked since George had last managed it in 1968, our ability to hold the ball up and the workhorse willingness to keep making split runs which burst holes in the defence meant we gave the onrushing Bryan Robson the space to shine. Having said that, I did score four times in our first five games of the 1982–3 season, the pick of which was my second against Ipswich at Old Trafford on 11 September. Before the game, it was said that Town's England international centre-halves, Russell Osman and Terry Butcher, would be the biggest test I'd faced so far. I was pleased enough to score our first early on, but four minutes from time I think I caused those who thought that my physique was my main weapon pause for thought when I deftly chipped the goal-keeper, Paul Cooper, from outside the penalty area. Ron was chuffed that his hunch had proved right and went beaming into the press conference. 'His potential is frightening,' he said. 'He's going to be a great player.'

Thank God he had that faith because I must have sorely tested him over the next seventeen games, when my goal-scoring tally went from Best to Birtles proportions. That spell was the first major setback of my career and because scoring had always come so naturally to me, the drought had a psychological effect. I had never taken scoring for granted, but to go through seven-teen matches without the respite of the rush of satisfaction that came from a goal was unpleasant. Ron persevered with me until I repaid his faith in the eighteenth match of my dry run and was always reminding me that young players had to expect dips in form. In one way it was reassuring, but I wasn't too naïve to notice that he was having a little look around just in case.

I liked Ron and I know he liked me, but I was also made aware by his fiercest critic in the team, Frank Stapleton, that the boss wasn't someone with a long-term strategy. Indeed, Frank compared Ron's way to the methods of his previous club and found our manager seriously wanting. 'If a player was struggling for form at United,' he later wrote, 'then you had to hope they came out of it themselves. At Arsenal, Don Howe would put on specific training sessions to help you get back to peak form. At United, Ron would look to buy a replacement.' You can argue in his defence that the huge expectation of our supporters denied him the luxury of thinking long-term, or, like Frank, you can see it as a flaw in his character. Whatever Ron's motive, Frank's cold-blooded description of his habits rings true: a dip in form would mean the boss looking at replacements. Beardsley was followed a year later by an experiment with Garth Crooks and six months after that he finally landed Brazil. I could appreciate the pressure he was under and see why he would opt to buy, but I was never happy about it. I saw it as a challenge and was determined not to let such a blatant threat to my future stand in my way. For the next couple of seasons, if I was ever dropped to the bench, it took me no more than three games to regain my place.

My resurrection that season came in the Cups, but not, as I'd hoped, in the UEFA Cup, where I renewed my acquaintance with Valencia's Miguel Tendillo, who seemed to hold me personally responsible for Spain's humiliation in the summer and reminded me of that by leaving my left leg coated in bruises in the two ties. Our 2–1 defeat on my return to the Estadio Mestalla knocked us out of Europe, but we put that behind us to go all the way in the two domestic competitions. I broke my duck on 1 December 1982, and it was especially pleasing to do so against Peter Shilton when we beat Southampton 2–0 in the Milk Cup. I was never one to go crazy after scoring – I was usually more concerned with conserving my energy – but when the ball flew past the England goalkeeper I'm sure the Stretford End could hear my scream of joy that night above the din of their own wild celebrations.

It didn't exactly kick-start my season and I never matched the strike rate I'd achieved at youth and schoolboy level, when a career spent scoring with an Ian Rush-type frequency had at one point seemed possible. The cliché goes that I was not a great goal-scorer, but a scorer of great goals. I don't know about that – I scored my fair share of scruffy goals too – but I did have the happy knack of scoring important goals in quarter-finals, semis and finals. I only scored eight times in thirty-nine League games during my first full campaign, putting me third behind Frank and the goal-plundering phenomenon Robbo, and if I was disappointed with that return, I could at least console myself with a fair proportion of assists and the role I played in two tremendous Cup runs.

The most remarkable thing about our Milk Cup semi-final first leg at Highbury was that United hadn't beaten Arsenal away for fifteen years. But on that frosty night we absolutely hammered them. I used to love going to Highbury in the winter because the marble floors in the dressing room were heated, which was a boon for me as I always changed my strip at half-time and put on a fresh shirt, shorts, jock and socks. At Old Trafford we only had people to towel us down after showers; this was real decadence! I scored the first after Remi Moses lofted a pass to me on the left side of Arsenal's penalty area. Pat Jennings was in goal that night and throughout the World Cup he had requested that I stay behind after training to work one-on-one with him. He told me I had the accuracy he needed and had me hitting six shots to his left and six to his right to test him. He wanted each one to be at the very limit of his grasp, so they weren't impossible for him to save, merely very difficult. It was up to me to gauge the extent of Pat's full stretch and feed that point. So, when the ball looped up to me that night and I opened my foot out to hit it with my instep in a neat tuck volley, I'd had six weeks solid in the summer working on his reach. It was as if he'd given me the tools with which to beat him, as I was quick to remind him: 'Cheers, Pat. If anyone knows how far you can dive, it's me.' Subconsciously, my memory of those workouts kicked in and I knew instinctively where to place the ball.

We went 4–0 up. Having given them a pasting, our powerful running pulled their defence out of position on numerous occasions and let Steve Coppell, who scored two, come in from the wing at will. Then, as we were thinking we were in the final, we conceded two in the last ten minutes, which put a real downer on the end of the match. At first the dressing room was quite sombre, but soon an almighty row broke out, as if we'd thrown it away. Ron stood there watching, not interrupting, and he told us later that he admired the anger we'd shown and the spirit to kill our complacency. Teams that win things, he said, were as ruthlessly professional with each other as we were that night. With our disappointment in ourselves still simmering, we comfortably won the home leg, despite an injury to Bryan Robson. Although we didn't know it at the time, poor Stevie Coppell scored his last goal for the club to seal a 6–3 aggregate victory before having to retire eight games later. Looking back, it would have been so deserved if such a fine player, and one who had scored six goals in getting us to Wembley, had won the trophy in one of the final matches of a wonderful career.

Unfortunately, it was not to be. Throughout our barren years in the seventies and eighties, Liverpool were often cast as our League Championship nemesis, winning the title eleven times across the two decades. But it was their consistency we could not match, although we actually enjoyed an impressive head-to-head record against them. We weren't, therefore, at all wary of taking them on in the Milk Cup final, even with our best player, Robbo, missing. Indeed, we had the lead for over an hour after my twelfth-minute goal made me the youngest scorer in a Wembley final. Gordon McQueen always claims the assist for the goal and, as the funniest man in football, has a unique way of demonstrating it. He was the master of the sharp, savage wit that fizzes around dressing rooms, once shouting to the coach driver when we were lost at Spaghetti Junction and went past the same point for the fifth time, 'Do we have to shake a six to get off or something?' A better example came when he was pestered by Martin Buchan for the umpteenth time in a month to sign a ball, this time for 'wee blind Joe, who is your No. 1 fan'. 'He's blind?' asked Gordon, lobbing the ball back to the club captain. 'What are you bothering me for? Just tell him I've signed it.'

Whenever we meet up now he re-enacts the goal. He takes an imaginary arrow from the invisible quiver on his back, moves his right hand from left to right to indicate he's setting his sights, then, to the accompaniment of whooshing sound effects, Gordon of Sherwood fires and preens before rounding off his mime with 'and all Norman had to do was put it in'. He's right about one thing. It was a beautiful, sixty-yard pass, but I had to control it on my chest, shield it from Alan Hansen, throw him off-foot by dipping my shoulder to turn him, and hit my finish into the bottom right-hand corner as Hansen fell on his backside. It was a very rare right-foot goal for me and that probably accounts for it lacking pace, which caused me a nanosecond of worry when Bruce Grobbelaar got his fingers to it. Thankfully, it was weak but accurate, more like a pass than a shot, and it tucked in the net by the frame of the goal.

During the question-and-answer sessions I do at supporters' club functions or when I'm at the bar having done a speech at a dinner, I am often asked what it feels like to score at Wembley. I usually say something glib like 'wonderful' because I realise a truthful answer would sound arrogant, even if it is not meant to be. I should say to the questioner that he would find it diffi-cult to understand because he hasn't done it. I'm not trying to be facetious or sound like I'm playing the Big Time Charlie. I say it because I find it almost impossible to articulate – each goal I scored felt different depending on the circumstances, just like the pride I experienced captaining Manchester United was not precisely the same as I felt when leading my country. I think if I equated scoring to orgasms it would get a laugh and also strike a chord as it is something easily recognisable, but it would be a silly answer – I was getting pleasure from goals long before I was having sex. The best way I can describe scoring is that you get a sudden rush of adrenaline and a jolt of pure bliss, but that doesn't adequately convey the thrill or address the subtle variations between a League goal early in the season and one in a semi-final or final. All I can say is when I scored against Liverpool I was as happy as I had ever been. But because we didn't win, the only pleasure I take from it was the buzz I felt when it went in and the nostalgic glow I get looking back at it since I retired. From the end of the game to the end of my career, I never thought of it with any sense of satisfaction.

If it had been five years later, when two substitutes were allowed, the result would probably have gone in our favour, but we were poleaxed by injuries to both our centre-halves, Kevin Moran and McQueen, in the last twenty minutes of normal time. We ended up clinging on to our lead, with Lou Macari playing at right-back, a central defence pairing of Mick Duxbury and Stapleton and Gordon hopping about on one leg out on the right wing. I still think we should have consolidated and hung on, even with our injuries, but tiredness and caution took hold and we dropped off and let Liverpool come on to our makeshift back four. Their equaliser, fifteen minutes from time, was a speculative shot from Alan Kennedy which hit the ground just in front of Gary Bailey, who let the bounce mug him. He got his hand to it and should have saved it, but they probably would have equalised anyway, even without his error. It was as if they could smell we were wounded and pounced on us.

In extra-time we were almost on our knees, but it still took a wonder goal to beat us. It came from Ronnie Whelan, when he tried to drill the ball through Stapleton's legs to Kenny Dalglish. Frank, however, refused to suffer the indignity of a nutmegging by his international colleague, quickly closed his legs and the ball rebounded to Whelan, who must have thought, 'I can't go through him so I'll go around him,' and hit a superb curling shot with his right foot which bent round Frank and went into the top left-hand corner of our goal. When the game finished I burst into tears, which to some emphasised my youth. But my age wasn't the reason I cried. I had been so determined to win that it was a mixture of profound disappointment, frustration and a wee bit of rage. Lou Macari came over to me and tried to console me. 'Don't worry, son,' he said. 'You'll be back here again in your career, that's for sure.' Thankfully, it took less than two months for his prediction to pan out.

Although the intense rivalry between Arsenal and Manchester United is a recent development, there was an undercurrent of bad feeling between the two sides when I was playing, even if it was not quite as inflammable as it subsequently became. Perhaps it developed from us beating them in the semi-finals of both Cups in 1983. Certainly, Ron Atkinson saw this as the reason for a brawl during our next League game against them. They were obviously sick of the sight of us that season, but the ill-will should not have stemmed from anything that happened in those three games because in each one we simply outplayed them. In the FA Cup semi-final at Villa Park they went 1–0 up against the run of play when Gary Bailey dropped the ball and, though we battered them, Arsenal went into the break with their lead intact. Our equaliser after fifty minutes was a prime example of Bryan Robson's leadership. He had this uncanny way of stamping his mark on the game when the team most needed it. He had no right to score that afternoon, but he strained everything to force his body past Brian Talbot and win what to most eyes was a 20:80 challenge, chested the ball down and somehow hooked a shot into the far corner, with the ball bouncing into the goal Dambusters fashion.

I hit the winner fifteen minutes later, a result, I think, of the fact that David O'Leary didn't like playing against me. I was very awkward, all arms and elbows, and O'Leary, like Hansen, was lean, elegant and not at all the traditional stopper with bruiser tendencies. Whenever I played against either of them, I always let them know I was there and though both were excellent players, I never got the feeling they were up for a scuffling, physical battle.

A couple of weeks later I came up against Graham Roberts and Paul 'Maxi' Miller of Tottenham and they were the complete opposite of Hansen and O'Leary. Their banter was all about intimidation. Even when the ball was nowhere near us, Roberts would brush the back of my head with his arm and ask, 'Do you want a long career?' intimating he could hurt me at any time so I'd better not try anything flash against him. I knew it was an idle threat, he didn't actually mean it and it didn't bother me in the slightest; in fact, it made me laugh. You have to stand up as a man in those situations, even if you are a boy, and that meant using my whole body — legs, backside, arms, shoulders and elbows — to protect myself, very often sailing on the border-line of foul play, sometimes crossing it. It was something I simply had to do to survive.

That was Spurs' approach; Arsenal were rather more scientific. What Arsenal did to counter me was to play on my lack of speed and maintain a high defensive line. O'Leary didn't want me knocking him all over the place, so they tried to keep me up the park because O'Leary knew he was ten times faster than me and could pick me off easily if the ball was hit over the top. They gambled on the theory that I couldn't do them any damage 'in behind' their back four and normally they would have been right. But they miscalculated on this occasion, when one of our set pieces broke down and the ball unexpectedly ricocheted out to Ashley Grimes by the left touchline. He hit a quick, lofted pass which I ran on to at the edge of the area, miles onside. I let it bounce and saw it sit up perfectly. By deciding to take it on the half-volley, I'd given myself time to look up and locate the goals and I hit it so sweetly I knew it was either going to hit the scoreboard or the back of the net. It was the latter and the photo of the match-winning goal, which captured just me on the left corner of the penalty area, Arsenal's goalkeeper, George Wood, leaping backward with his left arm stretched to its full extent and the ball further beyond him as it hit the inside of the side-netting, won an award for sports photograph of the year. If there'd been a photographer in the dressing room afterwards he may have won a prize for comedy shot of the year if he'd caught the moment when we threw assistant manager, Mick Brown, into the bath and he struck the already stitched-up Kevin Moran across the head as he flew through the air, reopened the cut and left the often-bleeding centre-half requiring further treatment.

Thankfully, he was fit for Wembley and the FA Cup final against Brighton and Hove Albion. Having been relegated at the end of the League season, they were big underdogs, but hogged the media coverage in the build-up. Brighton's manager, Jimmy Melia, went all showbiz during their preparations and was featured heavily in the newspapers with his glamorous girl-friend, Val Lloyd, his lucky white disco shoes and his gimmick of flying the team to Wembley by helicopter. By contrast, we stayed in the shadows, first at Bisham Abbey then at Oakley Court in Windsor, where we occupied ourselves with meals out at the Compleat Angler in Marlow, boat trips up the Thames and numerous press calls in the hotel's grounds. Melia's attitude was that Brighton had nothing to lose so they should go out and enjoy the game, putting the pressure on us, the clear favourites, to go out and perform. And, but for one of the most famous fluffed chances in Wembley's history, Albion's bald manager and his laid-back approach would have pulled off a coup.

We played poorly and went in one-down at half-time, but managed to get back into the game when Mick Duxbury went down the right, played a one-two with the surprise call-up Alan Davies and spun a cross to the near post. From his body shape, I could tell Mick was going to dink it up and I lunged past my marker, dived at the ball and got a glancing header to it — what Ron, with his unique way of speaking, called 'giving it the little eyebrows'. My touch made the ball flash across the goal-line, where Frank tapped it in with his left foot to score. Then Ray Wilkins scored a classic goal, shifting the ball from his right to his left foot, dipping his shoulder to throw the defender off and curling the ball up and around Brighton's goalkeeper, Kevin Moseley, who had drifted off his line. Ray had started the season as captain of England and United before his injury gifted both jobs to Robbo and he celebrated like someone who had emerged from a particularly dark place. He ran around the corner flag, vaulted the hoardings and went down to our fans. It took him about three minutes to get back.

Wembley was such a debilitating place to play. It's not that much bigger than the majority of pitches and is smaller than some, but the Cup final is a hell of a long, nerve-shredding day and is particularly exhausting when you've not been playing well and have to strain everything to go from 1–0 down to 2–1 up. Moreover, the pitch was sopping wet, conditions which suited my knee because it meant less jarring but sapped the stamina. That and the relief of saving ourselves from potential embarrassment probably accounted for our almost fatal mistake of retreating and trying to play keep-ball for the remaining fifteen minutes. We got our comeuppance three minutes from the end, when we gave away a stupid corner by trying to waste time with a back-pass to Gary Bailey, marking up with dreadful looseness in the box and leaving Gary Stevens free to equalise with a right-foot shot from about the penalty spot.

In extra-time both sides turned cagey and little of note happened until thirty seconds from the end, when Michael Robinson beat both McQueen and Moran and played in Gordon Smith to go one-on-one with Gary Bailey. The all-important thing in that position is not to give the keeper a clue what your intentions are and the best solution is usually to hit it first time. While Peter Jones on the BBC radio commentary was uttering his famous 'And Smith must score . . .' line, the player himself decided to take a touch, gave Gary the opportunity to read the probability of what he was going to do next and compounded his error with a weak shot. Understandably, Gary puts it down to a great save, but in truth it was a terrible miss. Either way, I didn't care. We were off the hook. Even though we had to go on a prearranged open-bus ride from Altrincham to Manchester city centre the following day with nothing to show, there was no lingering sense of anti-climax that we didn't win it on the day. We felt lucky to have another chance.

Ours was the third Cup final in three years to need a replay and though the media should have been used to it by then, we were left relatively undisturbed at the Compleat Angler for the two days before the Thursday night game. Perhaps Brighton wilted without the hype, maybe they needed the dancing manager all over the press and the helicopter to take their minds off the game, because they certainly weren't the same team we had faced on the Saturday. There was a grim determination about us in the dressing room and we absolutely steamrollered them. Their right-back from the first game, Chris Ramsey, was unable to play after I had injured him and whenever I touched the ball in the opening minutes of the replay the Brighton fans jeered and booed me. I'll admit it was a bad tackle, but I was convinced from the way he came into the challenge that he was going to 'do' me, so I went in a bit high. The boos didn't unnerve me at all and they didn't reappear after I scored our second goal, a header into the left-hand corner of the goal from Gordon McQueen's cross. At eighteen years and eighteen days, it made me the youngest scorer in an FA Cup final. Robbo got his second before the break, giving us a 3–0 half-time lead. I've never been in a dressing room like it — we'd forty-five minutes to go and we knew we had won the Cup. I wonder if AC Milan felt as calmly satisfied as we did during the 2005 Champions League final against Liverpool?

Unlike Milan twenty-two years later, we weren't going to give Brighton a way back. The only things of note that happened in the second half was Robbo's refusal to take the penalty he had won himself, which would have given him a hat-trick, and our supporters' relentless taunting of Brighton's captain after we went 4–0 up. Steve Foster had been suspended for the first game, but Ramsey's injury had given Melia the opportunity to shuffle his defence and restore his captain to centre-half for the replay. For the last half hour of the game our fans kept singing to him, 'Stevie Foster, Stevie Foster, what a difference you have made.' It was cruel but funny.

When I walked up the steps to get my medal from Princess Michael of Kent, it was as if nothing else mattered because we had won the Cup, so, like the rest of the boys, I passively let myself be garlanded in scarves and silly hats. Later on, the photographs taken make you cringe for the rest of your life – it's the greatest moment of your career and one of your key mementoes shows you wearing a big, daft grin and a big, daft hat. As often as you are advised by anyone who has played in a Cup final before to 'savour every moment', it is impossible. The hours before become a blur: you go from reading the telegrams put out by the kit man in the dressing room to looking for your family in the stand. The match flies by and the next thing you know you're up the stairs to the royal box, failing to resist the urge to stick the lid of the FA Cup on your head while pulling a face. You kiss your medal, glug champagne out of the trophy and then you're in the bath.

If I had thought to take stock at that moment, as I soaked and looked to the future, I would have had the rosy specs on.

United, I felt, were on the verge of sustained success and I was fortunate to have possibly fifteen years ahead of me with the club I loved. I was the favoured son, the home-grown player who had made enormous strides to establish myself as an integral part of United's future so quickly. Instead, within a month, I found they were trying to turn their investment, which amounted to little more than a fistful of return flights from Manchester to Belfast, into a £1.5 million profit.

CHAPTER NINE

A LITTLE LEARNING

The one minuscule downside to my World Cup adventure the previous summer was that it deprived me of the opportunity to take my girlfriend, Julie, on holiday, a situation I rectified by booking a trip to Florida for June 1983, on our return from United's tour of Swaziland. I had met my future wife shortly after I first moved full-time to Manchester when I was sixteen and she was twenty, and my first words to her were an embarrassing remnant of the mentality I'd been used to in Belfast. Our regular Saturday night haunts were Pip's in town and Sands nightclub in, of all places, Stretford's Arndale Centre. It was in the latter, a stone's throw from Old Trafford, that I first spotted Julie and after three weeks I made a move and introduced myself. In Belfast first names often reveal a truth about someone, but when she told me hers I was left none the wiser. So, romantic that I was, I came out with the ultimate in passion-killing chat-up lines and asked her straight out, 'Are you Protestant or Catholic?' The need to know was part of the cultural baggage I'd brought from the Shankill, but before you lump me in with the bigots I should point out that she answered, 'Catholic' and it made no difference at all to me.

We were together for the next twenty years. I was happy enough to go against my upbringing for the girl I loved and I was determined not to let the gossip back in Belfast make me deviate from my decision. And my parents did have to put up with a fair amount of stick. 'He's married a Roman Catholic,' they were told. 'He's mates with Moran and McGrath and he plays for a Roman Catholic club. Don't they have a chapel in the tunnel there? Does your Norman take mass before the games?' It never went much further than that, but no one likes being talked about or being made fun of and, even more so, no one likes their kids being talked about as 'traitors', so it wasn't at all easy for them to hear that sort of nonsense. 'Mixed marriages' were not popular in Belfast in the 1980s and occasionally proved fatal for one of the parties. My ma and da were worried that I was putting myself in danger and at one point advised me to break it off. But I refused to listen to their fears and dug in.

Over the next twenty years we travelled all over the world together, but of all the places and situations we found ourselves

in, none was as unsettling and strange as our first afternoon as
a holidaying couple in a hotel room in Orlando. As soon as I
opened the door to our room I could see a flashing red light
on the telephone and when I called reception was told that Mr
Ron Atkinson urgently needed to speak to me and would call
me again in an hour. I spent those sixty minutes racking my
brains and the only thing I could come up with was that it was
either bad news or some disciplinary measure, but I couldn't
think of a reason why he might want to fine me. When he
called back, the boss informed me that the club had accepted
an offer of £1.5m from AC Milan for my transfer and moreover, since I hadn't asked for a move, the club would give me
a lump sum of £100,000 if I agreed to go. The catch, if you
could call it that, was that I had no time to consider the deal.
If I said yes I would have to get a 10 a.m. flight to New York
the next morning and then the afternoon plane to Milan. If I
wasn't prepared to do that then the deal was off. Never mind
not having time to think, I barely had time to blink before
deciding my future. I sat on the bed for half an hour, dialled
Ron's home in Rochdale and said no.

The fee would have equalled Bryan Robson's domestic transfer
record and the golden goodbye on top of a salary of about
£150,000 a year would have made me one of the richest
teenagers in the world. When I'd signed my first professional
two-year contract in May 1982, I was given £125 per week,
but that had been doubled when I went to see the manager
after passing my driving test to chance my arm at getting a club
car. He gave me a Capri, £250 a week and extended the deal
to the end of the 1986–7 season. Asking for that car cost me

a fortune – by 1987, after £50 a week annual increments, I was getting £400, while some of the lads were comfortably clearing £3,000. It wasn't as if the Capri had solid gold bumpers. How's about that for being stitched up! In 1983, however, money wasn't an issue. If Milan had given me the option of flying over and checking out the city, I might have been persuaded, but the take-it-or-leave-it manner of the offer which hit me an hour after I'd come off a nine-and-a-half-hour flight was simple to turn down. I was only eighteen and, though I'd had a dream year since my call-up by Billy Bingham, I did not feel I'd achieved anything yet. Yes, I had scored some important goals, but I'd hardly started my career and there was so much more I wanted to win at United.

Longer term, my plan had always been to have a successful career at Old Trafford and then make my move in my late twenties, after I'd done my ten years with the club. Playing abroad was a definite ambition; I love to explore other cultures and sample different outlooks and lifestyles. With only a season under my belt, however, I hadn't satisfied myself that I had done enough with the club to warrant turning my back on it solely for cash. It was too soon. I would have been more disposed to it if I'd been older, but by 1985, when Lecce offered £1.3m, United weren't struggling so badly for finance and turned it down flat, and a couple of years later they priced me out of moves to Monaco, Paris St-Germain, Sampdoria, Bari and Olympiakos when I'd asked to go on the list and Fergie seemed happy to sell me.

Ron was rather more ambivalent than the man who replaced him and said that he was pleased I'd turned the move down.

He owed it to me to let me know, he said, and had to put it to me because the club had accepted the offer. But the decision was entirely up to me and there was no question of forcing me out. I'm sure the board would have preferred me to go; that's why they offered me the sweetie of a hundred grand straight off without any haggling. I was surprised by the boss's view that he wouldn't try to sway me either way, but took him at his word that it was the *club's* decision and as a club employee he could not sabotage their wishes and had to remain neutral. Yet I wasn't dumb enough not to recognise that he could have blocked it if he had wanted to, just as he would do on many occasions when bids were made for Robbo. He maintained that there would be no comeback if I opted to stay, however, so I called the club's bluff and the next day headed off with Julie to Disneyworld still a United player.

During the early weeks of the 1983–4 season, I scored only three goals in the first thirteen League games, which did nothing to dispel the uncertainty I'd felt about the club's commitment to me since they had agreed the deal with Milan, nor theirs about my viability as the best partner for Frank Stapleton. Internationally, though, things were much better. I had been injured at the beginning of our European Championship qualifying campaign in October 1982 and missed our opening defeat against Austria but returned to make my Windsor Park debut as a full international against West Germany in November. Perhaps the spirit of Spain had been reborn by the packed civic parade we had attended a couple of days before the match, I don't know, but we refused to be intimidated by the reputation of the World Cup runners-up and took the game to them. Even after Ian Stewart had given us the lead in the first half, we dominated them and the muscular energy we showed in the icy conditions was probably the best performance of the Bingham era. We just seemed to have this knack of playing well against the best sides.

Only one team qualified per group back then but, having scored my first goal for Northern Ireland against Austria in September 1983 and sat on a bus while we were bricked in Ankara before we lost to Turkey, I couldn't wait to face West Germany in Hamburg for the crunch tie of a particularly tough European Championship qualifying group because we were still in with a reasonable shout. Alan Hansen was probably the best centre-half I played against in England, but the guy who marked me in the Volksparkstadion, Karl-Heinz Förster, was even better. He was only one of many great players in a side which included Uli Stielike, the giant Hans-Peter Briegel, Lothar Matthäus and Karl-Heinz Rummenigge, and they had so formidable a line-up that I broke my usual habit and arranged to swap shirts with one of them before the game had even kicked off.

It was my worst performance so far for Northern Ireland and Förster never gave me a kick. He had, as we say in the game, tucked me in his back pocket through his phenomenally sharp anticipation and wiry brute strength. Ian Stewart had come into the team since the World Cup and the QPR winger had the astonishing knack of saving his best performances for West Germany. He had scored the only goal in our home game against the group favourites a year earlier and in Hamburg almost scored the goal of the season. Setting off on a run five minutes into the second half, he stormed past Matthäus and

Klaus Augenthaler, jinked away from Stielike on the edge of the area and opted to curl it past Toni Schumacher. For all the notoriety he gained following his brutal challenge on Battiston, Schumacher was an excellent keeper and he saved well, palming the ball away from the box. Paul Ramsey's eyes must have lit up as the ball fell to him, but the full-back, who was playing in midfield that night, reverted to the scoring instincts of his natural position and scuffed his shot, which landed at my feet. My only significant contribution to the game was the touch I took to control it, swivelling on to my left foot and placing it powerfully into the corner of the goal. For the only time in the game I had eluded Förster, who was temporarily preoccupied with the attempts made by Stewart and Ramsey. We somehow survived the next forty minutes and the euphoria of scoring must have made me forget my earlier arrangement. When I was sitting in the bath there was a knock on the dressing-room door and Karl-Heinz Rummenigge threw his white No. 11 shirt to Jim McGregor and said, 'For Whiteside.' Even though we had beaten them home and away and he must have been seething, he was true to his word, which showed the class of the man. Still, he had the last laugh. We had lost twice – to Austria and Turkey – but finished our eight-game programme on top of the group with a two-point lead over West Germany. Unfortunately, they still had Albania to play, and with a superior goal difference thanks to their 5-1 mauling of Turkey, they qualified at our expense when they beat Albania four days after I had scored my goal in Hamburg.

I knew that being the first side apart from East Germany to beat West Germany at home in a competitive match since the war was a big story, but I was still surprised to see a huge mob of reporters and photographers waiting for me at Manchester Airport the next day – this was England, not Belfast. It didn't even click when I came through customs and the rank of photographers bundled over to me and started shouting, 'Are you all right, Norman? You must be worried?' They had to explain what had happened: United had taken Tottenham's striker Garth Crooks on loan, with a view to a bargain £150,000 transfer. They didn't want a picture of me to adorn a story on our historic victory, but one of me looking pensive and shaken to run alongside their 'Where does teen sensation Whiteside go from here?' features. It was a stark reminder, if ever I needed one, that a petty story about United sells more papers than one of pretty momentous significance to a national team.

Impatience was welded into United's DNA in the eighties. The fans and manager wanted to win the title playing fast, attractive, attacking football in line with the traditions laid down by Sir Matt. Sending out a team with two strong, tall target men did not fit Ron's blueprint and he was tempted to solve his dilemma on several occasions by buying someone who more closely fitted his ideal. Ironically, his two most successful teams, in 1982–3 and 1984–5, both had a pair of orthodox 'No. 9s' – me and Frank in the first side, Frank and Mark Hughes two years later – but it was never what Ron had imagined for his dream team. He was always looking for a nippy poacher to feed off the main striker and over the years tried to replace me with Crooks and Brazil and Hughesie with Terry Gibson. The one thing he couldn't do, though, was dampen my desire and determination to get back in the team. He dropped me to the bench for a few games to try Crooks out, but our form during his seven appearances was just as hit and miss as it had been before he came. I was coming off the bench and making a point by linking up with the midfield more than Crooks, who wasn't a back-to-goal player, and by the time we went to Anfield on 2 January 1984, our roles had been reversed. Funnily enough, it was Garth, in his last game for the club, who set up my equaliser a minute from time, when the substitute's header fell into space in the penalty area and I drove the ball past Bruce Grobbelaar. Ron may have wanted a faster or more senior player than me, but he could never stop me doing my job whenever I got a chance. I always believed I deserved my place in the team.

If it sounds as though I'm having a dig at Ron, I want to emphasise that I'm not. His burden was far heavier than mine and I appreciated that even when I was eighteen years old and fed up with him yakking on about Alan Brazil or Charlie Nicholas to the press. I respected the pressures he was under, but we were in a position where we were two strong-willed characters and he held all the power. My aim was to keep proving him wrong, but there was never any tension on the surface of our relationship because I accepted he had the more difficult job. And behind the face he adopted for the public — jovial, wise-cracking TV Ron — was a football manager as serious and ruthless as any other. When he was fired, the papers used his easygoing style and supposed blind eye to breaches of discipline as the stick with which to beat him. But those writers never saw him at the Cliff on the Sunday after we, as holders, had been knocked out of the FA Cup in the third round by Third Division Bournemouth.

We had witnessed his rage only once before, when he had screamed at us in the dressing room at the Manor Ground when we had lost a Milk Cup tie in extra-time to Third Division Oxford United earlier the same season. This time was far worse. Normally on the way back from games, Ron would indulge his love of trivia by playing the quizmaster at the front of the coach and firing questions at us. But on the long journey back from Bournemouth the only words he uttered came right as we pulled into Old Trafford. They were the words all footballers dread: 'Tomorrow morning, 10 a.m., the Cliff.' It was unheard of to go in on a Sunday after a Saturday game. Even if we had been soundly beaten, he usually saved his anger for Monday morning, but the humiliation of being eliminated from both Cups by third-tier teams had clearly riled him. Having lined us up against one side of the gym, he pointed to the opposite wall sixty yards away and said, 'If you can't run on Saturdays, you're going to have to run on Sundays instead. Sprint over there and straight back.' When we got back, he said, 'No breathers. Do it again until I say stop.' It seemed like it went on for the whole day, but it was probably no more than an hour, which is enough flat-out running for anyone but a marathon runner. By the end, even Robbo was struggling and the rest of us were out on our feet, but the boss did not relent until we'd done a further couple of laps. At last he blew his whistle, turned on his heel and walked out, leaving his £10m magic circle strewn around the cinder floor like battlefield casualties. I don't think he had a game plan at all; it was pure punishment and he didn't seem to take any enjoyment from it. All the way through he had a face like thunder, the worst I've ever seen on him.

That was the other side of Ron, one far removed from the champagne-guzzling, Mr Bojangles image that the public saw. He certainly poured a lot of pink champagne for the guests he regularly entertained in his office after home matches, but he took ages to drain his glass and hid the fact that he was secretly drinking gallons of tea while his visitors were necking the sauce. It is true about the sunbed in his office, though, and he often conducted contract negotiations with players while lying beneath his lamp, dressed only in his briefs and a pair of red goggles. It was probably quite a good negotiating tactic when I think about it, as it had the effect of unsettling you. His assistant, Mick Brown, took a lot of the training sessions and we were always in hysterics on dark winter mornings when we'd ask Mick where the boss was and he'd say 'scouting' or 'talking to a manager' because behind him as he spoke was the tell-tale Close Encounters-style fluorescent blue light emanating from the window of Ron's office. It is his tragedy as a manager that if we had won the title everyone would have forgotten about all the showbiz stuff they used as an excuse to attack him. To me, it was just part of the showmanship of a naturally extrovert man.

Ron was at his best working with good players, an art that shouldn't be underestimated, as some managers are cowed by reputations. One of his tricks was to be very complimentary, and it endeared him to us because players love compliments – who doesn't? It was a massive ego-boost to be told after a match that your left foot reminded him of Ferenc Puskás'. Even now, when I see him, he always lays it on thick and calls me 'God' or 'the legend' and in the twenty-odd years I've known him I have no complaints other than the day-to-day gripes all players have with their managers. He gave me my debut, my first proper contract, made me captain on about thirty occasions and even let me take training some days. It would be churlish of me to criticise him. On the other hand, I wasn't blind or deaf. He wasn't every player's cup of tea and he used to infuriate the Scots, Welsh and Irish on a Friday morning when he set up the five-a-sides, naming himself captain of the England team and pointing at everyone else saying, 'It's England versus all you rubbish.' But perhaps getting us wound up was his intention; it gave an edge to those games and let him fulfil his fantasy that he was Bobby Charlton. He was always keen to show that he could play and he revelled in the competitive atmosphere he produced. If he could have moved as quickly as he came out with a one-liner, he would have been half decent, but sadly he never recognised that his brashness only played well with those of us who were already fond of him.

It must have been unnerving for Ron that we stuttered so badly during his third year in charge. He had always said that a manager's first year at a club was spent dismantling the team he had inherited and building a new one, the second was for bedding-in and the third for winning things. OK, we'd torn up his timetable by lifting the FA Cup at the end of the previous season, but our elimination from both domestic Cup competitions before the first Saturday teatime in January and Liverpool's occupation of their customary spot at the top of the table must have made him feel at times that we had veered wildly off course. That was probably the reason for his fury. At the team meeting the day after that Sunday beasting in the gym, he lay down a challenge: 'You owe it to the club, the supporters and yourselves to go hell for leather in the League Championship and Europe.' The 'or else' was left unsaid, but the look on his face adequately conveyed the threat.

I was having my best run of the season by the time we flew to Barcelona for the quarter-final of the European Cup Winners' Cup in early March, having scored five goals in five games to put us two points behind Liverpool in the title race. Annoyingly, I'd suffered a groin strain shortly after scoring our third in a 3–0 defeat of Aston Villa and had to go through a fitness test in an empty Nou Camp three hours before kick-off. Jimmy McGregor took me down to the ground in a taxi ahead of the team coach. The only two people in that vast, concrete arena were me and Jim and for about an hour I tried to prove to him and myself that I shouldn't miss out on the experience of playing in one of the great stadiums. I responded as he shouted out his commands to 'walk, sprint, turn, jog, stop, sprint, jump', but I couldn't work out whether I was actually still feeling the twinge or whether I just thought that I was. I kept asking for one more go after each routine and both he and Ron left it to me to decide. In the end, I decided that the one substitute rule meant that the risk was too great; if I'd lasted only ten minutes I would have let the team down. So I reluctantly put United's interests before my own ambitions. It is a great regret of mine that I was so close to playing there, and the small hope I had of having another chance was wiped out by the ban for English clubs following the Heysel disaster the following year.

It was awful to watch our 2–0 defeat because we didn't deserve it. Their first goal came from an unlucky miscued clearance by

my youth team-mate Graeme Hogg in one of his first appearances and although the second from Francisco Rojo was a
stunning shot, it did come in the ninetieth minute when we
thought we'd got away with a first-leg deficit from which we
could recover. Despite the odds against us in the home leg, a
4–0 victory over Arsenal which propelled us to the top of the
League four days before gave us the confidence to go all-out
against Barça. Our frailty against Third Division teams notwith-
standing, we knew we were a good Cup side and felt pulling
back two goals was difficult but not impossible. It was all about
what Ron, in his unique language, called 'going to the sound of
the trumpets', by which he meant death or glory. Indeed, it
turned into the greatest night Old Trafford would witness in
the entire twenty-five-year barren spell between 1968 and 1993
and those who were there still come up to me to say it is their
favourite ever match.

Before the game, Bryan Robson tried to warn me that their
centre-halves were two of the most hard and cynical players he
had played against and to watch myself. He must have forgotten
that I had faced one of them, José Alexanco, at the World Cup
and knew what to expect. I wasn't going to let him get away
with booting me all over the park as he had in Valencia back
in '82 and within five minutes of the start I found myself
racing into a 50:50 challenge with him by the touchline. I knew
that if I bottled it he would see it as a licence to take liberties for the rest of the game, so I went in wholeheartedly and,
with the full force of thirteen stone flying through the air,
bundled him over the line and smacked him into a perimeter
advertising board. That challenge might have played on his

mind a few moments later, when he must have seen me steaming towards him out of the corner of his eye, because he looked flustered when playing the ball back to the keeper, Javier Urruti, underhit the pass and gave me the chance to steal in behind him and lob it towards goal. Sadly, it hit the bar and went out for a goal-kick.

If my sights were marginally off that night, Robbo made up for it in arguably his best ever performance. He played so well so often that it can be difficult to pick one example as the definitive Robson moment, but those of us who were fortunate enough to play with him will never forget his dominance over Bernd Schuster and Diego Maradona, his inspirational drive and (red) devilish energy in that game. He scored his first when he got his head to Graeme Hogg's near-post flick from Ray Wilkins's corner and his second after I had bounded towards Urruti, who was trying to gather another back-pass. Ron used to call the type of tackle I used on Alexanco 'reducers' because they were supposed to reduce the contribution of skilled players. That night it certainly reduced a couple of the Barça players' courage and when Urruti saw me coming his way he probably thought I was going to trample on his fingers so he hacked it away with his foot instead. It went straight to Remi Moses, who teed up Wilkins to shoot. Urruti recovered to parry and Robbo belted the rebound in to square the tie. Less than a minute later we got the third, another 'little eyebrows' job from me, a glancing header to Frank Stapleton, who scooped the ball into the net.

The fact that we survived the remaining thirty-eight minutes had as much to do with what happened off the pitch as events on it. The Old Trafford crowd was simply magnificent. I had never before heard such fervour and I haven't experienced it since. It lifted every one of us, not just Robbo, and so inspired Graeme Hogg that he too reached a level of performance that he never again attained. This big rough-and-ready Scottish kid was all over Maradona – he shadowed him round all four corners of the pitch and did not once lose concentration and give the wee genius an opening. That said, they had enough top-class players to cause us untold problems in the last twenty minutes and Periko Alonso and Rojo bombarded Gary Bailey with shots. I was watching Barça's last-gasp assault from the bench and I was deafened by the noise of our fans, who were possibly teetering towards hysteria. Robbo and Ron both said afterwards that it was so loud they feared the roof would come off, but my memory is that it almost lifted me off my feet so that I could play at the very limit of what my body was capable of doing. Mind you, I wore myself out in the process and when the final whistle eventually came I was literally lifted off my feet when, in what must have been one of the last ever pitch invasions at Old Trafford, the players were hoisted on to supporters' shoulders and paraded around like trophies. It was such a great night that it even moved Bobby Charlton to stand up and dance in the stands. If only we could have bottled the euphoria, I'm sure it would have triggered a title charge and success in the Cup Winners' Cup. Not for the last time, however, we had done the donkey work but peaked too soon.

After the Barcelona high, our title bid fell apart and we ended up winning only two of our last ten games. Our dip in form coincided, as it often did, with an injury sustained by Robson.

I think there's a suspicion about the team I played in that we were psychologically dependent on Bryan, but Ron was always adamant when the skipper was out that we should not worry and that we were good enough to cope without him. And on many occasions we did win in his absence, but he was such an iconic figure that when we did well when he was not playing, the feeling outside the dressing room was that we would have done even better with him in the team, and when we lost or drew it was always because he was missing. I think his absence highlighted a failing, but not the one that is usually trotted out. Our weakness was that we had a good team but not a great squad.

With Robson out injured and Wilkins suspended, we had to take on Juventus in the first leg of the semi-final with a patched-up midfield comprising the full-back John Gidman and the inexperienced Paul McGrath. Not only were we deprived of our best player in Bryan, but Ray had been so outstanding in his last season at the club that he had won over the fans, who had underestimated his contribution for much of his five years at Old Trafford, and was named our player of the year. One midfielder who might have helped us compensate for their loss with his calm head and sublime passing was Arnold Muhren, but he too was ruled out. I loved playing with Arnie – he was such a cool and graceful footballer – but I used to get on his nerves by greeting him every morning with an extremely formal hello. 'Good morning Arnoldus Johannus Hyacinthus Muhren,' I would say. 'How are you this fine day and how is your father Arnoldus Pietrus Hyacinthus Muhren?' There was no real reason for it other than my love of long words and it really tickled me to come out with his full name all the time, even more so when I sensed he was getting fed up with it. I only wish I could have said it to him in the dressing room at Old Trafford before the first leg. We would have found any opposition difficult without our three talismen, but Juventus, with Platini, Zbigniew Boniek and five men who had won the World Cup two years earlier with Italy, were a particularly daunting prospect.

Having read those words, you may think, if you can't remember the result, that we got a shoeing, but we actually should have won. Graeme Hogg was the unlucky man again in the opening spell, when Paolo Rossi's shot deflected off him to give them the lead, but we held our nerve, kept possession and started to create chances. Alan Davies, playing his first game since the previous year's FA Cup final, came on as a substitute early in the first half and was what Ron called 'Johnny on the spot' when I blasted a shot from about five yards at the goalkeeper, Stefano Tacconi, and he prodded the rebound into the net. The atmosphere never reached the ear-piercing volume of the Barcelona game, probably because it was only the first leg and therefore lacked the 'kill or be killed' tension of a decider, but it was still loud enough to fire us on. Our left-back, Arthur Albiston, was fearless going forward that night, even though he was up against Italy's assassin, Claudio Gentile, and just as his cross had set up our equaliser, he made fine chances for Frank Stapleton and me at the near post, which, maddeningly, we missed. In the end, we had to settle for 1–1, a result, given the circumstances, which we would have seen as a small triumph had we not spurned the opportunities to win it.

By the time the away leg came around a fortnight later, I

had been dropped. Ron told the press that I'd taken a knock, but that was rubbish. I hadn't scored for six games, the boss said I needed a rest cure and he'd given Mark Hughes a start in my shirt against Coventry the Saturday before we flew to Turin. Just my luck, Hughesie got two goals and Ron decided to gamble on him making a greater impact than me in only his fifth start. Telling everyone that I was struggling for fitness then not springing a late surprise and picking me, rules out mind games with Juventus as his motive. I don't know why he did it; the only thing I can think of is that perhaps he was covering his back in case his hunch backfired. At least it was better than the Nou Camp; although I had to sit simmering in frustration and anger on the bench, there was a chance I could play a part and prove the manager wrong.

Playing a night match in Italy is an extraordinary experience. The crowds are bigger in Spain and louder and more raucous in England and Scotland, but the hostility and volatility of the Italians take some beating in creating an electric atmosphere. It was the only time in my career that I was tentative, and that was in the warm-up, when I had to go behind the goal to fetch the ball. As I approached the stand, about fifty firecrackers went off and through the smoke I could see the Juve fans looking like bandits with their scarves tied over their mouths. Common sense intervened and I left the ball where it was and went back on to the pitch to cadge a kick with another group.

Michel Platini's performance during the first hour of the game was a throwback to the one he'd given for France in Madrid. When he wasn't shooting, he was pulling our defence apart with cute through balls to Rossi and Boniek. He was the sort of player I loved, using his exceptional mastery of the ball to hurt the opposition rather than executing flashy tricks to woo the crowd, but at the Stadio Communale that night he put on the full show, embellishing his game with flicks and Ron's beloved 'lollipops'. Having gone 1–0 down in the thir-teenth minute, it took the boss another fifty to throw me on. Remarkably, and thanks to Gary Bailey, who had made six Jennings-like saves, we were still only one goal behind when Ron turned to me and said, 'Big man, put yourself about a bit and get stuck in.' I did what he said, made my runs, launched into a couple of block tackles and chased to close down the defenders so they had to get rid of the ball sooner than they had wanted. Twenty minutes from the end, Paul McGrath, who was a threat in the air but less prolific with his feet, slammed a shot across the penalty area. It wasn't the most accurate effort, but it had the power to cause panic and pinballed through their defence and came towards me. I stepped forward, blasted the ball into the roof of the goal and was mobbed by the beaming McGrath and Hughes.

The equaliser put us in pole position to win, as Juventus, fearing they were going to get mugged having bossed the game, went through a mini crisis of confidence. Their fans went quiet, the ball at last started to stick in our midfield and they looked absolutely deflated. But we couldn't finish them off and thirty seconds into injury-time the great sweeper Gaetano Scirea fluffed a chance and inadvertently set up Paolo Rossi to bundle home a winner. I think we had three more touches, including the two at the kick-off, before the referee ended the game. We could sit in the bath and lament our misfortune with injuries, congratulate ourselves on our bravery and curse the fact that we'd come so close, but it marked the end of a trophyless season, and that, as we were constantly being reminded, wasn't good enough for United.

At the back of the plane on our flight back to Manchester I was still following Ron's instructions, putting myself about a bit and getting stuck into some beers, when the boss tapped me on the shoulder and said, 'Tell you what. Don't have too many of those. I want you to have a run-out at Barrow tomorrow night.' In eighteen hours I went from swapping shirts with the best player in the world, Michel Platini, to the almost surreal experience of a pre-match hospitality tour of a nuclear submarine in Barrow-in-Furness dockyard. I scored in the match, making it two in two – one in front of 65,000 people at the Stadio Communale, the other before 300 at Holker Street. I'm not complaining, but it did seem a bit weird. There was some light relief, though, as Gordon McQueen was on the trip and he managed to leave Eric Harrison speechless with one of his quips. Eric had never played in the First Division, but was rightly proud of his 517 games in the Football League and had, as he told us on the bus to the harbour, hugely enjoyed his two spells at Barrow. He had been sold to Southport, but had come back to finish his career at the Cumbrian club. When we were doing the pre-match warm-up he was reminiscing, so Gordon, pointing to the dilapidated wooden stand behind the youth-team coach, shouted, 'Is that what they bought with the money they got for you?' I had never seen Eric look crestfallen before and although we tried, we could not contain our giggles.

I had the No. 12 shirt glued to my back for our last six

League games, as Ron gave Mark Hughes a run in the side. It was a tepid end to my second full season and gave the press ammunition to write stories about the teen prodigy who had fallen off his pedestal. It was a huge disappointment and left me wondering whether I had made a serious error in turning down the transfer to AC Milan. It would have been a rotten summer but for one thing. What I failed to achieve in a red shirt I made up for in green when Northern Ireland won the last ever British Championship by drawing with Wales in our final game in the 100-year-old competition. I like to think of our success as a blow to the arrogance of the English and Scottish Football Associations, who thought Northern Ireland and Wales weren't good enough for regular fixtures and were wasting their time. They didn't simply abolish it, but went off to have their own lucrative annual matches and left us for dead. It had a devastating effect on the Welsh and us, but we have the consolation and the last laugh, if you like, of being the final winners and, twenty-three years on, remain the undefeated reigning champions. It was a great fillip to my confidence and I knew that next season would be different. They could take my place but they couldn't remove my self-belief, and I left for my holiday determined to fight back and prove the doubters wrong.

CHAPTER TEN

SECOND COMING

If my decision to turn down AC Milan preyed on my mind during the summer of 1984, when some uncertainty about my place in Ron's long-term plans surfaced, it did not signal the end of the Italian club's influence on my career. Although it is easy to stereotype Atkinson as a chequebook manager, the previous two years had been characterised by stability in his first-team squad and he must have become frustrated by his inability to raise funds to bring in fresh blood. People forget that there was little money in the game back then – crowds were dwindling, the income from TV was paltry and given that the boss had blown the farm on Frank Stapleton, Remi Moses and Bryan Robson in his first few months at the club, he had very little leeway to strengthen his magic circle in his preferred fashion. All that changed in the close season, when Milan, who must have had a very narrow focus in their scouting policy for a couple of years, came back to him with a £1.5m bid for Ray Wilkins. When the club accepted the bid it did not escape me that it was the same money they could have had for me, and the way it was spent probably indicated how desperate the manager was to give the side a makeover and his unhappiness with our stuttering form at the end of the previous season.

I think the squad we had at the start of the 1984–5 season was probably the closest it ever came to the ideal in Ron's head. He was a great believer in the saying that chalk on the boots stretches defences, by which he meant that he loved old-fashioned wing play. By buying Gordon Strachan and Jesper Olsen, he at last got the width he had been looking for since Stevie Coppell's retirement and, with the change from the Wilkins windfall, he also bagged the striker he'd been trying to secure for three years by finally signing Alan Brazil. Strachan and Olsen were no direct threat to me (apart from making the magic circle feel somewhat crowded), but Brazil, combined with Mark Hughes's breakthrough, made the competition for one of the two forward roles the toughest it had been since my debut. Little did I recognise, with all the arrogance of someone who had been raised as a thoroughbred centre-forward, that AC Milan's purchase of Ray had created an opening as well as a log-jam upfront. It took me some time to switch my ambition from a stubborn determination to regain my No. 10 shirt into grasping the opportunity to make Wilkins's old No. 4 my own.

It was typical of Ron to claim before the season started that his three signings encouraged him 'to believe passionately that Manchester United are now on the very brink of becoming the major force in English football'. If it put pressure on us, I suppose he also heaped it on to himself, but it emphasised clearly that Brazil, whom he also called a 'match-winner', was going to get a run and, therefore, Frank, Sparky and I were all challenging for only one spot. When Frank went in for surgery during pre-season I thought I had a real chance, but the boss stuck with Hughes and I was back on the bench. It was a fitting start to a horrible six-month stop-start period of substitute duty, recalls, then a run in the team just long enough to shake off the rust before injury struck and the whole cycle started again. I did manage to become a 'match-winner' myself on a couple of occasions during that spell and got four goals in seven starts as a striker, but a swollen knee followed by a pulled hamstring meant that it was the beginning of February before I got a sniff of being named in the starting XI for the eighth time.

While I was out, Mark Hughes continued to score, Frank Stapleton returned to fitness and Ron kept giving Alan Brazil public votes of confidence to try to stop the barracking he had started to get from the Stretford End. He had begun to take stick partly because the crowd preferred home-grown players and partly because he'd been talked up so much in the summer but had failed to become what Ron had promised. It must have been difficult for him and I sympathised on a personal level because he was a likeable guy. On a professional level, though, I thought it was great that the fans wanted me to play. As I've said before, if I was not in the team that didn't mean that I wanted them to lose, like, for example, my colleague John Gidman says he did when he was dropped. At the same time, I didn't want the person in my shirt to have a good game. The treatment Alan received probably smashed his prospects of a long career with United and, in the short term, it backed the boss into a corner and he had to persevere with the player he'd raved about so much to save face. By the time my hamstring was ready, it seemed like the season was going to be a write-off. Of course, I would keep plugging away, waiting for a chance, and I was still confident enough to be convinced that I deserved a place in the side. It was dispiriting, nonetheless, to face up to the truth of the situation: for whatever reason — lack of goals, wrong blend, youth, a managerial hunch, PR and politics — I'd gone from first to fourth choice in a few short months.

Although Ron had the rare luxury of four international forwards chasing two places, the strength in depth upfront hid weaknesses elsewhere. With Wilkins in Milan, the boss reverted to the central midfield partnership that had helped make his name at West Bromwich Albion, bringing Remi Moses into the middle alongside Bryan Robson. Remi's career, like mine, was ended by injury at the age of twenty-six and I fear he's become the forgotten man of the Atkinson era. He was what used to be called a continuity player, a wiry, aggressive, buzzing defensive midfielder who did the unsung job which gave Robbo the freedom to make so many forward breaks. The other players used to rate his ability, but found his manner a bit odd because he never used to say a word. Yet we always got on very well, even though, like everyone else, I have lost touch with him completely in recent years.

Every morning he used to come into the dressing room at the Cliff, nod at me, put his head down, get changed and go off to the gym to do his warm-up, train and be the first one to be showered, dressed and out of the door. As he was leaving, he would often turn to me and ask if I was going to the snooker club. Those would be the first words he'd uttered all day. I'd go into town and meet him at the club a couple of hours later. We'd pay for the lights, set up the balls and then he'd start to quiz me: 'What's everyone been saying?' He wouldn't talk to anyone else, but he wanted me to be his informer and I would have to fill him in on all the gossip and banter and occasionally reassure him that no one was talking about him behind his back. From about 1985 onwards, the nights out after European games, in Paddy Crerand's Altrincham pub, The Park, became notorious, but in previous years I'd always be with Remi in the Marlborough snooker club in town, playing until 8 a.m., with only night-shift workers and insomniacs for company. Everyone would think, 'Whiteside's out on the sauce,' but in truth I was drinking pots of tea because the club didn't have a late licence. I never once thought, as we pottered around the table, trying to get rid of the adrenaline rush of a night game, that my snooker buddy's misfortune would hold the key to my re-invention as a player and revitalise my career.

My conversion into a midfield player, however, wasn't the foregone conclusion that Ron sometimes claims. The boss didn't turn to me and say, 'Because of your lack of pace, this is the obvious solution', as soon as the perennially unlucky Remi broke down in training with complications following what at first looked like a run-of-the-mill twisted ankle but which would eventually end his career when it began to affect his calf muscle. For a couple of games while he was deprived of Moses and Bryan Robson, who had dislocated his shoulder, Ron used Mick Duxbury and Paul McGrath to fill the hole and I stayed on the bench, but an injury to Kevin Moran during the first half of a League match at Highbury meant that Paul went back to centre-back and I went on as stop-gap. The game was like a dream and I immediately felt comfortable in the role. For the first time I was facing forwards for long periods and instead of getting tangled up with defenders, fighting for the ball with my back to goal, most of the field was constantly in my vision. Midway through the second half, I picked up the ball outside our box, laid it off to Jesper Olsen, ran sixty yards to pick up the return pass from the Danish winger and rifled a shot past John Lukic into the top corner which gave us a 1–0 victory. Afterwards, Ron spoke of the inevitability of the switch, how I'd fulfilled his vision, but that could have been a touch of hindsight-driven justification. It might have been fate or it might have been luck, but even if it was fortuitous, there was no arguing that it had worked out. Ironically, Mark Hughes had been a midfielder who had been turned into a centre-forward. Now I did the move in reverse, and I stayed there ever after under Ron.

The transformation worked because it gave me a broader canvas on which to make my mark. Those who have been kind enough to compliment my skill as a footballer – from Harry Gregg when I was thirteen, to Robbo and Gordon Strachan years later — always identify the same quality: I could see the big picture. From my studies at university, I know that sports psychologists talk about visualisation techniques, something I used to call 'imagery'. I have a very visual brain. For example, when I'm trying to get to sleep at night, I can conjure up pictures of sheep to count and see them in fine detail. I always had the facility to be able to run through a game the night before as I lay in bed and vividly see moves that might happen. And the next day we'd be playing and I would almost have a sense of déjà vu, as things I had envisaged the night before came off — little moves where a player goes here so I step in there. I could imagine parts of the game before it was played and then relive it when it was actually played.

It's known as mental rehearsal and a load of players would recognise the gift. I never went to bed before a match and just went to sleep. I would close my eyes and run through certain moves in my head. Just as basketball players sometimes stand in front of the net without a ball to visualise free throws and can see the ball that isn't there, bounce it and pop it through the net, some footballers can see a cross coming in and themselves heading the invisible ball into the net. Because of my lack of speed, I had to compensate in other ways and my instincts played a huge part in that. I could always see three moves down the chain: if Jesper Olsen had the ball in one place, I could tell by the shape of his body that he was going to play it to me, so I knew I could lay it off with a view to getting it back ten yards further upfield. The master of this was Eric Cantona, another player without speed. He would give the ball to Mark Hughes with the understanding that Sparky's best option was to play it off, say, to the third man run. He would know what should happen three phases down the line, so he'd pass it to Mark with the right weight for him to play it off perfectly to meet, say, Roy Keane's run. Eric would have calculated what Mark's dominant foot was and the speed of Roy's run and would play the ball accordingly, giving Mark the best opportunity to play the best option for the team. And it was all done in a split-second. I may not have shared all Eric's wonderful traits, but I was always capable of making instant calculations of how moves should unfold.

The switch in position also opened up a bigger area for me to play in. I was no longer confined to the rat-runs in and around the box, but would have eighty yards to play in. I may not have had the pace, but, as the old saying has it, nothing moves faster than the ball. I couldn't beat anyone on a fifty-yard run, but if you're an accurate passer, a fifty-yard pass is far quicker and more devastating than a fifty-yard run. The other thing that helped my game in midfield was the realisation that you don't have to move to make space. If the defender is back-tracking, you can often get ten yards of space by suddenly standing still. That understanding came without me thinking about it; it was an automatic answer to my perennial problem. But it was logical. If you look at Michel Platini or Zinedine Zidane, they didn't run about like whirling dervishes, but conserved their energy and had the confidence and technique to slow down. In midfield you have far more opportunities to buy time with intelligence than was usually the case when playing upfront. The position suited my strengths, and weaknesses, down to a tee.

I also had the supreme advantage, of course, that my usual

midfield partner was Bryan Robson, the best player in Britain. From the first day we teamed up, we used to have this little bet going — a competition really, as no money changed hands — on who would give the ball away the most during each half. We were deadly serious about it and it kept us on our mettle. I know it is something Bryan later introduced to his central midfielders when he was manager of Middlesbrough and West Brom. Even though there are eleven players out there, if two of them are having a little tournament based on professional pride then the team benefits. Every little thing like that helps. Yes, it's a team game, but every individual player should be competitive on an ego level to some extent. In my experience, good players always tend to be like that.

I wasn't a traditional holding player in the mould of Ray Wilkins and Remi Moses, so you would think Robbo and I must have had a set plan, at least at the beginning. But we didn't and left it to our common sense to read the game and trust the other's instincts. All you have to do is be aware and vigilant enough to look over your shoulder to get the complete picture. For example, if I was on the edge of the box when the ball broke from one of our set pieces, Bryan might be ahead of me, so I would become the holding player. It's purely logical and not the case that you have to take turns, like some people think. I can't tell you why Frank Lampard and Steven Gerrard don't work as a partnership for England. They are both clever and skilful enough to make it flourish. Perhaps there's a lack of communication and familiarity or maybe they find it hard to cope without the more orthodox holders — Claude Makelele and Xabi Alonso — alongside them. All I can say is that Bryan and I, in style at least, were similar players, with the same attacking instincts, and we made it work to the extent that we lost only one of our first twenty-five games together as a partnership. The one downside of playing with the England captain is that it was always going to be me who picked up the majority of bookings. If I was fouled, Robbo would get the player back for me and vice versa, so it didn't look like blatant retaliation, but because of his status, he was given far more leeway for 'hard' tackles than I ever was. There's a massive difference in referees' perceptions towards England internationals and the rest. Paul Scholes, for example, is a magnificent footballer who I love to watch, but over the course of his career he has probably made as many bad tackles as I ever did. It's me that has the reputation as a 'dirty' player, however.

It was only when I captained the side in his absence that I truly appreciated how great Robbo was at the job. I would try to get everyone to shine by dishing out praise and encouragement, but Bryan was never as shy as me at offering constructive criticism, and at times he administered some terrible rollickings. If a cross did not meet its target I would say, 'Hard luck. Keep going, it'll come.' But Bryan would be annoyed and eff and jeff like crazy. 'What the eff did you do that for?' was one of his more moderate statements. 'C'mon, get it right next time.' A good captain will always find time to have a word and will appreciate that whatever he says or does must not be just because he has the responsibility of wearing the armband. Every shout must be for a reason and if we were playing well, Bryan would get through a game and only have one or two digs at players. At other times, he'd give himself a sore throat.

I would never dream of saying, 'That was crap,' like he would, nor would I sit in the dressing room at half-time and get incensed by the manager's platitudes. If the boss said, 'Jesper, you're having a good game. Keep it up,' and Robbo disagreed, he would say, 'I think you're wrong, gaffer. He's playing useless. He needs to . . .' Most players just sit there and nod while they're being addressed, but Bryan always stood up for his opinions and so would Ron, and they would often have to have a meeting on Monday morning to thrash out their differences.

I don't mind physical confrontation, but I would never feel comfortable having a stand-up row with the boss at half-time. I wouldn't mind doing it one-on-one, but unlike the top captains, Bryan and Roy Keane, I wouldn't argue it out in front of everyone. It just wasn't my style. Having said that, Bryan and I hardly ever had a cross word on the park and it wasn't because we got on so well socially. I think he knew that I never shirked, even when I was playing poorly. Courage on the field doesn't mean handing out or withstanding physical punishment; it means accepting responsibility. If I was ever marooned in a nightmare period where two long passes had gone astray and my confidence had been affected, I still wanted the ball. The brave player never hides. I'd want it, but would have the wit to get back to basics, hit a five-yard pass and be back in the game. No amount of encouragement, praise or insults will help you regain confidence and composure. It's down to you to build it up again and if you go missing or try something spectacular and fail, you're potentially in difficulty for the rest of the game. If the captain recognises that you have that quality and respects your skill, then you're not going to receive too many tongue-lashings, especially if you're thriving in your new role and helping to drive the team towards a second FA Cup final in three seasons.

The quarter-final against West Ham was only my third game in my new position and it was played in a very volatile atmosphere which was captured on an ITV documentary about the Inner City Firm, West Ham's notorious hooligan crew, and their failed attempt to 'take' Old Trafford. There was some nonsense at the ground, as well as on the streets around it. Gordon Strachan was struck by a coin after thirty-nine minutes, with the score at 1–1. He was eventually able to take the corner, with police protection as cover, and found Paul McGrath, who headed it across goal towards me. I had my back to the net, but, by leaning back and stretching, I was able to get my head to it to divert it to put us 2–1 up. It was the first of a proper, 'pure' hat-trick – header, right foot, left foot – and the only one I scored as a professional.

The second came fifteen minutes from time, when Graeme Hogg took a free-kick just inside our half. I was going to take it myself, but at the last moment decided to go up and told him to wait while I made my way into the box. At my speed, that probably caused a delay of ten minutes, just enough to unsettle the defenders! Because I came so late, no one picked me up and Hoggy's ball fell into the perfect position to hit with my right foot. The pitch at Old Trafford that day, as so often, was rubbish, like playing on Blackpool beach, and though the direction of Graeme's delivery was fine, it squirted off the ground as it sat up. I managed to adjust and get to it. All I could ever do with that foot was get it on target and hope for the best, and it was such an unexpected intervention that the goalie had already gone the other way and the ball rolled into the opposite corner. At 3–1 up after seventy-five minutes, we should have been safe, but then Paul Allen got a goal back for them, which would have made the last four minutes nerve-wracking had wee Gordon not gone straight up the other end and been tripped to win a penalty.

Gordon had been on a woeful run with penalties and had missed three of his last four, so before the game there had been a discussion in the dressing room about which one of us would be willing to step up. It was felt that I was capable of taking a decent penalty and I was given the job before the match, but afterwards there was some speculation that I was only given the opportunity as a sentimental gesture, so that I could get a hat-trick. In fact, Gordon turned on his heel as soon as it had been awarded and said, 'Not me!' I wasn't a great penalty-taker and went on to miss two of the four I took, one excruciatingly against Arsenal, when I mishit my shot and dinked the ball straight into an astonished John Lukic's hands. But for my first, I just blasted it down the middle and West Ham's goalkeeper, Tom McAlister, obliged by diving away to the right.

When we left the pitch, the referee threw the ball to me and I got all the boys to sign it and, never having been one for memorabilia, then stuck it in my attic for fifteen years. It's now in the United museum. The following morning's headlines took me back from zero to hero, with 'Wonderful Whiteside' being the pick, but, judging from my post-match comments, it's clear that the uncertainty I'd had all season had not been banished. 'It's my first hat-trick,' I said, 'my first penalty at senior level, and playing in midfield has improved my fitness. But I don't know what the future holds.' Most nineteen-year-olds would have been happy just to get a game, but I was too aware of how fickle football and managers could be to put too much of a positive gloss on my immediate future after only three games as a converted midfielder.

While I was cautious but optimistic, Ron says my perform-ance against West Ham convinced him that the switch should be made permanent, and when Bryan Robson returned for the first time from the shoulder injury that was to plague him for the best part of eighteen months, I kept my place. For a few hours after our 5–0 League victory against Stoke City, when I got a bang on my weak right knee, I was worried that the old familiar soreness would deteriorate into something far worse and rule me out of the FA Cup semi-final against Liverpool, but the pain soon reverted to its normal, everyday nagging state, rather than the crunching, locking and grinding that would have meant surgery. The game at Goodison Park was another against Liverpool that should have been sewn up quite easily, but we were done by a typical late, late rally and it was again Ronnie Whelan who stole our thunder with an eighty-seventh-minute equaliser. In extra-time, we climbed back up the mountain and scored another, only for Paul Walsh to bring it back to 2–2 with half a minute to spare. We had played fantastically well and were raging with disappointment and anger in the dressing room afterwards. I seem to remember that some players felt that Gary Bailey should have stopped Ian Rush flicking the ball on at the near post, which set up Walsh, and we had one of those awful ten-minute sessions of bickering and bitterness. I'm sure they were common to all clubs, but at United it never seemed to stay in-house. Who the mole was, I don't know —

most players have the ear of a friendly or 'tame' journalist – but the press build-up to the replay at Maine Road was laced with stories of bust-ups and United's turmoil.

We harboured that fury at being robbed from the start of the replay and, though we went in a goal down at half-time, felt we had established a grip on the game by playing at a very high tempo and constantly harrying their midfielders to deny them time to hit passes through for Ian Rush. At one point, even Kenny Dalglish began to look a little flustered and, shortly before the break, he came flying into a challenge with me and got booked. Both our second-half goals were classics. The first, from Robbo, came as a result of Liverpool's defensive line being too high. Our captain played a one-two with Mark Hughes, broke clear through and belted an unstoppable shot past Bruce Grobbelaar. Then Sparky won it with another long-range shot, when he raced on to Gordon Strachan's clever pass and smashed it in from twenty-five yards.

The thing I'll always remember about that game, apart from the pitch invasion at the end and Ron having kittens when Robbo was hauled on to the fans' shoulders, petrified that his talisman might fall off and damage his own shoulder again, was the success of a huge bet. Phil Black, a massive United fan and friend of the players, was, I think, £85,000 down with his bookies before the match because he was always on the gamble. He had the most ridiculous flutter that night, based on something like the half-time score, full-time score, that type of thing. He even predicted both goal-scorers. He ended up winning £90,000 to get himself off the hook at the last possible moment. No wonder he partied so hard when we got to Wembley!

You never get jaded by the experience of playing at Wembley, and the second time is just as good as the first. In truth, it's probably better because you have the incentive of knowing how much you enjoyed it the first time. Being certain of how good it's going to be beats guessing at it and makes your sense of anticipation more realistic than dreamy. The other major difference between my two finals was that we were overwhelming favourites for the first and underdogs in the second. Everton had won the title by a margin of thirteen points, had beaten Rapid Vienna in the Cup Winners' Cup in Rotterdam on the Wednesday night before the final and were the pundits' choice to beat us and win a treble.

The pre-match analysis focused on Neville Southall and how difficult we would find it to score past him and talked up the great midfield partnership between Paul Bracewell and Peter Reid, which was said to be too good for Whiteside and Robson. The only thing in our favour, it seemed, was their tiredness after the Wednesday game and the fact that they would have celebrated their midweek European trophy win in traditional Everton style, something I knew nothing about at the time, but learned all about when I went to Goodison. But we didn't capitalise on that at all and if you've ever had the misfortune of watching the entire match from start to finish, you'll know it was a terrible game.

The only thing of note that happened to me in the first hour or so was that I had a great chance to score when I saw a gap in their defence, broke from midfield and bustled into the gap. Mark Hughes, who could hold the ball up all day, saw my run, shielded the ball from Derek Mountfield and played me in to go one-on-one with Neville. It was on my right foot and it's one of the two chances I had in my career – the other being the one against Stoke on my full debut that I mentioned earlier – that I relive a lot in my mind. Having got in front of the defender, I was faced by Southall rushing towards me and stretching to dive. Instead of realising I had got the upper hand because I'd turned the defender and so could have switched it to my left foot, which I could do anything with, and making the target bigger by changing the angle of my approach, I kept it on my right and clipped it. I didn't hit it properly at all and hit Neville on the shoulder. I should have been cleverer and I hate the mistake I made. I always fast forward that bit if I watch that game again. Still, my one excuse is that he was player of the year that year!

No, it was truly a dreadful spectacle and rather like a lot of recent Cup finals where two decent teams cancel each other out. And you could still pass it back to the keeper in those days, which meant that the ball was in open play for far fewer minutes than is normal now. Some commentators have said that the game was made by Kevin Moran's sending off, but in truth it didn't improve all that much afterwards. His straight red card on seventy-eight minutes for upending Peter Reid was definitely unfair by the refereeing standards of the mid-eighties and may even have only earned a booking today, as Paul McGrath, who had given the ball away to Reidy, was haring back to cover. Peter would never have got to the ball and, to his credit, he immediately protested to the referee that Kevin didn't deserve it. Peter Willis, however, was not going to be swayed by character witnesses and made his mark in his last game, going out on the biggest note of all by sending off a player in the FA Cup final for the first time in history. To be a bit selfish for a moment, it also stole some of my thunder. Loads of players have scored winning goals in Cup finals, but only one could be the first to be sent off. I didn't care at all, but Kevin was very sheepish about it on the train coming back the following morning when we opened the papers and most of the reports were about him!

It certainly made a drab game more exciting, not particularly in the quality of play, but because two tired teams, one reduced to ten men, eventually began to make mistakes and leave spaces. I suppose we would have been happy to settle for a draw and have another go, just as we had two years before, but during extra-time we gradually started to create a few difficult chances. Robbo always says that it was a sense of injustice that drove us on, that Kevin's sending off had made us defiant, but if that was the case, I must have been too tired at the time to stash those thoughts in my memory bank because I honestly can't remember us turning it into a crusade for Kevin.

By the second half of extra-time, I was absolutely shattered. My body hadn't fully adjusted to the huge physical demands of playing as a central midfielder yet, and the extra burden of being one man down had started to take its toll, or so I thought. Shortly after we kicked off for the last period, Mark Hughes, who was playing as a lone striker with Frank filling in for Moran at centre-half, got free up the left wing, drew Gary Stevens, did a step-over and headed towards the byline to send over a cross. I was the obvious target, having made most ground to the edge of the six-yard box, but, as I pivoted to shoot, I

kind of lost balance, the ball became tangled between my legs
and I fluffed the shot, which was blocked. Bryan told me after
the game that he had shouted for me to leave it, as both he
and Gordon were better placed and if I had dummied and let
the ball go through my legs, he would almost have had a tap-
in. Unfortunately, I didn't hear him. I lay on the floor for a
few seconds, with my head in my hands, annoyed that I'd missed
a rare opportunity.

My memory of what happened when the ball immediately
went up the other end is that I was so tired that I trotted back
quite slowly and was loitering on the right wing to give myself
a breather. But when I looked at the tape, I realised I'd done
myself a disservice and that I'd actually got back into position,
ten yards outside our box, by the time the second phase of
Everton's attack had broken down and Frank headed Kevin
Ratcliffe's cross to Jesper Olsen's feet. I was parallel to the Dane
when he received the ball and he waved his hand to signal us
to get forward, so I started to advance. Jesper played a short
pass to Mark Hughes by the centre-circle and it was then that
I lengthened my stride, passed Sparky and veered right, bending
my run so as not to stray offside. Mark hit a beautiful curling
pass with the outside of his right foot right into my stride and
on the ITV commentary Brian Moore became more excited
than he had been all day, shouting, 'Whiteside's onside!' I must
admit that when Mark played the ball, a small part of me
thought, 'Great, more running. Just what I need!' but, far more
positively, I could see that Everton's offside trap had fallen
apart.

I was running down our right, their left, so Everton's right-back, Gary Stevens, was the furthest away from me and he should have stepped up to play me offside because he could see across the whole line and that his three back-four colleagues had already gone up. In fact, he was the one who played me onside. I took the ball by the touchline, knocked it forward with my right, advanced and saw Pat van den Hauwe tracking back rapidly to try to close me down. Strachan, who had kept pace with me – no mean feat! – pulled out of the middle, came around me and started to overlap on the outside. I knew exactly what I was going to do because I had done it often enough in training, but I had to have the patience to wait for the perfect moment. That's why I did the little shimmy and step-over with my left. I had to wait until I had manoeuvred van den Hauwe into the right position, when he came into a perpendicular straight line between the ball and the goalkeeper. My intention was to stop Neville seeing the ball for as long as I could and I wanted to use Pat as a shield to block his vision. As soon as Pat obstructed my view of the far post, and, consequently, Neville's view of me, I hit it. And the distance the ball took to travel around Pat, the extent of Southall's blind spot if you will, was the same distance the keeper's hand was away from the ball as it crept in and hit his glove bag inside the far post.

Over the years, people have asked me whether it was a cross, but it must have been a terrible one if it was, as no one was near it. So when I'm offered the option of crap cross or great goal, I always go for the latter. Of course, it was a shot and was something I used to do all the time in practice matches. I never had the tricks or pace that Cristiano Ronaldo has, but I did have what his predecessor on United's right wing, David

Hat-trick hero, aged eight, for the 72nd Boys' Brigade.
Wonder if the bloke to my left had had a flutter on me scoring four?

After failing to qualify for Argentina '78, the England selectors opted for youth over experience… actually my Cairnmartin School team in May '79.

I obviously can't count. This is my second Schoolboys' cap.

I might have been on my way to the World Cup, but it could still be unnerving being swarmed by older fans.

It was hard to get into the Northern Ireland squad for Spain '82, but it was harder to get out.

Back home the
tension was mounting.

Mum and Dad
hired a video…

…Mum's workmates
got carried away…

… and Mrs Armstrong
and Mrs Whiteside became
pundits, predicting scores.

As for us, we were focused
on the job to be done.

I put my finger on what we were after. The press put their finger on my selection: 'If he's good enough, he's old enough.'

Training was going well …

… and we were ready.

'Belfast Boy Beats Pele'. Well, his record as the youngest player in a World Cup. In fact, here I'm beating Yugoslavia's Zajec on my debut.

Northern Ireland 1, Spain 0.

Our greatest achievement.

What a journey we'd had. But the French were just too good for us.

Beating West Germany in their own backyard was a huge achievement.
I scored the winner. But I wonder who cut that defender's puppet strings.

We couldn't quite repeat our heroics
against the Spanish in the Mexico '86
World Cup.

And the Brazilians outclassed
us. But I am proud to have
played for my country against
them in a World Cup.

Playing for the Blues in the 1989–90 season, I felt I'd rehabilitated my fitness and my reputation. I had a lot to look forward to... but it wasn't to be.

Above: Getting the better of Norwich's Andy Townsend in October 1989.

Right: Back at the Theatre of Dreams in March 1990 and determined not to be distracted.

I wonder if they'd have made me form captain if they'd known what was to come...

Marrying Julie in October 1987.

Walking back into the classroom was one of the hardest things I've ever done. But it was all worth it.

The Whiteside clan – Clodagh, Della Beau and Blaine.

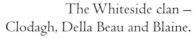

Beckham, had: good timing, an eye for a good angle, the ability with one foot to deliver a ball with precision and the vision to pick the best option. Dennis Bergkamp hit similar finishes to the one I scored in 1985. If you get it right, it's unstoppable because the ball's on its way before the keeper sees it. Moreover, if you're close enough to goal, he's never going to be able to get there.

Before I hit the shot, Gordon was screaming his head off at me for the ball. He had made a great run, drawing two defenders away from me, and he had the intelligence to see that if he had overlapped on the inside, my space would have gone, so he went on the outside. It was very much like the run made by Brazil's Cerezo for Falcão's equalising goal in that wonderful match against Italy at the 1982 World Cup. The two finishes were different, but if you wanted to teach a young player how to take defenders away, you would use wee Gordon and Cerezo as arguably the best examples ever. All the same, Gordon's main intention wasn't to create space for me; he actually wanted the ball, as I could tell by his screaming commentary as I shaped to shoot: 'Give me the effing ball, effing hell, effing pass it, come on you effing . . . great goal, big man!' The other funny thing was the sight of the BBC's Tony Gubba behind the goal. I didn't know before I scored that he was a big United fan, but it was pretty clear afterwards because he jumped backwards and started celebrating as wildly as we were. So much for the Corporation's neutrality!

All I remember about the last ten minutes was repeatedly giving the ball to Jesper Olsen and hoping he'd run upfield with it and keep it there as long as possible. That seemed the best tactic to hold Everton away from us and they never got close enough to make a clear-cut chance. At least this time, when we went up to collect the trophy and our medals, we avoided putting the silly hats on, so there are some shots of us that don't make us cringe. That didn't last long, though, and we were soon parading up and down the pitch in all manner of caps and scarves. Some of the photos of us celebrating on the field could be used as definitive images of eighties footballers: every single one of us, even the sensible ones like Gordon and Frank, had mullets poking out from under our polyester red-and-white United flat caps and we were all wearing these tiny, tiny shorts. We looked ridiculous and, thanks to Kevin Moran's foresight, were about to act ridiculous too.

A week before the Cup final, we'd been playing at Loftus Road against QPR, who were sponsored by Guinness at that time. Kevin, as a Republic of Ireland international, was invited as a guest to their corporate box, because he was injured, and I tagged along. Kevin is an astute businessman and told the top man about the players' post Cup final party and asked Guinness to come on board and set up a bar at the Royal Lancaster hotel for the players' pool after the game. So from 7 p.m. onwards that night we were drinking pints and pints of the stuff, forgetting that it was traditional for *Match of the Day* to do a live broadcast from the hotel after showing the highlights at 10 p.m. By that time, everyone was happy and I'd certainly had a few when Jimmy Hill came over to interview me. I sat there with a big, daft grin on my face, with Ron standing behind me, and Jimmy's first question was about the goal and if I'd meant it or not. My reply did not find favour with the boss.

'You know everything anyway, Jimmy,' I said. 'What do you think?' And with that Big Ron whacked me around the ear, slapped me on live TV, like a teacher with a naughty kid, and said, 'Eh, you, behave yourself. Mr Hill's asked you a question, son. You give him a proper answer.'

Later, we went on to Tramp. I was very drunk, but people were making a fuss of us and didn't seem to mind. At one point, we were invited to join George Best and Rod Stewart at their table. Rod was going out with Kelly Emberg at the time and in the VIP area they had lights that came down from the ceiling and you could adjust their height and bring them down so they were hovering over the table. I thought it would be hilarious to pull one down and shine a light straight in Rod's face and address the stunning Texan model in pure, slurred Shankill: 'Can you shee all the wrinkles on Rod's face?' Well, Bestie thought it was funny!

The celebrations continued for some time afterwards and after the city-centre parade on the Sunday, we went off on tour to Trinidad and Jamaica, where I had a bit of a run-in with Ron's assistant, Mick Brown. On a previous trip to Israel, we had carried a dead turtle we had found on a beach up to Mick's room, put one of his beloved cigars in its mouth and left it in the shower. It took five of us to carry it up there and it stank so bad that they must have had to fumigate the hotel when we left. But Mick had lost his sense of smell and didn't notice it at all. I don't think he had a go at me to get his revenge for that escapade, more that I think he had a tendency to read the mood wrong. One night in Trinidad, I was still on the Wembley high and really went to town on the drink. At one point, probably between too many beers and far too many beers, I got up to go to the toilet and walked straight into a plate-glass door, thinking it was open. I must point out that I didn't break it, just banged my head and, in the state I was in, I was fairly amused by it. Mick was at the bar with Ron and heard the bang and said, 'Look at the state of him. He's an absolute disgrace.' It was symptomatic of his attitude towards me and unfortunate timing. I often felt he let things go at home when he might have stepped in. But when he wanted to mouth off and be the disciplinarian, he had the knack of doing it at the wrong time. Why coat someone for being drunk when he's on a money-spinning jolly for the club? Fortunately, Ron sprang to my defence and I clearly heard him say, ''Scuse me. He's just scored the winning goal in the Cup final. You leave him alone and let him enjoy himself.' For turning around a season that was heading nowhere, I think I was entitled to that.

CHAPTER ELEVEN

OFF THE RAILS

The question that always lingers about Manchester United under Ron Atkinson is whether we realised our potential. 'All right,' our critics say, 'they won two FA Cups, but they never won the title.' It's not only with the benefit of hindsight, either, that our achievements have been demeaned. From the beginning of my time with the club, the fact that we had not won the championship since 1967 was etched on our minds. There was never a season that went by when it was not brought up a thousand times, none more so than 1985–6, when for spells it seemed we were at last going to end the jinx after eighteen long years. If you had told me on 2 November 1985, after our fifteenth unbeaten League match of the season, which put us ten points clear of Liverpool, that it would be another seven seasons, two years into my retirement, before the club would actually win it again, the news would have sent me to find comfort in a stiff drink. That we faltered then, as before, is said to tarnish our reputation, but to me now it is more of a disappointment, an unfulfilled ambition, rather than a regret. I can't look back on my career as a failure or torture myself because I don't have a League Championship medal. I will always be sorry that I wasn't part of a team that broke the hoodoo, but I am too secure in the knowledge that I did my best to give myself a hard time about falling short. However, if I ever have cause to be introspective about our inability to conquer our frustrating inconsistency, it is always the memories of that season that flicker through my brain.

Our first ten matches, all won, were like a carnival of attacking football, as we scored twenty-seven goals and only conceded three. Funnily enough, though, during the first game of that run, at home to Aston Villa, we were booed when we went in at half-time because the scoreline was 0–0! I always got the feeling that the crowd expected us to be gung-ho all the time. We developed a very open, fluid game that clicked during the second half, when our one-touch passing and movement tore Villa to shreds. Because of a dispute between the Football League and the BBC and ITV, the early games of that season were not broadcast and it's a terrible shame for Ron that little footage exists of the matches when our execution of his ultra-confident, flamboyant philosophy came close to perfection.

In previous seasons, we had always failed to cope when struck by injuries, but it looked as though this time things were going to be different when we carried on winning despite the loss of Olsen, Strachan and Robson. Indeed, when Robbo strained his hamstring, it was me who captained the team for three games of that unbeaten spell. I was still the youngest player in the team, so I never expected it, but that wasn't the worst shock for my team-mates. The boss sent Billy Watts, the Cliff's odd-job man, to summon me to his office before training one morning to tell me the news. 'I'm going to make you captain,' Ron said, 'and now you should assemble all the players in the big gymnasium and take the training session. It's your respon-sibility, so get over there. They're all yours.' You should have seen their faces when I walked in and in my best Bruce Forsyth voice declared, 'I'm in charge.' It took them about ten minutes to accept that I wasn't taking the mick. I didn't do anything revolutionary – the usual warm-up, some one- and two-touch exercises and a seven v seven match, but it was typical of the manager to make such a public show of faith in me. He must have thought something of me to give me the armband and the coach's job on the same day.

I'd better point out that it wasn't my coaching session that knocked us off course! We actually drew the first game, at home to Liverpool, and won the next two under my captaincy, but our defeat to Sheffield Wednesday in the sixteenth game and then a run of only two wins, two draws and three losses to finish the year brought back the familiar accusations about our durability. Even so, we still had a five-point lead and a game in hand over both Merseyside clubs on 1 January, not quite the supposedly unassailable cushion we had had at the end of October, but one that should have been good enough.

Instead, we won only six of our remaining eighteen games, and if you compare our thirteen victories in our opening fifteen matches with a record of nine wins and ten defeats in our last twenty-seven, it shows how steep the slump was. Criticism of that team, from Gordon Strachan in particular, focuses on the fact that we had a lot of ball players who were relatively light-weight and who were out-muscled on the heavy mid-winter pitches. But I don't agree. Apart from Gordon, Arthur Albiston, Jesper Olsen and his deputy Peter Barnes, the rest of us were big and strong enough to battle against teams such as Wimbledon, who might try to bully us. In Moran, McGrath, Robson, Hughes, Stapleton and myself — the centre-halves, central midfielders and strikers — we had a formidably tough spine who should have been able to kick on and defend our lead.

Yet we simply didn't have the consistency of champions. We could beat Liverpool but then lose to teams like Leicester, Southampton and QPR. Ron could never put his finger on the problem and many of my colleagues and our fans must have driven themselves crazy trying to come up with an answer. It must have been infuriating that we were always up for the fight against the big guns but then couldn't steam-roller teams such as Sheffield Wednesday in the same manner that Liverpool always seemed to manage. That opening sequence of sparkling form and ten straight victories seemed to suggest that we were finally cured of our maddening inconsistency, but it was a false dawn. Of course, we were weakened by injuries, but collectively, as a club, we failed to keep our foot on the pedal. Ask any of my team-mates why that was and you'll see that there isn't a consensus which identifies one single issue. The mid-season announcement that Mark Hughes was being sold to Barcelona is one candidate, as well as the same old culprits – a slap-dash approach, lack of mental toughness and, most notoriously, the 'drinking culture' that was allowed to flourish during this period.

Let's deal with Sparky's transfer first. I remember him telling me quite early that he was joining Barcelona at the end of the season, long before the news had emerged, while we were on a night out. I couldn't believe either that he had accepted the move or that United had been willing to sell a player who had scored sixteen goals the previous year and thirteen so far during the current campaign. He didn't need to tell me that, as a home-grown player, he felt that the club took him for granted financially. Money only started to matter to me when the club began to publish the salaries in the annual accounts, giving the figures, if not the names of the recipients. I didn't have to be a math-ematical wizard to work out that I was being majorly hard done by when I read that one player earned £150,000 a year, another £125,000, two more £100,000 and a further three £75,000, while I was stuck on £250 a week. After much haggling following the 1985 FA Cup final, I had finally settled on a £60,000-a-year deal, a great wage for a twenty-year-old. But the difference between what those of us who came up through the ranks took home and those who were bought in did was staggering. Mark obviously decided he was not going to stand for it.

I suppose the tea boy who becomes managing director of a company always tends to earn less than a headhunted recruit, but it was distinctly unfair that our salaries, often a quarter of the going rate, were cast down from the big table in a patronising fashion, as if they were saying, 'Take this and be happy, and never forget we made you who you are.'

The other factor was that the club wanted the money and, like with the sale of Ray Wilkins, Ron felt he could sacrifice a star and still strengthen the squad. What they hadn't bargained for, and no disrespect to Ray, was that our fans adored Mark and when the news leaked out in February they went berserk. The whole saga was an important factor in Ron's demise the following season, as it looked like the club was cashing in. He was under pressure from then on because he had sanctioned the sale of one of our best players, one we had nurtured and who was so young and full of potential. It was a funny business and God knows what it was like for Sparky psychologically to have to play when he knew for certain that he was off at the end of the season. It must have been dreadfully tough for him. It affected the rest of us too, especially those of us who had come through the youth system, as it underlined once again that we were commodities. It didn't matter what the players thought or the fans or what harm it might do. It was like AC Milan all over again. If the deal was right, any one of us would be sold. Having to accept that such a key player was here today but gone tomorrow wasn't the biggest boost to our title chances.

Then there was the booze. Tales of our excesses in the mid-1980's are legendary and if you believed everything you read, you probably wouldn't be surprised if I told you we went training with hip flasks tucked into our socks so we could have a quick livener every time the boss's back was turned. Of course, that's not true, but it is the sort of myth that has sprung up about the so-called lax discipline under Ron and about the group of players, which included me, that was said to be out of control.

First off, let me say that I come from a place where heavy social drinking was commonplace and it was not unusual for people of my da's generation to have a drink at 7.30 a.m. in one of the many Shankill clubs on their way to work every morning. But during my first few years at United, I was relatively moderate in my habits. After training I played a lot of snooker with Remi Moses, as I've said, or would meet Julie in town on her lunch hour. Later on, when she'd stopped working, we would often drive out and explore the countryside. We even joined the National Trust and would often go out to Chatsworth for lunch or drive up to the Lakes. It was hardly a routine that justified my reputation for being constantly in the pub.

When I was seventeen and eighteen I would have Saturday nights out, doing a minor crawl around town and we would always end up in a famous Chinatown establishment in the early hours drinking lager out of a teapot to get round the licensing laws. As I got older I'd go out a bit more regularly, but if you look at the schedule of a typical week, it's clear that we had a lot of time on our hands and the way we filled it reflected the difference between what was deemed acceptable in the culture of professional football then and now. Later, we would go out with the wives and partners on a Saturday night to somewhere like the Four Seasons hotel out by the airport and then have a boys' drinking session on the Sunday. The usual suspects – Bryan, Paul, Gordon McQueen and me – would be joined by others such as Mark Hughes, Alan Brazil and Kevin Moran, depending on their commitments, and we'd stay in The Park all day, gassing about the game, steadily knocking back pints in front of the big fire and joining in a singsong with the Irish musicians in the evening.

On Monday morning we would have a good, hard couple of hours of physical work to blow the cobwebs away, from 10.30 a.m. to 12.30 p.m. On Tuesday, having got the Saturday night and Sunday sessions out of our system the previous day, we would do an hour and a quarter, maybe an hour and a half maximum, from 10.30 a.m. again. If there was no midweek game, we would have Wednesdays off and do an hour and a half on Thursday; if we played on Wednesday night we would have Thursday off. On Fridays we'd do an hour at most of five-a-sides, with perhaps some finishing to end with. Then we'd play on Saturday and have Sundays off. It was either four and half hours of training plus three hours of matches or six hours of training and a ninety-minute game — a seven and a half hours working week.

Usually, if we didn't have a game on a Wednesday, and from 1985 onwards there were fewer than before because of the European ban, Robbo would convene a team meeting on Tuesday afternoons that would often go on for twelve hours or more. I'm not pointing the finger at Bryan — if he hadn't given us the nod (and done it with the manager's approval, I must add) some of us would have gone out anyway. Why? Because we loved it, thought it was normal and honestly felt it had no detrimental effect whatsoever on our form and fitness. After I'd given up the all-night marathon snooker sessions when I was about twenty, we would go to one of our mate's pubs on

Wednesday night after games. Even if we'd played away, we could knock him up in the early hours and he would let us sit in the bar, unwinding over several pints, and would allow us to carry on if he called it a night and trooped off to bed. Then we would sleep it off on Thursday and go back to training pretty fresh on Friday. Whenever I was fit enough to be picked, I never once had a drink from Wednesday night until Saturday night and would always stick to water, even though we were allowed a glass of wine with our Friday dinner when we were in hotels for away games.

Another thing I never did was socialise with the opposition players after a game. I would never go for a drink in the players' lounge at an away ground unless I felt obliged to put in an appearance because of an international colleague's invitation. I would much rather go and sit on the coach on my own. I needed some time out after a match and I was very happy to sit there in isolation with my own thoughts and wait for the boys. I was a bit anti-social I suppose, but I just couldn't face a discussion about the game immediately after it. I would save it for Sunday.

In the Old Trafford players' lounge, Mrs B, who used to run the place, always had a tray of chocolate bars put to one side for me to tuck into straight after I'd got changed because I'd be ravenous. But I couldn't face a drink for the first couple of hours after a game. Big Paul would get through five or six pints before we'd even left the lounge, while I'd struggle to get one down in a couple of hours because my body was so wrecked and I felt so exhausted. By seven o'clock I was back in the ball game, but for those first two hours I was in slow-motion, waiting for my heart-rate, brain and emotions to calm down.

I've always been honest about the fact that I drank and have not looked for any excuses or tried to blame it on anyone else. But I don't have the demons that my friend Paul McGrath suffers from. For Paul it's a constant struggle every day, dealing with the dependence he had on drink. He would come out of the taxi for training having drunk half a bottle of Southern Comfort just to make him comfortable enough to talk to the taxi driver. He is even more shy than I am; I have never needed a drink just to say 'hello' to a stranger or to meet my team-mates for training. Similarly, he had no self-esteem and never believed he was good enough. I'd like to think that I wasn't arrogant about it, but I always knew I could play and self-belief for me didn't come from getting slaughtered. I've always been able to take booze or leave it and when I do have a drink, it doesn't change my personality. It's the ritual and process I love — being out, a good meal, a few bottles of wine and the company. I don't ever drink to reach oblivion, as Paul often did. I didn't know it then, but he would have been on a flier by the time we met up, having hit the vodka at home or even in his car, and then he would neck pints in the pub until he blacked out. At that time, I was in my early twenties and didn't have the experience to know the trouble he was in. But I never drank like that and even today, when I've got all the opportunity in the world to drink as much as I like, I will have a few glasses with my partner Denise over lunch some afternoons then go home and be delighted to put my 'jamas on and go to bed to watch telly at 8 o'clock.

There is a difference between people who enjoy drinking heavily on occasion, binge-drinking as they call it nowadays, and alcoholics. I've got another friend who is in recovery and, as well as his alcoholism, is battling chronic gambling and anger problems and addictions to cigarettes, cocaine and sex. One day he said to me, 'Norman, you're just like me.' When I protested and pointed out that I have never smoked or taken drugs, have never slept around, rarely had a bet and never once been violent (off the field!), he came back with, 'You like to get drunk.' Perhaps it's the therapy that has driven him to see the addict in everyone, I'm not sure, but I remain adamant that liking a drink and enjoying its effects does not make you dependent on it. Just because some people project their own problems on to you, it doesn't mean that you're the one who's in denial.

I know that by today's abstemious standards our drinking sounds horrendous, but I must stress that we weren't the only ones who had a carefree attitude to nights out. Liverpool did it, Everton certainly did it and you only have to read Tony Adams's accounts to know that Arsenal were up to it too. I'm not saying it was right, but on the other hand I cannot see that it was all that wrong either. I feel that I always prepared properly for games. What happened under Fergie, when I was injured for almost a year, is a different matter and one which I'll address shortly, but when Ron was the manager I honestly don't think we abused his trust or took liberties with the club's chances of winning the title.

Ron's attitude never changed towards us and his take on the notoriety of Whiteside, Robson and McGrath was that as long as we were doing it for him on the pitch, he'd still pick us and we could do what the hell we liked off it. Paul and I, for instance, were often the ones who would do the rounds of supporters' club dinners and discos at Old Trafford after a Saturday game. The club actively encouraged us to go and the two of us built up a terrific rapport with the fans, which often involved sharing a drink with them. I don't think we could have done much more to interact with United's supporters. We were always willing to do a couple of hours and we didn't have to be forced to do it. I think my many appearances in those club function rooms account for the warmth with which I'm still greeted at Old Trafford and, because I came through the ranks, I have always felt I was taken to the fans' hearts. So, we were in the position where some of our fans wanted us to have a drink with them, while others would complain that we were boozing.

I think Ron felt that there was no point tying yourself in knots trying to please everyone and he maintained that as long as you were fit and ready for business at 3 p.m. on a Saturday, you would be in his team and that's all that mattered. Obviously, he was hearing gossip because some supporters were, and still are, always ready to phone in to the club to report what the players were up to off duty. He was not in the slightest bit interested in that. He was only interested in football. 'You turn up for training, you train, I pick you for the team.' That was his view. Looking back, perhaps he should have cracked the whip more, but if he had instituted an alcohol ban, we would have found a way around it because when you're twenty years old and as fit as you'll ever be, you're never going to be persuaded that a night out is going to do you any harm.

Yes, the same whispers that went back to Fergie were heard by Ron years earlier, but they were dealt with in a different way. I doubt that if Ron were given a job tomorrow, he would do things differently. It's not in his nature. And anyway, it wasn't as if we were rolling into training drunk or going out on the lash the night before a game. Those of us who were privileged to play for Manchester United owed the club the responsibility of making sure we trained hard and played as well as we could whenever we pulled on the shirt, but in the 1980s that did not entail living like monks. Attitudes have changed with the times, but it's pointless to condemn the boys of '86 using today's moral standards. The most hurtful fact of all is that, during that year, like previous ones, Liverpool once again proved that over the course of a forty-two-match season they had more consistency, durability and strength in depth than we could muster. Even our record-breaking early-season form should not obscure that truth.

I should mention here that there's been a lot of talk about the rivalry between United and Liverpool in recent years, with the Gary Neville songs and what happened when Alan Smith broke his leg at Anfield in 2006, but it was even worse during the 1985–6 season. Throughout my time with the club, I was only on the losing side twice in those 'East Lancs Road derbies', the first time at Wembley in the Milk Cup final in 1983 and then when they were awarded a dodgy penalty in the fourth round of the same competition in 1985. While they were winning titles, we often had the measure of them in head-to-head games and it obviously incensed their fans. When we played them on 9 February 1986, the atmosphere was the worst I ever encountered.

As soon as our coach came through the gates at Anfield, a

brick hit the window right next to where Mark Hughes and I were sitting. It didn't shatter, but caved in and momentarily spooked us. Two minutes later we got off the bus and were walking through the entrance when a Liverpool fan threw a CS gas canister at us and we had to run straight on to the pitch because our throats had started to burn and our eyes were watering. It's amazing that the game went ahead and, though Ron had to re-jig his starting XI because one or two of the lads had been seriously affected by the smoke, we still emerged with a draw, which kept us equal on points with Everton at the top of the table. From then on, though, we must have suffered a kind of delayed choke and took only twenty points from a possible forty-two to finish in fourth spot for the third year in succession. To rub it in even more, Liverpool went on to win the Double.

At that stage of my career, my summers seemed to follow a cycle whereby, every other year Northern Ireland would compensate for any disappointments with United. In 1982 I went to the World Cup and in 1983 won the FA Cup, in 1984 the British Championship and in 1985 the FA Cup again. In 1986 it fell into place once more and my second World Cup offered the hope of some consolation for the frustrations of my domestic season. The draw for the group stage had been extremely tough on us, throwing up Algeria, Spain and Brazil, but we departed for our training camp in Albuquerque with the confidence we still wore from Spain and satisfaction in our achievement in getting to Mexico from another seemingly impossible group containing England, Romania, Finland and Turkey.

The atmosphere at the two England games lives longest in

our fans' memories, but it was our performances against Romania, who had the young Gheorghe Hagi bossing midfield, where we were at our most resilient and which sealed qualification. England drew with them home and away, but we beat them twice, first 3–2 at Windsor Park, where I scored our second with a firm header and was booked for celebrating the goal, and then in Bucharest, where our goal was under bombardment for an hour after we took the lead. I had already missed a good chance when Jimmy Quinn put us ahead and I didn't get another sniff, as we were constantly on the back foot and had to retreat in a ten-man rearguard lined up on the edge of our penalty area for the rest of the game. After the match, there was a general feeling among the Romanian officials that because we only needed a point from our last match at Wembley, we and England would take it easy and stitch up the draw which would guarantee qualification for us both. Nothing could have been further from the truth.

Pat Jennings had retired from domestic football at the age of forty in the summer of 1985, but was training with Tottenham reserves at Billy Bingham's request so that he could continue his international career until the end of our qualification campaign. He had one of the matches of his life at Wembley that night in November 1985, almost as if he was determined to save his last hurrah for his home patch in North London. Time after time, he stopped Kerry Dixon opening the scoring and our fans, who had come over in their thousands on the Larne-Stranraer crossing, serenaded the Chelsea striker with 'Kerry Dixon, you're a w*****r, you're a w*****r' for about an hour after his first miss.

I couldn't match Pat's performance and had one of my poorest games for my country. At one point, Glenn Hoddle, who was magnificent, ran towards me, dipped his shoulder and went past me as if he'd sent me off to fetch a bottle of milk. As I turned to watch him crack a shot towards the top corner, it gave me a tremendous feeling of relief to see that forty-year-old man in a bright yellow jersey leaping through the air and palming the ball away with one of those dustbin-lid-sized hands.

After the game, which ended 0–0, our centre-half, Alan McDonald, responded to the taunts of the Romanians and the England fans' ironic chants of 'It's a fix!' to the tune of 'Here We Go' by getting wound up in an interview and almost shouting, 'If you think this was a fix, come and see me and I'll sort yous out!' He's famous for that statement back home because it echoed everyone's thoughts, but the mad-eyed way he delivered his threat was hilarious. If it had been a fix, how come no one told Dixon or Gary Lineker? No, it was Pat, and Pat alone, who fixed qualification for us and thus ensured that his move into full-time pipe-and-slippers mode would have to be postponed until the following summer.

Billy Bingham had chosen Albuquerque because of the opportunity it gave us to do altitude training. Coming to terms with the height and the heat made it the most difficult ten days of my career. My knee had got progressively more sore as the season drew to an end, but I was determined to get through the World Cup before I sought the inevitable surgery I needed to clean the joint out and stop the pain.

There were two circuits, one near our base camp, the other further up in the mountains, and the latter, which took six minutes to complete, tortured my knee as I pounded out the hour that we spent on the stony ground every day, trying to acclimatise to running in the thin air. Practice matches at such a high altitude were just as difficult as the pure fitness work and we all found the adjustments we had to make to the weight of our passes and shots very tricky. At first, the ball flew all over the place, but gradually we got the hang of it and by the time we had a couple of games at the bottom of the hill, we found that we were bounding about like supermen in the oxygen-rich air down there. But there wasn't much to do in the evenings and about the most exciting thing that happened was when a pal of mine, an Ulster TV electrician, who made heads turn because his name was Albert Kirk and he was in Albuquerque, tripped and fell on a training run and chipped his ankle. I ended up helping him hobble about the hotel and even washed his hair one night.

Things weren't much more exhilarating in Guadalajara where our three group matches were scheduled and, though the camaraderie in the squad was still strong, the task of topping, or even matching, our achievements in Spain proved too tough a call. In contrast to four years earlier, we hadn't been written off this time and Jeff Powell of the *Daily Mail* summed up the general mood of optimism about our chances. 'Bingham has organised some of the most patriotic footballers from any country in the world into a proficient machine which is difficult to break down while being willing to attack anyone at every opportunity,' he wrote. Patriotism, however, was not enough and, the first half of our first game against Algeria apart, we didn't have the experience of the 1982 team to cope with the heat and superior individual abilities of the opposition. I scored against Algeria after five minutes and twenty-two seconds, when I took a free-kick outside their box, opted for power and it deflected off the wall and went in. In 1982 Bryan Robson had scored the quickest goal of the competition and had been awarded a very fancy gold watch, and it would have given me a great chance to swank about in front of my friend had the one against Algeria stayed the quickest of 1986. I was praying during every game I watched on television that no one would overtake me, but in our second match against Spain, Emilio Butragueño scored after sixty-five seconds and I eventually ended up in ninth place. I was still given a watch for it, which I continue to wear, but Robbo retains the bragging rights, as well as the flashier model.

We ended up drawing the game against Algeria and Spain took their revenge for Valencia by beating us 2–1 in the Estadio Tres de Marzo, but because it was a tournament of twenty-four teams there was still a chance we could qualify for the last sixteen as one of the four best third-placed teams if we could get a draw against Brazil in our final group match. As a kid I'd heard so much about Brazil that to play against them seemed like the ultimate international football could offer and we were not overawed by the prospect as they had only racked up 1–0 victories against Algeria and Spain. I went in with the attitude that they may be the best team in the world, but a ball might fall to me in the box, I might get a deflection, the keeper might have a nightmare and I could end up scoring the winner. Why not? It had happened before in West Germany. However big the odds stacked against you, it's always possible to nick a goal.

Indeed, I nearly did in the second half, but fired my shot from a tight angle straight down the goalie's throat. By that stage, we were 2–0 down and had been given a hell of a runaround. We hardly got a look in as they tore us apart with graceful one-touch passing. We tried to shore up our defence by leaving Colin Clarke alone upfront and I played in a five-man midfield, but every time we tried to press the ball and close down the man in possession, he'd just lay the ball off into space for one of his team-mates to pick up. I almost felt like tapping Socrates on the shoulder and asking if I could have a kick of the ball. When Josimar scored their second with a rasping shot after a twenty-touch move that probably would have been the tournament's best goal but for Diego Maradona's wonder goals against England and Belgium, we could have been forgiven for feeling relieved that we were going to get two touches at the kick-off.

They had so much control of the tempo, and were seemingly able to ratchet the pace up at will while gliding around looking as fresh as daisies, that it became one of those games that seemed to last three hours. I was substituted shortly after the hour; a combination of my knee, the heat and the punishment inflicted by a midfield of Junior, Socrates, Elzo and Alemão had reduced me to walking pace. They got a third when Zico came on and set up Careca, but if it hadn't been for Pat's heroics on his forty-first birthday, we could have let in ten to ruin our goalkeeper's last ever match. I don't think there was anything we could have done to match them that day, they were simply too good for a team that they outshone in skill and class. Despite the drubbing, though, I am proud that I played a match against Brazil in the World Cup finals, yet I'm rather pleased that I didn't have to face them every week!

When I'm asked if I'm bitter that my career was over at such a young age, I can sincerely give the answer 'no' and one of the reasons for that is the opportunity Northern Ireland gave me to get two World Cups under my belt by the age of twenty-one. Look at George Best. He never got the chance, and there are countless other great players whose careers reached full maturity who haven't had the privilege to play on the game's highest stage once, never mind twice. I had to admit, on the flight back from Mexico, that it was unlikely that I would get a third opportunity, given the age of our squad and the retirements that followed our exit from the tournament. It's interesting to think, though, that if all had gone well and we had made it to Italia '90, I would probably have captained the side, as I'd worn the armband in several of the group games. Captaining my country at the World Cup finals would have been the greatest experience of my life, but I'm level-headed enough to accept that you can't have everything. We weren't close to qualifying for Italy, and even if we had been, when West Germany lifted the trophy in Rome, my right knee had barely an hour of first-team football left in it.

CHAPTER TWELVE

FERGIE AND ME

It wasn't the arthroscopy I underwent five days after returning home from Guadalajara that suggested my days were numbered but something the physiotherapist, Jim McGregor, said as he drove me back to Old Trafford after the operation. It's a relatively straightforward procedure which entailed opening up my knee and literally flushing the debris out and was one that I'd gone through several times before. The relief I felt after the flakes of bone had been removed and the knowledge that I could start running again without those painful pieces of grit in the joint always left me in a positive mood. But when I asked

Jim, who had watched the surgery, for his opinion of how it had gone, his disconcerting answer piddled on my parade. 'It'll be all right for now,' he said, 'but you'll only have another five years. Your knee won't last.'

I can usually banish fear to the back of my mind. I've even been known to do it to a ridiculous extent, like the afternoon Denise and I were driving to an after-dinner engagement in Peterborough and I heard an alarmingly loud banging noise coming from the back of the car. I just cranked the radio up and drove on. When I eventually plucked up the nerve to turn down the volume, the noise had disappeared and never returned. But I never had the same luxury with Jim's words. I actually, quite literally, laughed it off when he delivered his verdict, but there was no one whom I trusted and respected more than him, so I couldn't continue to successfully fool myself for very long. According to his prediction, which proved to be bang on, I was about halfway through my career at the beginning of the 1986–7 season. Because the bleak inevitability of early retirement was now loitering at the back of my brain, I had little time to waste and hoped like mad that this would be the season when United would crack the lack of consistency and win the title on the twentieth anniversary of the club's last championship. Instead it turned into a season which exposed our flaws like never before and cost Big Ron his job.

The recovery from surgery slowed me down at the beginning of the season. Two weeks before then, I played back-to-back warm-up matches within twenty-four hours in Amsterdam I could barely walk. Jim had to teach me how to run again and I was nowhere near fit enough during the opening three games of the rebranded Today First Division. However, so many of my colleagues were carrying injuries from the World Cup that I wanted to help out. It was like the previous season had never ended, though, and we lost our first three games, drew with Leicester, then rallied to beat Southampton 5–1 to give our fans hope that the blip was over, then lost the next three on the trot.

It had become clear that time was running out for Ron. Old Trafford's capacity was 55,000 that year, but when we were mired in that rotten sequence of results only 33,340 turned up to watch us lose 1–0 to Chelsea. That small crowd was the hard core of our support and they let Ron know that it was time for him to go. A combination of shoddy, disjointed performances, embarrassing defeats, a place in the bottom three of the table and what, by the end of October, amounted to a full year's inconsistency made for a very cold and eerie atmosphere about the place. You dared not crack a joke in training as the crisis deepened. I'm sure Ron, for all his bravado, must have been hurt when he lost the crowd. He pointed out the number of players yet to recapture full fitness, but the club had no time for sentiment or excuses when it was haemorrhaging 5,000 entrance fees every fortnight.

The final nail came in a 4–1 League Cup defeat to Southampton at the Dell on 4 November 1986. I had been named captain, but went off after thirty minutes when I bashed my knee in a tackle and couldn't run the pain off. Sitting on the bench was dreadful. To see Ron wisecracking at his press conference two days later, you might have expected him to have shown the same gallows humour while a young Matthew Le

Tissier tore us apart and the goals kept going in, but in fact he looked distraught and winced whenever something else went wrong. The mood on the journey home was understandably frosty and subdued, but when I went in on the Wednesday for treatment while the other players were on their usual day off, I didn't get the feeling from the staff that the boss had passed the point of no return.

On the Thursday morning at the Cliff, after my regimen of ultrasound treatment, ice and massage, I was walking through the car park to make my way home when Ron arrived in his Mercedes. He wound down the window and I could tell immediately that something was up because he looked gutted and was very glassy-eyed. He asked me to go with him to his office and as soon as he had closed the door he turned and said, 'Tell you what, I've just been up to Old Trafford and they've sacked me. You're the first to know.' Obviously, I expressed my regrets and then he asked me to go round the corner to the other training pitches on Littleton Road and fetch them all back to the gym. So I became the messenger of doom, told Brian Whitehouse what had happened and led the squad back to the gymnasium, where Ron, who had recovered his composure, made a short announcement with a couple of characteristic quips, thanked everyone and shook us all by the hand. With that he was gone, the magic circle was broken and his beloved sunbed began to gather dust until the new occupant of his office got rid of it and the blue light that once lit up Broughton was seen no more.

Quite typically, Ron did not bury his head in the sand, but threw a leaving do that night at his home in Rochdale. I felt that I owed him my presence and often your initial kind instincts have their own reward. Four years later, when Colin Harvey was fired from his job as manager by Everton, I immediately rang him to tell him how sorry I was and to thank him for taking me to Goodison. The next day he turned up in his new role as . . . assistant manager to Howard Kendall, so it worked out that I had made the best possible political move the day before without having the slightest inkling of how things would unfold.

The only other players at the Rochdale party were Bryan Robson, Gordon Strachan and Gary Bailey. We were injured and knew we weren't fit enough to play on Saturday so we got stuck into the drink – Strach not so much because he was too busy playing the DJ and spinning Ron's Shirley Bassey LPs. Ron was back to his bubbly self and even took it quite well when our friend Phil Black ribbed him about his new unwanted status and interrupted the ex-manager's discussion of certain players with, 'Is that the layman's point of view?' Wee Gordon's reaction when Ron confirmed that Alex Ferguson would be taking over the following day should have made us slightly wary about the revolution ahead. 'Och no!' he said and told us about the discipline and the rage to win he had experienced under him at Aberdeen. Instead of being frightened, we thought that the wee man's trepidation was hilarious.

The new manager gave me a name-check in the first sentences he uttered the next morning, when he called the entire playing staff into the gym to address us. 'Good to see you, boys,' he said. 'I'm Alex Ferguson and I don't care who you are, whether you're a Robson, Whiteside, Strachan or McGrath. I'm the boss. There'll be no favourites. You all start on the same level and if you train well you all have a chance here. Let's hope we enjoy it.' Of course I was hungover from Ron's party the night before and it probably wasn't the wisest move to meet the new man when I looked rough and reeked of beer. In my defence, I was injured and couldn't even train, let alone play.

It would be a month before I was fit enough to make my debut for him, by which point he had won one and lost two of his opening four games. I already knew that he rated me, though, because he was purring after at last seeing me in full training, a positive impression he later confirmed in his auto-biography. 'I felt the excitement that is felt by watching a player of the highest class,' he wrote. 'I would never have appreciated how good he was without the advantage of studying him at close quarters.' He immediately told me that I could best serve the club by going back upfront, a move I was happy to make, and I proved that Alex's instincts were sound by scoring three times in the first four matches.

My start couldn't have gone any better and I capped it with the third goal in that run, which enabled us to beat Liverpool 1–0 at Anfield on Boxing Day. It gave my fan club on the Kop even more reason to break out into that old standard: 'Eff off, Whiteside!' My performance also registered with the boss. 'He had self-assurance that was extraordinary in a twenty-one-year-old,' Fergie said. 'The excellence of his technique gave him easy mastery of the ball and he had the gift of making time for himself that is the stamp of quality. He was an island of compo-sure, looking up and unhurriedly making his decisions. He rarely surrendered possession and he increased the angle and weight of his passes so well that the receiver never had to fight

the ball. His eyes were as cold as steel and he had the tempera-
ment to match. As a player he was close to the genius category.'
Do these really sound like the words of someone who, according
to the many media myths, doesn't like me?

The biggest myth of all is that we never got on, and because
I turned down the many newspaper offers to slam him when
I left, which Paul McGrath regretfully accepted, there's this
feeling that I was gagged. I've lost count of the number of
times I've been asked at functions for the 'real' story of my
relationship with Fergie and the innuendo is always present that
I'm covering something up, as if, like Sherlock Holmes and the
curious incident of the dog that didn't bark, the absence of
something is in itself somewhat fishy. But the truth is we got
on fine. Sure, there were run-ins, and at times my behaviour
and wilfulness infuriated him. More often, though, it exasperated him, which is a different thing. We're not talking about a
catalogue of misdemeanours, just a few incidents when we didn't
see eye-to-eye over my liking for a night out. I always paid him
the respect his position and character demanded and to this
day, whenever I see him, and that's fairly frequently, there's a
lot of affectionate banter but no rancour and no grudges. The
press like labels and so his 'hairdryer' temper is seen to define
him, but that's only one part of his personality. He's also warm
and witty, a genuinely caring and kind bloke, thoroughly decent
and so unlike his public image that I laugh when I see him
portrayed as this one-dimensional rage monster.

But I can't deny that I found it difficult to come to terms
with the swift change from the latitude Ron gave us to Alex's
less liberal approach, and I wasn't alone. Shortly after he arrived,

we went on a pre-arranged trip to Bahrain for an exhibition match which we won 1–0 with me scoring. For some reason, we stayed on for a couple of days after the game and one afternoon, when Fergie went out shopping, the entire squad got stuck into a few beers. As the session unwound, the singsongs and loud banter eventually became so rowdy that it must have caught the boss's attention on his return from his trip in the early evening. He stormed into the bar, still clutching his bags, and told us all to get to his room at once. With fifteen of us crowded into his bedroom, he read us the riot act for the first time, shouting his head off that we were 'a disgrace to the club and yourselves. You're an absolute irresponsible bloody nightmare.' When he finished his tirade and we filed out of his room, breaking out into beery giggles as soon as we escaped his gaze, I turned to Robbo and said, 'But he didn't actually say we couldn't go out, did he?'

We sloped off to a bar and then went on to a nightclub a few miles away, thinking that we were safely out of Fergie's range, but as soon as we ordered a drink in the club I turned round and clocked the chairman, Martin Edwards, with some friends. We knew we'd been busted and that he'd be on the phone to the boss, but boozy bravado took over and we quickly ordered another round before the inevitable happened. Sure enough, fifteen minutes later, the manager and his assistant, Archie Knox, careered through the doors as if they were raiding a Wild West saloon, grabbed the pair of us and dragged us out. The boss let us have it. 'I've only been in the job a couple of weeks,' he bellowed. 'I haven't even signed my contract yet and here we are with my two best players behaving like this.

Look at the bloody state of you!' I apologised immediately and said, 'C'mon, boss. We're really sorry. Let's get a taxi back to the hotel.' That was the red rag that set him off again. 'Effin' taxi?' he cried. 'Bollocks! You can walk.' And he marched us the three miles back to the hotel, with me and Robbo swaying from side to side. I tried my best to calm him down by saying sorry repeatedly. 'Sorry, boss,' I squeaked in a slurring but contrite high-pitched voice. 'I'm really sorry. I'm out of order and I accept that. You can fine me a week's wages because I deserve it. I'm sorry.' Bryan, a person, shall we say, who is rather more careful with his pennies, was having none of it. 'Shut up, you,' he hissed. 'No one's effin' fining me a week's wages!'

I might as well get the other incident out of the way here too, which came essentially from the same misunderstanding or, more accurately, difference of opinion about what 'time off' constituted. To me it meant time away from my job and responsibility, time to myself to do whatever I wanted to do, but the boss saw time off during the season as a rare opportunity to rest. Our contrasting interpretations of what rest was came to light when we were preparing to go to Parkhead in March 1987 to play in Roy Aitken's testimonial match. No one knew better than the boss, a proud Govan lad, that a kid from the Shankill Road would not be made particularly welcome by Celtic fans and, with some sensitivity for their feelings and mine, decided it would be better if I didn't go. It wouldn't have bothered me, it couldn't be any worse than the reception that usually greeted me at Anfield, but when he dangled the carrot of a couple of days off, I didn't protest at being forced to sit out a friendly.

It ended up with me having St Patrick's Day off, which is

also my ma's birthday, but I couldn't claim with a straight face that I was toasting my mammy as an excuse when later collared by Fergie about the day's events. I spent the day, it was a Tuesday, with my friend Michael Beresford and we started off in The Park, where Paddy Crerand succumbed to an enormously embarrassing Paddy's Day disaster and ran out of Guinness. He formed a posse of his regulars and sent us off to one of his mate's bars to get some more and I helped him load a barrel into the back of his car before going off into Manchester for a few more drinks and a Chinese meal. When we came to the end of our midnight feast, a nightcap was suggested and then we were struck by inspiration: if we went over to Gorton market, the pub that catered for the porters would be opening at 4 a.m. and we could kick on for a couple more hours. Even though the place was rammed with City fans, who gave me plenty of stick, we had a couple more pints before I jumped into a taxi and finally went home to sleep off the epic eighteen-hour session.

As soon as I walked through the door at the Cliff on the Thursday morning, I was met by the sight of a silent but clearly fuming Fergie beckoning me to his office with the curly finger. I doubt he could have been better informed if he'd been out with us himself. He knew every single detail and he looked increasingly bewildered as he listed my movements: Paddy's, moonlighting as a drayman, the bars in town, the Chinese restaurant and the fish market. He seemed to be particularly perturbed that I'd been spotted in Altrincham loading a barrel of Guinness into the boot of a car. I tried to explain that I was only helping a friend out, but he kept returning to how bad it looked. He was furious that he'd given me two days off 'and all everybody does is ring in about you'.

That was always the way when you played for United. The manager didn't need to employ his own army of informers; there would always be enough volunteers to help the boss keep tabs on the players. Having said that, however, I once spied Fergie and Archie Knox executing a pretty hasty and flustered three-point-turn when they got stuck up the cul-de-sac past my house during a surreptitious attempt to check out where I lived. I was lucky they didn't spot what I was up to when they drove past, as I had just returned from Costco and was busy laying down several cases of wine in the garage. Now, of course, Alex is an even bigger wine buff than me, but back then I'm sure the sight of all those bottles would have sent him round the twist.

If you discount the odd managerial drive-by, the level of scrutiny we faced was highest from the press and we usually dealt with it by frequenting only the places where we felt 'safe' such as Paddy's, the Roebuck or the Four Seasons. When 'United's booze culture' became a newspaper story, we learnt that some reporters did a circuit of the pubs of Hale, Bowden and Altrincham on our days off, hoping to catch Whiteside, Robson and McGrath off the leash and on the lash. It paid to keep your head down because privately offered 'intelligence' from insiders or 'concerned fans' was one thing, but we knew that public coverage and criticism from 'outsiders' in the press would understandably embarrass the boss and probably irritate him beyond a point from which an apology or even our talent and performances could save us. On this occasion, though, he delivered a stinging reprimand, fined me and we started afresh.

It may seem odd that I didn't stop going out after that verbal warning. The boss can be so intimidating at times that people seem surprised that I didn't just bend to his will, but I couldn't simply switch all the characteristics that made me a first-team player at sixteen on and off at will. I can be just as stubborn, determined and selfish at times in all aspects of my life, not just my career. The bottom line is that, at the age of twenty-one, I fundamentally disagreed with his view that drinking was harming my football. I wanted to enjoy myself and I wouldn't stand for anyone telling me what to do. If I wanted to go to the pub, I went to the pub. Yes, I could have sat at home and been the most miserable fella around and not got on with my team-mates, but one thing that would not have made me was a finely tuned athlete. Any chance of that happening went out of the window with the operations I had before I turned seventeen. If I had done as I was told, would I have recovered from injury quicker, or been a better player or better person? The answer to that is I don't know and there's no definite way of knowing. The injuries would have got me anyway and not one of those was caused by drinking. I didn't look after myself properly in the way players do now, but neither did anyone else and when you're coping with a knee that's been reduced to bone-on-bone from the age of sixteen, your whole career is on borrowed time. I think it's pretty pointless to speculate whether a few pints less would have meant a few games more. Ultimately, who's to know?

Although Fergie's quest to change our lifestyles was the most noticeable aspect of his revolution, he also brought a far more meticulous approach to training, so much so that we used to joke that during his first few months at the club, a meeting would be called to tell us when the next meeting would take place. His first diagnosis, that we were not fit enough, led to far more running than we had been used to and we did much more work on set pieces and strategy than had been the norm with Ron. Archie Knox took a lot of the sessions, but you could tell that everything had been thought out upstairs in the office and planned to an intricate timetable, so that every routine was sharper and more intense. Nothing was ever off the cuff again. Alex was great at delegating responsibility, but cleverly understood that although players try to give their all for the coach, something kicks in subliminally when the boss is watching. He always seemed to know the right moment to approach or intervene and you didn't even have to spot him yourself to realise he was near, the quickening of the pace and your team-mates upping the ante was always a dead giveaway.

The immediate focus of his first few months in charge was to steer us clear of relegation and once that had been achieved with our unbeaten League run in January and February, he took stock of the squad he had inherited, gave a lot of fringe players a chance and made his plans to remould the team in the summer. I always remind Fergie's first signing, Viv Anderson, that he should thank me for his move to United. I should point out that Viv and Brian McClair joined the club on the same day, but Viv likes to claim precedence on alphabetical order!

Arsenal were top of the First Division and had been unbeaten for seventeen League games when they came to Old Trafford in January 1987 and, because Robbo was out injured, the boss decided to move me back into midfield to stop Steve Williams and Paul Davis overpowering us. The famous twenty-one-man brawl that took place when United played Arsenal in October 1990 is often cited as the one which sparked the bad blood between the two clubs, but this one, three years earlier, was just as ferocious and ill-tempered and was probably only a punch-up away from notoriety.

David O'Leary has always identified me as the chief culprit for the antagonism that followed, saying, 'He was like a wild nutter throughout the whole match. He was allowed to run around like a lunatic.' It's true that I did dish out a few robust tackles, but the lateness of some of them didn't come from a desire or intention to hurt anybody, just from too much commitment and too little pace. Hard tackles are not the same as dirty tackles: the former are designed to rattle the bones and make your opponent think twice about the next one, the latter to injure him. If I ever crossed the line that separates the two, it was because I tried to use the full weight of my body to win the ball and if I took the man as well, too bad. If the player was too quick for me and offloaded the ball when I'd pulled the trigger to go into the challenge, I had no way of pulling out and it often looked appallingly late. But I never lifted my foot to hit someone studs-first or raked anyone or stamped on them. I was hyper-aggressive and used all the physical advantages I enjoyed, but I was never deliberately dirty.

The incident that convinced Fergie that Viv was his type of player occurred in the second half, shortly after we had gone 1–0 up. I'd been booked for a tackle on the late David Rocastle, God bless him, before the break and when I went in hard on him again he kicked out in retaliation as we both stood up and was sent off. When the game restarted, play moved down towards Arsenal's goal, but Viv, the right-back, did not retreat and came over to me, sticking his face as close to mine as he could without touching it, and, using words you wouldn't believe, unleashed a storm of abuse. 'What you doing getting a young kid sent off you dirty effin' c****?' He was so agitated the veins on his neck were standing up like cables and I thought they were going to pop. His right arm, meanwhile, was twitching as if he was trying to restrain himself from hitting me. It was all great ammunition for a wind-up and I began whispering very softly to him while I had a big, greasy smile plastered across my face: 'Punch me, go on. Please hit me. I dare you. Be a man, you know you want to. Come on, knock my lights out.'

I wasn't trying to get him sent off, just needling him to see how much more annoyed I could make him, the sort of games-manship you use to try to force your opponent to lose his composure. But he didn't bite and Alex was impressed both by the fact that he'd stood up to me and that he'd had the coolness not to be pushed over the edge by my goading. His behaviour that day earned him a place at the top of the boss's list and he proved to be an excellent signing, even though he played very few games. He had the sort of strong personality Alex was looking for: fearless, loud and very upbeat. A merciless mickey-taker, he kept the dressing room bubbling, so, for example, if you ever wore a new suit, he'd be straight over to inform you that your tailor had gone blind and offer you his sympathy.

Viv and Robbo had been mates for years, a friendship forged on international duty, and on the first day of pre-season training in the summer of 1987 it was Bryan who showed him around the Cliff. It was common knowledge that Viv hated me and was forever banging on to Robbo about 'dirty effin' Whiteside', so when he strode over to my peg to be introduced, Bryan turned to the full-back and said, 'C'mon, Viv, tell Norman what you say about him when we're away with England. Now's your chance to tell him what you think about him.' It was a good way to break the ice. Viv's face was a picture, but we shook hands, had a joke about it and have been friends ever since.

One of the things that Fergie always asked me to do was to show the new boys around, perhaps because he ruefully realised that no one knew the pubs and restaurants of the area better than me, so I took Viv and his wife out for a meal that night and Brian McClair a few days later. I also did the same for Ralph Milne and he occasionally joined me and Paul McGrath on a night out, once he'd become a part-time member of what he dubbed the '£80 boys', the amount he claimed he always spent on a session with us. I mention it to disprove the suggestion that Bryan, Paul and I formed a clique that excluded the others, a glee club which the manager ordered our team-mates to avoid. It was never like that and though the boss was frustrated by our refusal to go on the wagon during the season, he always trusted me to be a good influence on the new signings and show them the friendly face of his club.

It has largely been forgotten that we finished as runners-up in the First Division after Fergie's first full season in charge. With hindsight, you can look at the fact that he added only a couple of players – Viv and Brian – to the players that were there when he took over as his 'quick fix' solution, before he had the finance to rebuild from scratch. It was his misfortune that Liverpool had the resources for more extensive remodelling and spent the money they got from selling Ian Rush to fashion yet another devastating attacking partnership by buying Peter Beardsley, John Aldridge and John Barnes. We won more games and lost fewer than we ever had in a season under Ron, and Brian McClair scored twenty-four League goals and made the boss look like King Midas in the transfer market. Brian was a good, opportunistic striker who used his intelligence and anticipation to read the game superbly and had a priceless awareness of always being where the ball was most likely to fall.

I played twenty-four games upfront with McClair and though I scored only seven goals, I did set up a fair few for him, including one at Highbury in January 1988 when I dispossessed Tony Adams just inside their half, ran towards goal, drew John Lukic out and squared the ball to Choccy, who rolled it into the empty net. At that point, things seemed to be going well, but in truth our title challenge was more show than substance, as Liverpool, playing a scintillating brand of one-touch football that had the critics purring, never looked like faltering. At the beginning of the season I was one of three United players in the Football League side that celebrated its centenary by beating the Rest of the World XI 3–0 in the Mercantile Credit Classic at Wembley. I came on as a substitute and scored one of the goals, Bryan scored two and Paul outshone Michel Platini and Diego Maradona to be named man of the match. I always joke that whatever it was the three of us were drinking, it must have been good stuff. After such a decent start to the season and those clear signs that the club was making steady progress, it may seem odd that a fortnight after the Arsenal game I scored my last ever goal for United in a match against Derby at the Baseball Ground and I had become preoccupied with the idea of putting in a transfer request.

I had never entertained thoughts of leaving before that season and my change of heart wasn't a petulant response to the sterner discipline under Fergie. In fact, it was quite the opposite. I was impressed with the way he had set about breathing new life into the club and wanted to commit myself to playing a part in the exciting future that seemed guaranteed. But when the club first initiated talks about a contract extension two years before the expiration of the one I had signed after the 1985 Cup final, I was not just perplexed when they withdrew the offer after all the details had been agreed, I was furious. This was pre-Bosman, remember, and it was explained to me that Fergie had decided that new contracts would not be awarded until a player reached the last year of his current deal. I had no quibbles with his new policy – in fact, it made perfect sense – but I was annoyed that they'd come to me in the first place, put me through the charade of lengthy negotiations, agreed to redress the imbalance that meant I remained one of the lowest paid players at the club, then walked away.

I brooded on it for a few weeks, nursing my disappointment and nurturing a bit of resentment during chats with Paul McGrath, who had long felt unwanted by Fergie, and came to the conclusion that I'd never have the same bargaining power as a bought player. Prove that I deserved a new contract? Hadn't I done that often enough? No, I thought, the club had traded on my loyalty for too long. I called their bluff and went through the formalities of asking for a transfer. You sometimes read of 'disgruntled' players 'slamming in' transfer requests, and it conjures up the image of a frowning, chuntering man striding into the manager's office and whacking a piece of paper on his desk with an almighty thud. I doubt that ever happens and my experience was certainly less dramatic. I had a very friendly chat with Fergie, told him my concerns, admitted that I'd started to feel a little stale before Cup games and asked to go. He explained that his contractual policy was a point of principle, one that he wouldn't be changing solely for my benefit, and informed me that if someone came in with his asking price (which was subsequently revealed to be a ludicrously high £1.5m) then he would reluctantly sell me.

I was slightly concerned that my act of defiance might lead to limbo in the reserves while a transfer was arranged, but the state of my left achilles, which had been flaring up with tendonitis since the grounds had got harder in January, solved the manager's dilemma of whether to pick someone the tabloids now called 'wantaway Whiteside'. At that stage, although my ankle kept swelling up, it was more a constant discomfort than the debilitating condition it later became and twice daily ultra-sound treatment got me fit enough for a place on the bench for our match at Anfield on Easter Monday 1988. The oddest thing about that game, my last for United against Liverpool, is that our fans, particularly the diehard ones, make more of my thirty-nine-minute cameo than they do of anything else I did in my career. Supporters still come up to me and say, 'Thanks for that day at Anfield.' I always think, 'Why are you thanking me for that?' A 3–3 draw was hardly important in the scheme of things, but it seems to have struck a chord with them as the quintessential Whiteside moment.

We were 3–1 down when Fergie told me to go on and I was not at all happy. My return to the squad had coincided with the news that I'd put in a transfer request and I'd heard some of our fans use the words 'traitor' and 'Judas' about me that afternoon. I was blasé about the insults from the Kop, which I always interpreted as praise – if they were that bothered about me, they must have felt I was a real danger to their team – but our supporters' abuse made me angry and determined to show the depth of my commitment. My bad mood was exacerbated by my loathing of being a substitute and when I belatedly gate-crashed the game I wasn't going to let anyone stand in the way of me demonstrating what United were going to lose when I went to another club.

Within five minutes of getting on, I had put both of Liverpool's best performers on the day, Steve McMahon and John Barnes, on the deck. Barnes was the victim of an Alan Shearer-style elbow to the throat, when I'd flung out my arms to shield the ball and unintentionally, but highly effectively, poleaxed him with a blow to the Adam's apple. That I wasn't booked for it drove the Kop barmy and they were even more outraged moments later when McMahon tried to exact revenge on me and ended up in a heap on the floor. I said afterwards that I had merely trodden on his little toe, but you have to remember that this was a couple of years before I took my biology O Level, so I may have been mistaken! I absolutely bulldozed him, in fact: I hit him with a boot loaded with thirteen stone, and got the yellow card I probably deserved. It looked worse than it was, though, and McMahon played it up to the crowd and referee, hyping up their disgust at one lateish tackle. It wasn't at all premeditated, but it worked like a dream. I'm sure he would deny it, but McMahon, who liked to dish it out but wasn't the greatest guzzler of his own medicine, was very wary of me from then on. From bossing the game and with us down to ten men following Colin Gibson's fifty-eighth-minute sending off, Liverpool cracked.

My fit of rage at the slander about my treachery transformed the tempo of the game and I screamed 'Come on, let's go and do this' at my team-mates. A couple of meaty challenges turned Liverpool upside down and when Robson scored our second, I knew we were going to get another. Sure enough, on seventy-seven minutes, I squeaked a pass through their defence that put wee Strachan clear to equalise and we scared the pants off them in the last few minutes as we dominated possession and turned their penalty area into the Alamo. That draw was celebrated like a victory, but the turnaround had been so drastic that I remember feeling slightly disappointed that we didn't actually win. I think that what I did that day became such a vivid memory for our fans because it was one of those games when both local and national humiliation were imminent and it appeared that I did exactly what the supporters dreamed themselves doing in my position — kicked lumps out of Liverpool. I became their representative on the pitch, as if I'd shaken up McMahon on their behalf, and they've never forgotten it. Some of them still booed my name when the team was announced over the tannoy at our next home game, but I didn't leave the bench again that season, so I never got the chance to test if the 'traitor' taunts would always light my fuse in a similar fashion.

Liverpool were an obsession for the boss around that period and, ironically, given my performance which aggravated their fans' hatred of me, they became the focus of my biggest non-drink-related disagreement with Fergie shortly after the match. I was in Belfast, preparing to play for Northern Ireland, when I did a short interview with *Match* magazine in which I agreed that Liverpool's attacking play that season had been admirable. When the reporter asked if I fancied playing in a team *like* that, I gave what I thought was a standard, bland reply. 'Of course,' I said. 'Who wouldn't want to be playing entertaining football, scoring hatfuls of goals and winning League titles?' There didn't appear to be any hostages to fortune in those words, but if I was playing now, media training would have taught me either to have spurned the journalist's request to talk or to trot out something even more banal such as 'I am playing for the best club in the world and that's all I'm interested in.'

When I returned to the Cliff a few days later, Alex was waiting for me. I obeyed his order to 'get upstairs now' and followed him into his office, where he had gathered his coaching staff. He then threw a copy of the *Daily Mirror* at me, which was open at a page with the headline 'Whiteside wants Anfield move', and he began to yell. 'Tell them!' he shouted. 'Tell Archie and Nobby [Stiles] what you've said. Go on, tell them you want to play for that effin' lot down the road. Effin' Liverpool.'

Before I'd even said a word to defend myself, he told me that I owed our fans an apology and that I'd better get myself on the radio and in the *Manchester Evening News* to beg for their forgiveness. I tried to explain what I had said and how it had been picked up from a kids' magazine and twisted by the newspaper, arguing that if I had said that I would like to play for a team like Brazil, it wouldn't mean I wished I was Brazilian. I had lived in Manchester since 1981, I told him, and, believe me, I knew precisely what our fans thought of Liverpool. I wasn't dumb enough to be so provocative. He, I said, more than anyone, should know how the media can misrepresent the mildest things. But he wouldn't drop it and did everything but fine me. I turned on the stubbornness, though, told him repeatedly that I had done nothing to apologise for and refused to back down. In the end, he had to give way and let me leave his office with my pay packet intact, but he was steaming mad about a trivial made-up story because it was about Liverpool, his bugbear. In retrospect, I think he was more irate about that than he'd ever been about the booze up to that point.

The drinking antagonised him more the following season, when my achilles trouble deteriorated from chronic soreness to a partial tear and culminated in a full rupture which meant a gap between first-team matches of 363 days. The thing that frustrated me most was that I knew something was wrong months before I could convince anyone to operate. I had to go through the whole rigmarole of injections, massage, cycling and swimming before resuming training and broke down again a couple of times before they put me under the knife. But that didn't solve anything either and I had to demand a second opinion. It wasn't until December 1988, a full year after my self-diagnosis, that I made it to Harley Street at my insistence and found a specialist who repaired it properly.

The six months from the beginning of pre-season training to Christmas, when I finally got rid of the crutches, were my worst days at United. I couldn't bear the wait-and-see approach of rest and recuperation and endless laps of the swimming pool. I wanted radical treatment from the start to get me back playing as soon as possible, but was steered down the softly, softly road which failed time and time again. I can't tell you how exasperating repetitive rehab is, particularly when you suspect that it's all futile because the ankle still doesn't feel right. It was during that period of intense frustration that I began to really drink. I didn't recognise then that I was drinking to escape, but it is obvious now. Every day I'd go in for treatment and it became far too easy for me to give Paul the nod once or twice a week, say, 'See you down there,' and head for Paddy Crerand's once I'd finished my daily routine. Instead of going home, I would try to fill the hole in my life by having a bit of fun while I was sat on a bar stool with a plaster of paris boot stuck on the end of my leg. I was trying to enjoy myself before going back to the grind. I usually intended to go home after a couple, but then we would have a last pint, then another, then just one more, and I'd get carried away with it, trying to lift myself out of the dumps.

It was probably around then that Paul, who had had three operations on his knee during the autumn, and I started to edge clear of Robbo in the boozing stakes. He didn't shun us and we certainly didn't ostracise him, but there is always a barrier between a fit player and an injured one. His days had a purpose, ours didn't, and we compensated for the boredom and isolation of our predicament by throwing ourselves at the solace drink seemed to offer. It didn't take long for Fergie to get wind of our afternoons out and when I turned up for treatment, the first thing Jim McGregor sometimes said to me was, 'The boss knows where you were last night.'

Unlike Paul, who laboured under the false impression that Alex hated him and therefore found it impossible to look him in the eye and confide in him, I would go and knock on Fergie's door to pre-empt the inevitable bollocking. 'Boss,' I would say, 'I was out last night. Sorry. Let me tell you what happened.' He told me a few years ago that he used to get phone calls telling him what we were up to and would lie awake in bed brooding and working out what he was going to say to me, but before he could deliver his carefully constructed dressing-down I'd breeze in with my apologies and explanations. 'You used to stun me,' he said, 'and take the wind out of my sails.' I was never surly or defensive with him and perhaps my honesty and the good-natured, wayward-son manner of our conversations spared me the full might of his wrath. 'He was intelligent and would hold his hand up when called to account over his drinking,' the manager wrote of me. 'My rebukes did little good but at least in our talks I felt I was communicating with Norman.' Yes, I irritated him, but there was fondness there too.

I managed to keep a fairly low profile when I went out, probably because I had a higher tolerance for alcohol than Paul, but the second of two highly publicised incidents with McGrath caused such embarrassment for the boss that it signalled the end of beer-fuelled escapism for the so-called Booze Brothers. The first episode happened a few days before my wedding in October 1987 when Paul joined us at the Four Seasons where

I was entertaining my future father-in-law's workmates who had put up a marquee in my garden for the reception. When Julie came to pick me up at the end of the evening, she offered Paul, who was clearly wasted, a lift home. He refused and quite forthrightly protested that he was OK to drive the few miles home, yet while Julie and I were in the fish and chip shop, he careered off the road in Hale, clipped the kerb and somersaulted his car into someone's garden.

As soon as we got home, his wife, Claire, rang us to say that he was in hospital. The nurses, seeing that I'd had plenty to drink, wouldn't let me near him. It was the talk of the staff's pre-training breakfast get-together at the Cliff the following morning and Fergie was absolutely furious, even more so when he learnt that Paul had turned down a lift home. I had to deny a rumour that had already started to circulate which put me in the passenger seat before I was supposed to have legged it from the scene. He was angry with me, but knew I wasn't a liar and he believed me even before he saw the photographs of the caved-in left-hand side of the car, which confirmed that anyone foolish enough to get in the car with Paul would have been torn in two in the crash. The manager saved his real scorn for my mate, but his understandable disgust at Paul's cavalier disregard for those he may have hurt or killed by his decision to drive drunk didn't snap Paul out of it, as Alex had intended. Instead it pushed my troubled friend towards another spell of gloomy introspection and self-loathing.

Although that incident was far more serious, it was the second time we put 'drunken Manchester United players' back in the media spotlight, more than a year later, that had far bigger consequences. Again, it started with an act of kindness, when I agreed to do a mate of mine, who had moved from the BBC to ITV, a favour and took Paul with me to be interviewed live on Granada on the Friday night before our third-round FA Cup tie against QPR in January 1989. We met in the pub, had two pints, then drove to Old Trafford for the broadcast. While the technicians were setting up, Paul disappeared and I later learned that he'd been up to the Trafford pub to sink a few shorts and give himself the courage to face the cameras. The interview was a farce. Paul was totally out of it and started pulling faces and saying 'Cooee' straight into the camera, which set me off in a fit of giggles. It looked terrible and the clip has haunted us for years, as it is still dug up for television list shows which catalogue footballers' bad behaviour. In my defence, I wasn't drunk, was off duty, as I hadn't played for eight months, and hadn't even started jogging again. But Paul had played the previous game and, though now injured, had been put on stand-by for the following day's match. I'm sure he didn't know that he might be needed when he started drinking on Friday afternoon – he wasn't so far out of control that he would get hammered the day before a match – but Fergie never really forgave him for his befuddled public display and his subsequent refusal to play the next day.

I was oblivious to the fall-out from our appearance until Monday morning, when I was called in to face the manager. Paul was already in the office when I arrived and when Alex eventually came in with Gordon Taylor of the PFA I knew it was serious. It transpired that the boss and chairman had called in the union and made a proposition to Paul that they should call it quits, pay him off on account of his chronic knee injury and award him a testimonial in Dublin to mark his retirement. It wasn't so bad for me. Martin Edwards did most of the talking, read out the charge sheet and confirmed that I would be fined the maximum two weeks' wages, despite my protests that I hadn't been drunk on the telly. I was told to go home and pack a bag, as I was being sent to the FA's rehabilitation centre at Lilleshall for an intensive fitness programme.

After some deliberation, Paul turned down their suggestion, sobered up and got back in the team for a run of eleven games towards the end of the season. But the Rubicon had been crossed and neither Paul nor the boss ever really trusted each other again. Our actions had allowed the club to be ridiculed and it's probably fair to say that from that point on there was no chance of resurrecting a long-term future for either of us with United.

I went to Lilleshall for three weeks and shed the stone and a half I'd put on during my long spell of inactivity. Some of that timber was down to Fergie's instruction that injured players should go to Old Trafford to entertain corporate guests at lunchtime. When he saw the result of several weeks spent eating five-course meals, he quickly put an end to that initiative. We slept in dormitories at Lilleshall and apart from a spot of TV in the evenings, the only thing to do was get fit. Ally McCoist and Ian Durrant were there with me and were in hysterics at the Cuban-heeled boots I had to wear to stop my achilles stretching. I even had to wear them in the shower, with plastic bags wrapped around them, but it worked and when I was finally given the go ahead to run, I could manage it without pain for the first time in more than a year.

Long months stuck in the gym and the treatment room had driven me towards a bleak, claustrophobic mood, but within days of getting back out into the open air on the training fields at the Cliff, I found I couldn't wipe the smile off my face. I was tingling with energy and optimism. Doing the thing you love most after being denied it for so long is better than any psychiatrist's couch for sorting out your head. I was so upbeat and confident that I didn't even dwell on my misfortune when my comeback in the reserves was curtailed when I contracted chicken pox. I was told to stay at home in quarantine for two weeks, but I was so desperate to get some miles in my legs that I would go in on my own in the afternoons to work. It took me six reserve games and the evidence provided by emerging unscathed from a ground-shaking 30:70 tackle against a Huddersfield Town trainee to convince the boss I was ready for the first team.

I played six games in all during April and May, partnering Bryan in midfield, but United had endured a dreadful season and I returned to a makeshift team which featured the first few of the forgotten band of 'Fergie's Fledglings' – Lee Martin, Russell Beardsmore and Giuliano Maiorana. We had been runners-up the previous year and should have kicked on after the return of Mark Hughes in the summer, but Mark and Brian McClair managed to score only twenty-four goals between them, the same number that Choccy had got on his own the year before, and by spring we'd fallen into a rut of dour, error-strewn, disjointed football and team morale was dreadful. I couldn't contain my enthusiasm at being back, but I failed to spark any life into a season that was petering out to an ominous chorus of boos from our livid fans.

It was pretty clear that the boss was unhappy and that his attempt to cobble together a competitive side by tinkering with it was at an end. It was time for phase two: the wholesale rebuilding of the first team. I was in two minds whether I'd be a casualty of his desire for mass changes when I headed off for my summer break, as he had said before my first game back, 'We can forget the speculation about transfers or whether Norman still wants to leave. He isn't on the list. He never was. All we said was that we would listen to offers because he said he wanted to go. It's in the interests of the club and the player that he regains his old form.' It gave me hope that I had a place in his plans, but on the other hand, no player can enter the last year of his contract with any certainty concerning their future.

With Sparky and McClair creating a roadblock to a regular role as a forward, the acquisition of two midfielders, Mike Phelan and Neil Webb, in June was all the evidence I required to realise that the chances of once more becoming an auto-matic choice at the heart of midfield were as slender as the opportunities upfront. Moreover, United were being heavily linked with moves for Paul Ince, Gary Pallister and Danny Wallace and it was pretty obvious that if Alex was going to pursue his three targets, then he would have to realise some income from fringe players, a category to which my injury-ravaged year had consigned me. They turned down £500,000 bids for me from Osasuna and Sheffield Wednesday in early July, then took £450,000 from Aston Villa for Paul McGrath. I was running my soccer school in Northern Ireland when I got the half-expected phone call from the boss to return to the Cliff immediately. Having hastily arranged for Steve Bruce to fly over and deputise for me, I took the Belfast to Manchester shuttle that I'd taken so often from the age of thirteen onwards for one last time as a United player.

When I met Fergie in his office and he told me that the club had accepted an offer from Everton, we had a long and amicable chat about my situation. Their bid was for £600,000, with a further £150,000 to follow once I had played fifty games, and he told me that my medical history made it too good to turn down. Because United knew every minute detail of my physical state and had heard Jim McGregor's prognosis that I'd be finished at twenty-six, I understood that it would be financially negligent of them to give me the sort of contract I might get at another club. I'd been with United since I was a kid, he said. It was time I went off and made some money. He gave me enormous help and great advice, telling me exactly what he was paying Webb and Phelan, and outlined the sort of sum I should ask Everton for. He basically sorted out my deal for me and I will always be grateful to him and Everton because I earned more in my two years at Goodison than I had in eight years at United. I went to meet Colin Harvey armed with Fergie's crib sheet, spent a night at home mulling it over and was spared no sadness at the realisation that I was about to leave the club I loved. But my better judgment told me I was begging for a fresh start, so I leapt in my car, drove to Bellefield and signed a four-year contract with Everton the next day.

Contrary to the gossip doing the rounds of Manchester pubs at the time and since, I wasn't shipped out of the club because of my drinking. Robbo was as fond of the ale as I was and had as many run-ins with the boss about it, but he stayed. Perhaps he was considered indispensable, I don't know, but it is also pertinent to point out that although he was wrongly seen by the public as injury-prone, he wasn't suffering from the same sort of debilitating condition that I had. I left because the boss wanted a new team and the state of my knee suggested that I was not a long-term prospect. Of course, when I was out for a year and there were interludes when I couldn't see much further than the bottom of my glass, Alex became extremely frustrated by my habits. On the whole, however, we had a warm relationship. The proof of that is that I've worked for United for the past ten years. Everyone knows how much of a say he has at the club and if there was any animosity between us, I know that he would have vetoed my employment in the hospitality department and would never have invited me to his testimonial dinner or collared me in the corridor at Old Trafford when we won the title in 2003, dragged me into his office and thrust a bottle of wine in my hand with the injunction to 'get this down you'. The £50,000 I was offered to slag him off the day I left would have come in handy – it was as much as my annual salary at United – but the truth is it offended my loyalty to a man about whom I had no complaints. I didn't have the material to delight the headline writers. There's not much sensation to be made out of my opinion that he's as decent a man as he is a manager.

CHAPTER THIRTEEN

A KIND OF BLUE

If you view Manchester United as the pinnacle, as many players do, it can be easy to be condescending towards other clubs, as if the moment you leave is the first slip on a downward spiral. But the truth is that Everton did not represent a backward step for me. Although I had denied them the Treble with my goal in the 1985 FA Cup final, Everton had been far more successful than United during the five years preceding my transfer, having won two titles, the FA Cup and the Cup Winners' Cup, and been runners-up in the League and Cup twice more. They retained a hard core of players from the twin title triumphs when I joined and had a year earlier invested heavily in remodelling the team, with exciting signings such as Tony Cottee, Stuart McCall and Pat Nevin. I was part of the second wave of Colin Harvey's rebuilding programme, designed, as he explained, to add some steel to the flair. I was one of five summer transfers and I arrived for my Goodison Park photocall to pose alongside Mike Newell, Martin Keown, Stefan Rehn and Ray Atteveld in a group photograph given the pithy if somewhat overcooked caption 'The Famous Five'.

I was delighted that such a prestigious and competitive club had come in for me, but, if truth be told, I would have forced United to sell me to one on the continent had it not been them or, unlikely as it may seem, Liverpool. It was a brilliant move for me and, though hindsight would suggest to the charitable that it was an Indian summer or swansong, while the cynical might call it a payday, you have to remember that I was only twenty-four-years-old and optimistic that the doubts about my long-term fitness prospects could be overcome. In any case, I sailed through the medical, which focused more on my recovery from the recent surgery on my achilles than the more serious concerns about the durability of my right knee which had prompted Jim McGregor's pessimism. By that stage, I had nursed the damned thing through seven operations in seven years, knew how to cosset it and had learnt to bear the constant ache. Properly managed and with a bit of good fortune, I felt I should be able to eke another four years' service out of it. I looked at the opportunity Colin Harvey had offered me, therefore, as a fresh start rather than a last hurrah. I was fit, happy, ambitious and highly motivated, from a determination to restore my career to the heights it had once reached. If, in putting it back on the upward curve, I succeeded in proving that United had been wrong to let me go, then so much the better.

By a strange coincidence, my first match in the royal blue gave me a chance to remind them. In the days before I left Old Trafford I had been inoculated for United's pre-season tour of the Far East and if I had bothered to read the itinerary I'd been sent, I would have known the jabs were not in vain when I signed for Everton. Only forty-eight hours after collecting my boots and saying my goodbyes at the Cliff, I faced all the 'turning up like a bad penny' jibes of my former team-mates when we boarded the same flight to play an exhibition game against each other in Japan. The trip was most memorable for the fact that my first child, Della, was born while we were away. It shows you how much football has changed over the past twenty years, and me too, when I say that even though Julie was nine months' pregnant, it never occurred to me to try to bail out of the trip. It simply wasn't the done thing, nor had there been too many New Men on the Shankill Road to set a good example when I was growing up. Even if it had been allowed, I must confess that I was so desperate to get out on the field and impress Colin Harvey and show the football world that I was not yet dead that I would have insisted on going anyway. It's a hard thing to admit to your daughter, especially since I was retired when my two younger children, Blaine and Clodagh, were born and I was present at both births. By that time, of course, injury had exiled me from the grip of my obsession with football.

I played in all four games on tour and was thrilled to score a goal in our 3–1 victory against my former club in Kobe, which prompted the small band of travelling United fans to give Fergie a bit of a rough ride over my transfer. We went on to defeat the national sides of Japan, Thailand and Malaysia in our three other games and, though the heat and humidity were making me tire before the end of the matches, I struck up a good understanding with Stuart McCall in the centre of midfield. Colin explained to me that he wanted to use my confidence and strength on the ball as a platform for the team and that I should hold as the anchor player and use my creative passing to release Kevin Sheedy, Pat Nevin and Stuart on bursts upfield. I was all for it, but also found some latitude to get forward myself, rather as if freed from the shadow of Robson I assumed all the responsibilities as the hub of the team that I had once subconsciously deferred to him. I thought then that my reduced mobility was a fitness issue caused by a year out of the game and that it would gradually fade away, not be the first signs of the terminal state of my knee. But the compensations I had to make to get by in terms of judgment and timing actually enhanced my game. Over time at Everton I reinvented myself as an old-fashioned playmaker, albeit one who could make a rhino flinch in the tackle. I was stuck with being one-paced, so my vision took over, engineering a role where accurate passing and my positional sense could still flourish. My spell at Goodison Park has largely been forgotten, but I maintain that, in technical terms, I played some of my best football there, an old head on young shoulders counterbalancing creaking and battered legs.

My pre-season form was good enough for Andy Gray to write that 'Colin Harvey has pulled off a masterstroke in capturing Norman Whiteside.' My debut away at Coventry, however, was a disaster. I would have never given it a second thought had William Hill not festooned their shop windows with a picture of me in the yellow strip, grimacing while challenging Lloyd McGrath for the ball – a reminder that has remained on show for the past eighteen years! We lost 2–0, but rallied to win our first two home games and I scored in the second, a 3–0 victory against Southampton. The former Liverpool player Tommy Smith wrote a weekly column in the *Liverpool Echo* and even he thought I'd made a pretty big impact in those games. He had never liked me much before and had written after United's 3–3 draw at Anfield in 1987 that 'he's so late so often in the tackle that he's an embarrassment . . . so late that I've wondered how he's managed to catch the train on United away trips'. But he shed his tribal dislike of Manchester United to concede that I was 'giving the Blues more power and possession' and 'could be the bargain of the season'. We won six of our opening ten games, not a bad record for a team in the throes of transition, and my partnership with Stuart McCall was praised for bringing stability and adventurousness to the side. Stuart was a great foil for me, a bustling ball of energy, and if I have one minor gripe it's that we could both play equally well but he would always end up winning the man of the match award because, I joked, his red hair made him so recognisable to the sozzled voters in the corporate lounges!

You often find when there's a great influx of new signings that the dressing room ends up splitting into cliques and I've heard criticism that Everton suffered from that malaise during my time with the club. There's always going to be a little bit of resentment from the 'seen it all' boys who had achieved so much in previous years, and they had become somewhat defensive about the standards that had been set and feared the club's spirit had been diluted. I always got on well with both camps – my record gave me the stripes to earn the respect of the old guard, while my relative youth and sociable outlook kept me in with the new boys. The one person whose wavelength I did find it difficult to find consistently was Martin Keown, who lived near me in Cheshire and used to cadge a lift into work with me most mornings. He had talent and was a wiry, strong stopper, but although I was only a year older than him, he was still unbelievably raw. He seemed to have the uncanny knack of always saying the wrong thing and wound people up with his moaning. I don't think he meant to be so tactless, but he was teetotal and steered clear of the regular 'bonding sessions', which left him incapable of overcoming the unfavourable first impression he'd made. He would have been less of the eternal outsider had he given the mellower side of his personality, the one I knew from its occasional appearances during our car journeys, freer reign when he was with the lads.

You couldn't find two players with more different personalities than Dave Watson and Pat Nevin, yet I hit it off with both of them and was as happy sharing a pint with Waggy in his local in Warrington as I was entertaining Pat at my house in Bowden after he had received a rare invite to visit my reclusive neighbour, the singer Morrissey. I even got on well with the captain, Kevin Ratcliffe, who had the oddest and most unsavoury pre-match ritual of them all — he used to pee in the tunnel before leading the team out. He became a good friend, despite an altercation a couple of years earlier. Everyone in the game knew I had a dodgy knee and some tried to take advantage of it. One such example happened when I was still at United and playing against Everton. The Rat and I went in for a ball that was more mine than his to win, and when I was on the point of making my lunge to nick it, I realised his six studs were going to rake down my knee and shin. I thought, 'No, I'm not letting you have that' and in the split second I had to evade it, I adjusted slightly and was OK, by an inch. If a tackle came from in front of me or was in my peripheral vision from either side, I could read the script well enough to avoid injury. It was the ones I couldn't see, the ones from behind, that did all the damage.

I never had any bother with the so-called hard men of my era — Vinnie Jones, Graeme Souness or Jimmy Case. Some players were frightened to go into challenges with them, but I didn't give a hoot. I was never intimidated by anyone and would enthusiastically fly into a tackle with someone like Souness. Obviously I would know which club we were playing against, but I often wouldn't know the make-up of the team until we were on the pitch. Even when I was captain and exchanged team sheets with my opposite number, I didn't read it before handing it over to the manager. I didn't care because I didn't think that any specific opposition player could influence the way I played. One thing that Fergie brought to my attention after witnessing a number of examples was my propensity for getting booked in the first fifteen minutes of a game, a good and a bad trait – bad because it gave him palpitations for the rest of the match, good because I would make my mark and then hold myself in check for the rest of the game without getting sent off. He said that thinking that I might get a red card used to drive him mad with worry for the remaining seventy-five minutes, but I was cool-headed enough for it never to happen, at least not while a United player.

Despite my notoriety as a clogger, I was only ever sent off once, and that was in an FA Cup fifth-round replay against Oldham at Goodison. It seemed to me that the referee, Mr Ward, for some reason had it in for me that day. It felt like that because normally I had a very good rapport with officials generally. That was back in the days when they could exercise their discretion, but Mr Ward was a letter of the law merchant and had that annoying schoolteacher-like way of addressing you. 'Player, state your name,' he would say, even though he knew full well who we were. He dismissed me for two bookable offences, the second wholly justified, when I caught Mick Milligan in the groin area under the ref's nose while challenging for a bouncing ball. The first, however, was never a yellow card, just a bog-standard block tackle. Like Ratcliffe, Milligan subsequently became a great mate of mine when he signed for Everton the following year. By that time I had been banned from driving, shamefully caught over the limit from a session the night before, and Milly used to pick me up and drive me to training every day, just as I had chauffeured Bryan Robson and Paul McGrath when they were suspended a couple of years earlier.

My first term at Everton went well and I scored thirteen

goals in the thirty-five matches I played. The highlight for me, inevitably, came against United at Goodison in our fifth game of that 1989–90 season. I played a part in all three of our goals – threading the ball between Gary Pallister and Steve Bruce for Mike Newell to finish; winning possession and passing to Kevin Sheedy, who played Pat Nevin in to lob Jim Leighton; then beating Mike Phelan to a header to start the move which led to Graham Sharp's diving third. We were 3–0 up when my hamstring went and I had to leave the field and, though United rallied to score twice before the end, we held on for an extraordinarily satisfying victory which led to equally memorable headlines on the Monday. I was gratified to read the *Guardian*'s 'Whiteside The Silent Avenger' and the *Manchester Evening News*'s 'Whiteside Makes United's Faces Red', but they overstated the notion of revenge. My motivation was never vindictive – I just wanted to prove the point that I wasn't washed-up and still had something to contribute.

This non-existent grudge factor, which was made up then played up by the press, probably contributed to the poor reception I got when I went to Old Trafford the following March. It was uncomfortable and slightly bewildering to be booed so vehemently when I ran out, and when I upended Mark Hughes I doubt I could have been more of a pantomime villain in the Stretford End's eyes had I been running around twirling the ends of my moustache. The match petered out in a dull 0–0 draw. At least I got a better welcome from Fergie than I had from the people who had raucously sung my name for seven years or worn pictures of me done up as Rambo on their T-shirts. 'I bear no ill will for Norman,' he said. 'It's a fact of football life these days that very few players stay a lifetime with one club. Norman was a smashing player for us and I hope he continues to have a successful career with Everton.'

Everything seemed to be going well. I enjoyed working with Colin Harvey, a thoughtful and innovative coach who was one of the pioneers of using videos to analyse games and illustrate his tactical plans. If I have any criticism at all of a man who was renowned in the game for his kindness and intelligence, it was that at times he could be too nice. He dropped me to the bench once for a game against Wimbledon and I was hacked off because I had scored four goals in the previous five matches. I wasn't the sort of player to make my protests at a time when it might cause embarrassment or ructions, so I waited until the Monday morning after the game to knock on his office door. Instead of bawling me out for questioning his judgment or telling me to mind my own business, he just gave way, admitted it had been a mistake and quite nervously assured me that I would be in the starting XI for the next match. I'm sure my reaction could lead to accusations that I wanted it both ways, for while I admired his honesty and was grateful for the recall, I couldn't help thinking that the very top managers would have defended their right to pick the team and firmly told me to eff off. I stayed in the team for the rest of the season and we ended up in sixth place, a pretty useful staging post for a side with so many new players, even if we had relied on the excellence of Neville Southall a bit too frequently for my liking. Still, I was enormously encouraged by the progress we had made and by the last weeks of the campaign I felt that I had rehabilitated both my fitness and reputation. How wrong I was.

I looked forward to resuming training in the summer of 1990, as I always did, with the desperation of a football addict relishing the prospect of a fix. My transfer from United had come so late the previous summer that I hadn't yet experienced a Bellefield pre-season, yet what happened on those impacted, concrete-like pitches that scorching July ensured that it was unlikely that I would get to 'enjoy' another.

One of Colin Harvey's coaches, Everton's former captain Mick Lyons, was a fitness fanatic and because I was always at the back of the field on training runs he would keep me behind afterwards to do more running work. The fact is I hadn't been able to run properly since 1979. The physio, Les Helm, would look out of his treatment-room window and shake his head, believing this sort of work was only making my condition worse. Les knew, just as Graham Taylor appreciated with Paul McGrath at Aston Villa, that you had to manage a chronic knee condition carefully. He knew that if, like Paul, I stuck to gym work on the exercise bike and just played matches, my career could be prolonged, but it took him a while to convince Lyons. In the meantime, I continued limping around the course, doing untold damage, until my knee grew so sore that I said to him, 'Mick, I can't do this.' I can't blame that pre-season for ending my career, but I do suspect that it fatally weakened an already damaged knee. It certainly robbed me of the enjoyment I usually experienced on the training park, and left me in no fit state to start the season. I went through a cycle in August and September of trying to play in practice matches and for the reserves, but every week or so my knee would swell up to the size of a ripe melon and I would have to sit it out and wait for it to return to normal before trying again. It was during one of those practice matches, on 20 September, that I was clipped by the apprentice professional as I mentioned right at the beginning. As soon as it happened I knew I'd have to have the operation that had been postponed for so long. I had made only one substitute appearance for the first team so far that season, but I was confident that another arthroscopy would do the trick, as it had always done before. It was then that Mr Johnson had his first look inside the joint, flushed it out and made the comment when I came out of surgery that I would probably end up in a wheelchair. But I ignored him, hobbled on, got through two and a half reserve games, enough to convince the new manager, Howard Kendall, to give me a run out, and managed to trudge through an hour against Wimbledon at Plough Lane in late November. It didn't feel like the end, but when I struggled to get out of bed the following morning and felt like an arthritic seventy-year-old, I was not capable of dancing a jig about my future, nor inclined to neither.

The nine most depressing months of my life followed, while I tried to fight off the inevitable. But however much I tried to ward off the bitter truth with a fug of alcohol, my plight would seem just as desperate the following morning. The swelling would go down, I would tentatively start training, get through, say, a week's sessions and feel a bit of hope returning. I would declare myself fit for the reserves, play a match with no reaction and the doom would be replaced by a crumb of confidence. This could go on for a fortnight, but then I would face the reality check when the knee would begin to click and clunk while running. I'd tell myself I was imagining it, but then the telltale swelling would come back and I'd have to start the process again.

When it happened for the third time, I had to accept that it was hopeless. I left Bellefield almost ten years to the day since I began my first pre-season at the Cliff. The obsession that had consumed my life from the moment I joined the Boys' Brigade at the age of seven was finished. Perhaps I should have consoled myself that I was walking, or more accurately staggering, out of the door and not being pushed in a wheelchair. But that was no comfort at all to me then.

CHAPTER FOURTEEN

THE CHANGING
MAN

The feelings of desolation and emptiness that dominated those first few weeks of my retirement do not torment me any more. But for quite a time I was nagged by a question that kept reverberating around my head: if football is what I was made for, what am I supposed to do when I can no longer undertake the primary purpose of my life? My friends in the game did their best to keep me involved by inviting me to join them on nights out, and for a while it helped raise my spirits. Soon, though, I started to find the company a little uncomfortable, at least at the beginning. I realised that it wasn't the pub trips I missed, but the game itself. I no longer had an outlet to show the very best part of me. I had always seen myself as a working man, very much like my father, and I found it difficult to cope with the exile from my ideal workplace. I used to love listening to the boys telling stories of what they had been up to the night before, that sense that there were no secrets between us. I could go into work every day and just, literally, play, then lounge about with twenty blokes who would battle to come up with the best mickey-take or riotously amusing, self-mocking anecdote.

That was the worst thing about packing the game in, the feeling that I had nowhere to go. I may still have been friends with my former colleagues, but I felt like an outsider and it just wasn't the same. There's a ruthlessness to the camaraderie of football players. If you're not a player there's a barrier there, even if you were a player only a few weeks before. Your membership is revoked when you retire and you're excluded from the banter and craic. That sense of togetherness in a unique common cause and the sheer exhilarating enjoyment of what we did for a living was lost. Don't get me wrong, I remained close to the lads and we had fun whenever we met up, but when the day-to-day involvement ended and the daily buzz disappeared, it was like an unusually harrowing and enforced cold-turkey cure for an addiction.

The first of my former team-mates to call offering practical advice and support was Sammy McIlroy, who had been so kind to me from the moment I first met him when I was fourteen. He had heard that I'd passed the FA's physiotherapy diploma course and was back at college, starting on the long slog through GCSEs and A Levels to get the qualifications that would secure acceptance on the degree course. He was manager of the Cheshire side Northwich Victoria in the Vauxhall Conference and asked me if I fancied some on-the-job experience as a physio looking after his players. For a few months I went along after college on Tuesday and Thursday nights, when the semi-professionals trained, and attended matches on Saturdays. Then, Sammy's assistant, Gordon Clayton, died and I was promoted to the role of assistant manager/physio for a couple of months and took some training, as I already had all the FA coaching badges, as well as carrying the sponge and spray.

I was grateful for the opportunity at first, but it caused a lot of tension at home because I'd be out two nights a week and often all day on Saturday. For Julie it was like I was carrying on as I always had, but the difference this time was that I wasn't getting paid. Well, they used to give me £20 a week in expenses, but I could easily spend that on a round of drinks at the bar before setting off for home. I was lucky to get work experience like that, but in effect I was subsidising it and I couldn't afford to continue doing that indefinitely; it just wasn't viable. Moreover, I could be setting off at 6 a.m. to get the coach, where I had to read my textbooks for a test on the Monday, to play Yeovil, say, or Welling, and it would be a ten-hour round trip. While I was happy to help Sammy out and even enjoyed joshing with the crowd, who used to give me a bit of stick when I limped on with my medical bag, the facilities at non-League level were a huge shock to me and the travelling quickly started to do my head in.

One night as we drove up the M6, I realised that I had seen enough of that road in my career to last me a lifetime. I had been on United's or Everton's coach for a decade, hurtling up and down that bleak and frequently congested motorway, and I knew every tiny feature of it. I'd sit there in the dark, on a less than luxurious bus, counting off the junctions – Keele, Sandbach, Knutsford – and could accurately forecast to the nearest minute, from more than a hundred miles away, the time of my arrival at home. In the end I had to accept that if I carried on driving up and down every fortnight to Colchester, Farnborough and Cheltenham Town I'd not just be out of pocket, I would be out of my mind as well, so I quit after four months in March 1992.

I was in dire straits financially throughout my spell at Northwich Victoria and the loose change I could put on the table late on a Saturday night was of no help whatsoever. I'd moved into the house in Bowden in 1985, under a scheme run by Manchester United whereby they had purchased the place and I paid them rent. When I left the club in 1989 I either had to leave or buy it at five per cent above the price United had paid for it four years earlier. While I was at Everton, on the best contract of my career, the mortgage repayments could be comfortably met, but by the summer of 1991, when my salary payments dried up, I found it a hell of a struggle to fund a £200,000 mortgage at 1991 interest rates, which were above ten per cent. We had the lifestyle to match the house too, and my savings took a real battering after I'd paid for the cleaner, au pair and gardener on top of the household bills. It took so long for the insurance payment to come through that I was almost wiped out by the time it finally fell through the letterbox.

While I was accumulating O and A Levels, therefore, I had no source of income. When my compensation arrived, I used it to pay off some debts and a lump sum of the mortgage, which reduced my outgoings but didn't redress my lack of incoming funds. United were kind enough to offer a way out of my predicament by awarding me a testimonial in May 1992, but circumstances conspired against me and I ended up with a gratefully received but nonetheless small sum. When the match against Everton was arranged in February, United were well on course to end their long title drought and they remained in first place until a disastrous run of successive defeats against Forest, West Ham and Liverpool in the space of a week let Leeds in to win the championship. Instead of my day giving a packed Old Trafford the chance to see the team parading the trophy for the first time in a quarter of a century, it was the biggest ever anticlimax. I understood fully why United fans, sick beyond words, couldn't face another match a week after their greatest ambition had been thwarted, but it was still a huge disappointment that only 7,434 made it to my farewell. Cursed by bad timing, like one of my tackles towards the end of my career, it was one of those occasions when you either hit the jackpot or you don't. Unfortunately, I didn't even come close on that sombre afternoon.

Salvation came from the unlikeliest source, given my low embarrassment threshold. Midway through 1992 I was asked if I fancied making an after-dinner speech at a forthcoming function. Nerves got the better of me and I refused, but I was persuaded to go along and do a question-and-answer session as a warm-up for the main act. It went surprisingly well and I even managed to have a few laughs, despite the sort of pre-performance anxiety I had never once experienced before a match. I must have done about a dozen before I was invited by a member of the audience at one of the dos to deliver a full speech at a football fundraising dinner. Surprising myself, I agreed to do it. Because of the Q&As, I now had a feel for what people wanted to know and my answers had grown progressively longer over the previous few months which gave me the basis of an act.

Gradually, it took off and I received more and more requests for bookings. I'm not a comedian and I focus on telling my story with a few anecdotes. I have done it so many times now that I riff off my prepared script and feel quite relaxed once I've overcome the nerves that flutter through my stomach from the moment I arrive until my name is announced and I stand up to speak. I've certainly confounded a few preconceptions held about me by the time I've sat down again. Given my reputation, some members of the audience think I'm going to roar in effing and jeffing, telling blue stories about players and then get royally tanked up, but when I've delivered my speech without swearing people often come up to me afterwards and tell me how different I am to their expectations.

I couldn't have sustained it without the help of my friend and confidant Geoff, who has supported me for the last decade. He is a divisional officer in the fire brigade but accompanies me when he can. We have been everywhere together – as far afield as Australia, Singapore, Canada and Spain – and he can turn his hand to anything. I am extremely grateful for the way he's looked after me because as the guest of honour you usually have to stay late into the night, meeting and greeting people. There are times when I've needed rescuing, when one last drink is thrust in my hand, and he has long had the knack of discreetly ushering me home. He even puts up with my snoring!

The after-dinner circuit was a godsend to me while I was at college and university. I had taken the decision that I had to go backwards to go forwards and the money I earned gave me the leeway to pursue my studies, even if some weeks I was absolutely shattered as my days became a procession of changing from one uniform to the next – the white lab coat for college at 7 a.m. and the dinner jacket and dickie bow in the evenings to pay for my education. I had always intended to do a physiotherapy degree once I'd finished my A Levels and was told by the University of Ulster that they were prepared to give me a chance. It had been the plan that if I got my qualifications, there would be a place for me at Jordanstown and I would move back home after thirteen years in England.

I didn't do as well as I had hoped in my exams, but I did well enough for Ulster University to uphold its side of the bargain, so Julie and I went to Belfast and started looking for a house and schools for Della and Blaine. But when I went to the campus to talk to the physiotherapy department about preparations for taking up my place, I was totally put off by their attitude towards me. Their opening line was, 'These aren't great results.' I knew that, but the way I was spoken to, it was as if they were doing me a favour, which wasn't the case at all. I'd gone away and worked hard for two years to get the right qualifications and the grades asked for. Then they said, 'If you don't like the course after six months, you can always go back to Manchester.' Such lack of faith in me was the ultimate discouragement. I wasn't some fly-by-night celebrity going there to have a bash at being a physio and if it didn't work out I would saunter back across the Irish Sea and resume my life. I was deadly serious about it. I was going to sell my house, relocate my family and, remember this was before the ceasefire, live in Northern Ireland as a Shankill Road Protestant married to a Catholic. They had no belief in me. When they saw I was getting annoyed, they tried to be more positive and said, 'Look, Norman, all the students are really excited about you coming here,' which rubbed me up the wrong way. It made me feel that they would take me on sufferance because I was a publicity coup for the university. My stubbornness returned and I bombed them out and called the move off.

The day I walked out of the office at the University of Ulster it looked like my dream of becoming a physiotherapist had died. Whenever an obstacle has been put in my way, however, I have always managed to get past it somehow. I don't have prolonged bouts of doubt and self-analysis. I certainly couldn't afford to at that time, so I adapted and moved on. While I'd been at the FE college, I had done a day course in podiatry at Salford University and really enjoyed it, so I contacted them, applied and won a place on the degree course there. Three years later, having supported myself throughout with a hectic schedule of evening functions, I graduated with a Bachelor of Science (Hons) in podiatric medicine. I'm probably more proud of my achievements at university than I am of anything else. Football came so easily to me, but academia was tough. I'm not a natural student at all and I had to work so hard to get through that course and the postgraduate one I did at Manchester Metropolitan University in sports science. Through college and university and by overcoming the pressure I felt attending classes with kids half my age, I made a second career for myself. I can't say it was more thrilling than playing in the World Cup or scoring the winning goal in the FA Cup final, but it was enormously satisfying to achieve something I never thought I was capable of.

I qualified in 1996 and, having done my thesis on 'the role of the podiatrist in the ninety-two professional football clubs' and received feedback from eighty-eight of them, I approached the PFA with my findings and a proposal. They agreed to back me and offer a service to the sixteen-year-old first-year professionals at the clubs. I started out with ten clubs and gradually got the provision for all ninety-two.

I did that for eight years, visiting seventy or so clubs a season, providing the same quality of service for Liverpool on one day as Exeter the next. Podiatrists specialise in the leg, from the thigh to the big toe, and my job was to make a biomechanic assessment of the way youth players moved, correct their posture and make insoles to cure them of complaints ranging from flat feet to shin splints. I did that until the end of the 2003–04 season, when the clubs, I think short-sightedly, reduced their contributions to the PFA and we ran out of funds to provide a free service. I had a good time, particularly if I was visiting seaside clubs, as I could load Della, Blaine and Clodagh into the car and take them with me. There was always someone at one of the clubs – a player, a physio, a coach or a manager – who knew me, so once I'd done my work for the day I would often go out in the evenings and escape the monotony of life on the road in Travelodges by having a plate of pasta and a few drinks. It kept me in touch with football in a totally non-pressurised way. I was sad when it ended, but I set up a private practice at 11 St John Street, Manchester and still get a lot of referrals from northern clubs to treat their trainees. It allows me to stay involved, even if my role is not as prominent as it once was.

I don't know where I would be now if Julie hadn't taken hold of me and convinced me that my life wasn't over during those tortuous days when the consequences of my retirement seemed so distressing. She encouraged me so much. It was as if she and the children became my new team-mates to support me through the next stage of my career. We were together for twenty years, but the marriage ended in 2001. There is no animosity at all between us and I see the children all the time, occasionally ferrying them about to dance classes, piano lessons and football. Julie and I had some great times together, but, and I know this is a cliché, we drifted apart, and became more like old friends than husband and wife. We are still best mates. Sometimes you can spend half your life with someone and that can be enough.

We were married in 1987 on Sunday, 4 October, the day after a 1–1 draw at Luton. Fergie was ecstatic when I told him about the wedding, telling me all about the stability a wife would bring to me and praising the virtues of settling down and family life to the hilt. We stayed at Mottram Hall on the Sunday night, went up to Windermere for a couple of days' honeymoon and, though Alex had given me the week off, I rang him and insisted that I be selected for the Wednesday night Littlewoods Cup tie away at Hull City. We were 5–0 up from the first leg and Fergie told me not to bother, but he loved my desire to play and was easily persuaded. The funny thing was that when I was warming up at Boothferry Park that night, nothing felt right. I couldn't kick the ball properly, I felt imbalanced and my timing had gone to cock. After about ten minutes of confusion and frustration, it dawned on me that the problem was my wedding ring. I went back to the dressing room and slipped it into my jacket pocket, where it stayed for the duration of that and every other game I played. When I took it off permanently fourteen years later, I still hadn't settled down in the way that Fergie had envisaged and was out most evenings earning my living. But we had three beautiful, well-adjusted kids to show for our marriage. Ultimately, it didn't work out, but I have no regrets at all.

From 1981 onwards there had been three constants in my life: Julie, Manchester United and a battered right knee. When Julie and I split up I was left with two, and when I bow to the inevitable and have a knee-replacement operation, I'll be left with United as the single thread that runs from my adolescence to middle-age. The knee still throbs like mad after I've done a session at one of my soccer schools, when the irresistible temptation of a ball rolling towards me momentarily transports me back to the functional but enchantingly romantic playing fields at the Cliff. I pivot on the frail joint and whack the ball goalwards with my left foot, as I used to do almost every day for almost twenty years. Suddenly I'm sixteen again and I can almost lose myself in that warm feeling. But then

I notice the limp and start to feel the grinding pain.

It's a shame that it stopped me from fulfilling another of my ambitions. As a patron of Guide Dogs for the Blind in Northern Ireland for ten years, I wanted to do an Ian Botham-type walk around the edges of the state, up the coast and along the border. My two-hour practice session soon put paid to that idea as I couldn't cope with the juddering impact of the roads, so I reluctantly had to switch to a bike. I enjoyed it and was greeted by crowds and local dignitaries wherever we went, but it was another example of how much of a constraint it has been on me.

Being self-employed all these years has made me slightly insecure when my diary isn't chock full of engagements. I know how seasonal both podiatry and the after-dinner game is and have more than ten years experience of knowing when the bookings come. But not having a conventional job leaves you constantly open to irrational fears about your future. Thank God, then, for United, where I've worked since 1994 on match days for the corporate hospitality department. It's been an enormous privilege to be welcomed back into the family at United and I'm immensely thankful for the opportunities that my continued association with the club has opened up. Over the years, as the corporate side has expanded beyond belief, Wilf McGuinness and I have been joined by Stuart Pearson, Frank Stapleton, Denis Irwin, Clayton Blackmore, Lee Martin and even Robbo and Neil Webb on occasion. We go around the suites, tell a few stories, have a couple of beers, then watch the game. I always get a lovely, warm reception from the fans, but it's far less intense than the days when I played and had to take two suits to the match as the one I wore when walking across the Old Trafford forecourt would be covered in felt-tip pen marks from the tight huddle of autograph hunters who escorted me from the door of my car to the players' entrance. Because I get embarrassed by adulation, I feel far more comfortable with this more low-key approach towards me today. I still get recognised and get a buzz from the kind things people say, but I've always felt no different to the supporters, not a star at all. I'm a normal person – I just haven't led a normal life.

All the time at functions guys come up to me and say, with an obvious note of disgust in their voices, 'Look at the money they're earning today.' It's always assumed that I must be jealous, but I'm genuinely not. I'd much rather look back and say I had a wonderful ten years than dwell on speculation that if it hadn't been for this operation or that one then I could have earned £1,000,000 a year. Yes, I wish I hadn't had to reinvent myself so many times, that fate had allowed me to be the footballer I was supposed to be, perhaps one of the elite few at the very top of the world game. I wish it hadn't all ended so quickly either, that I could still do the thing that defines me as a human being. Ten years ago I went to HMP Maghaberry on the outskirts of Belfast to coach the prisoners and afterwards did a question-and-answer session. After the usual stuff about whether it was a cross or a shot in 1985, one fella stood up and said, 'Norman, do you remember the time me and you robbed the Post Office up the Shankill and you got away with it?' Cue uproar among the prisoners and alarmed double-takes from the prison officers. Of course, it was only a wind-up, but I did recognise the joker who said it. He and I had been to school together and played football many times over the cobbles and puddles that littered the cramped back streets packed between the Falls and Crumlin Roads. Like so many of my contemporaries, he had gone the other way and was in prison at the age of seventeen, while I was at the World Cup in Spain. How can I have any significant regrets, let alone bitterness, when I compare my life to his? As I sit back with an open bottle of wine before me – red, naturally – I can honestly say that I will always look on the bright side of life, the Whiteside of life.

CAREER STATISTICS

Norman Whiteside, born Belfast, 7 May 1965.

West Belfast Schools, Northern Ireland Schoolboy International, Manchester United Schoolboy September 1978. Became an apprentice June 1981. Turned professional July 1982. First team debut v Brighton & Hove Albion as substitute on 24 April 1982. Transferred to Everton July 1989, £600,000 (plus £150,000 after fifty games). Retired through injury. Appointed Northwich Victoria assistant manager physio October 1991 until March 1992.

Club Honours

FA Cup winners 1983, 1985.

- Youngest player to score for Manchester United first team, 17 years, 8 days
- Youngest FA Cup final scorer at 18 years, 18 days v Brighton & Hove Albion 1983 replay
- Youngest League Cup final scorer at 17 years, 323 days v Liverpool 1983

International Honours

Northern Ireland: 38 full caps, 9 goals

1982 v Yugoslavia, Honduras, Spain, Austria, France, West Germany, Albania

1983 v Turkey, Austria (1 goal), Turkey, West Germany (1), Scotland (1)

1984 v England, Wales, Finland, Romania (1), Israel (1), Finland

1985 v England, Spain, Turkey (2), Romania, England

1986 v France, Denmark, Morocco, Algeria (1), Spain, Brazil, England

1987 v Israel, England, Yugoslavia, Turkey

1988 v Poland, France

1989 v Hungary (1), Republic of Ireland

- Youngest World Cup finalist at 17 years, 41 days 1982

Club Record

Season	League		League Cup		FA Cup		European		Others	
	Apps	Goals	Apps	Goals	Apps	Goals	Apps	Goals	Apps	Goals
MANCHESTER UNITED										
1981–2	2	1	-	-	-	-	-	-	-	-
1982–3	39	8	9	3	7	3	2*	-	-	-
1983–4	37	10	6	1	1	-	6+	1	1#	-
1984–5	27	9	1	-	6	4	5*	-	-	-
1985–6	37	4	4	2	5	1	-	-	5##	1
1986–7	31	8	4	1	2	1	-	-	-	-
1987–8	27	7	5	2	3	1	-	-	-	-
1988–9	6	-	-	-	-	-	-	-	-	-
EVERTON										
1989–90	27	9	2	1	6	3	-	-	-	-
1990–1	2	-	-	-	-	-	-	-	-	-
TOTAL	235	56	31	10	30	13	13	1	6	1

* UEFA Cup
+ Cup Winners' Cup
# Charity Shield
One Charity Shield, four Screen Sport Super Cup, 1 goal

Football League v Rest of the World 1987 (1)

INDEX

INDEX